The Origins of Social Work

Also by Malcolm Payne:

Modern Social Work Theory (3rd edn)*
*Teamwork in Multiprofessional Care**
Anti-bureaucratic Social Work
What is Professional Social Work?
*Social Work and Community Care**
Writing for Publication in Social Services Journals (3rd edn)
Linkages: Effective Networking in Social Care
Social Care in the Community
*Working in Teams**
Power, Authority and Responsibility in Social Services: Social Work in Area Teams

*Also published by Palgrave Macmillan

The Origins of Social Work

Continuity and Change

Malcolm Payne

Consultant editor: Jo Campling

First published 2005 by
PALGRAVE MACMILLAN
Houndmills, Basingstoke, Hampshire RG21 6XS and
175 Fifth Avenue, New York, N.Y. 10010
Companies and representatives throughout the world

PALGRAVE MACMILLAN is the global academic imprint of the Palgrave Macmillan division of St. Martin's Press, LLC and of Palgrave Macmillan Ltd. Macmillan® is a registered trademark in the United States, United Kingdom and other countries. Palgrave is a registered trademark in the European Union and other countries.

ISBN-13: 978 0-333-73790-3 hardback
ISBN-10: 0-333-73790-3 hardback
ISBN-13: 978 0-333-73791-0 paperback
ISBN-10: 0-333-73791-1 paperback

This book is printed on paper suitable for recycling and made from fully managed and sustained forest sources.

A catalogue record for this book is available from the British Library.

Library of Congress Cataloging-in-Publication Data

Payne, Malcolm, 1947–
    The origins of social work : continuity and change / Malcolm Payne.
        p. cm.
    Includes bibliographical references and index.
    ISBN 0-333-73790-3 (hardback) — ISBN 0-333-73791-1 (paperback)
    1. Social service—History. I. Title.

HV40.P333 2005
361.3'09—dc22   2005045731

10   9   8   7   6   5   4   3   2   1
14   13   12   11   10   09   08   07   06   05

Printed in China

For Margaret

Contents

List of Figures and Tables

Figures

Tables

Foreword and Acknowledgements

I have written this book partly because of my experience of students asking historical questions. They have difficulty in disentangling the story. To them, the 1948 welfare reforms in Britain, which finally broke up the Poor Law, seem similar to the 1971 Seebohm reorganisation, which created the modern administrative structure of the English social services. This again seems not too different from the 1989–90 child and community care reforms which legislated for the present pattern of services. More changes are expected soon.

Every generation, it seems, views history from its own experiences. My grandparents were born in the 1890s in Victorian times, the Edwardian era was their salad days, the First and Second World Wars were at the centre of their lives and they often talked of all these times. My parents experienced the Depression of the 1930s, the Second World War and the creation of the welfare state in the 1950s. All this is a vivid part of my experience of the past, but to many current students it is as distant as medieval feudalism. So I have written this book partly for my students and others like them to provide a longer perspective on their modern professional preoccupations.

This book is interpretive, rather than a delving into archives to exhume the detail of particular events. Obviously, its interpretation of continuity and change in social work relies on the efforts of people who have done the detailed work in every locality and country and in relation to particular aspects and specialisms of social work. I am grateful for much toil by others in being able to draw upon detailed evidence, and there is much more of great value to be done. As it is done, I am sure that the interpretations made here, provisional as all such interpretations are, will develop and change in the future.

I am grateful to the many colleagues recently and over the years who have given me information or discussed this project with me, the many libraries that have helped me to write the book and check its contents and the commentators and reviewers who have helped me to improve it.

MALCOLM PAYNE
Sutton, Surrey

Every effort has been made to trace all the copyright holders but if any have been inadvertently overlooked the publishers will be pleased to make the necessary arrangements at the first opportunity.

CHAPTER 1

Introduction: Social Work's Histories

Social work: changes and continuities

When someone next to us stumbles, we may stretch out a hand to steady them or shove them stumbling to the floor and take their means of living. One action symbolises personal help; its alternative symbolises competition and conflict. Compassion, benevolence, love, disaster, war and oppression are character-istic of all human societies. If social work is *social*, it must repre-sent and respond to all these aspects of society. If social work is *work*, it must represent an action within society in response to them.

All human societies express humanity and anxiety about potential disorder. Social work emerged in the late 1800s in some Western European and North American societies as a way of expressing that humanity and anxiety. I argue in this book that social work as an idea and a practice emerged and devel-oped as a way of implementing welfare for those societies during those particular times. Previous societies have offered charity and provided welfare, but I do not see what they did as social work under another name, or as a precursor to social work.

The current idea and practice of social work is only of its time, our time. It includes help with personal troubles, often associated with programmes of more general social provision, such as education, health and social security and connected to general social policies supporting the welfare of citizens and good social order. Social work is part of those wider programmes. However, it is different from them, in its focus on individuals, families and communities who need personal help to gain benefits from social policies. The personal help is

1

provided by employing professionals with particular expertise and training in interpersonal communication and support and in organising the delivery of complicated patterns of services so that they are relevant for individuals. By connecting the personal help with wider social policies, social work has become both a part of delivering wider social provision and also of social movements seeking change or development in that provision. The emphasis of social work varies depending on the society that it serves. In societies and communities with poor resources, its focus is social development: working with people to develop social cooperation and facilities, often allied to economic development. In richer societies, its focus is social assistance or social education (in Europe, this is sometimes called 'social pedagogy', emphasising its educational element). Social assistance offers problem-solving where someone has complex difficulties or distress, or personal growth and development where someone seems unable to fulfil their potential. Much social work focuses on population groups who share particular difficulties, because of poverty, family disruption, illness, disability or old age.

Most societies' values assume that people will manage their difficulties and fulfil their potential without help outside their family or local community. People calling on professional social work, therefore, are often stigmatised for needing help, adding to their already marginal status in their society. Social work often seeks to combat stigmatising attitudes and help families and communities develop to become self-helping. At times, as in the Poor Law and other social movements of the mid-1800s, stigma was emphasised as part of the service to encourage people to help themselves. At other times and in other places, as in some socialist welfare states, personal help and social welfare have been offered as social rights to avoid stigma. Issues of stigma and self-help are, therefore continuities in all social work services. Examining histories of social work allows us to see how changes in these continuities and others continually recreate social work and the services and policies in which it plays a part.

This book considers and interprets the histories of current social work because looking at how these continuities and changes interact illuminates what social work is, what has been attempted and what might be possible in social work. It shows that social work provision emerged from both war, conflict and disaster and also from caring and charity. It is a means of enhancing social order through concern for others, providing care for people in difficulties and controlling undesirable behaviour that comes from people's difficulties. Those difficulties have often been the product of human failings, sometimes personal, but often the failings of the society surrounding individuals in difficulty. The bubonic plague (the 'black death' of medieval times) and HIV/AIDS (the epidemic disaster of the late 1900s and early 2000s) both stimulated efforts at social control and new ways of helping. Poverty, natural disaster and famine have led societies to organise help to the people afflicted and make sure that their distress does not lead them to cause disruption to the social order through crime or revolution. War and conflict have always raised the need for help to displaced civilians or disabled soldiers, often pushing caring services forward. However, war and conflict also lead to the control of populations and the destruction of their life chances, making demands on caring services and sometimes negating their value.

I have argued that understanding change and continuity in social work helps to understand the nature of possibilities of social work, but it also helps in social work practice. To practise successfully, social workers need to understand their purposes, aims and activities. To follow up the example above, if stigma and self-help are continuities in all social work, to practise well, we need to understand what effect a policy or practice might have on stigma and self-help. For example, in the 1970s, 'intermediate treatment' developed in the UK to provide opportunities for self-development for deprived and delinquent young people. This seemed a beneficial example of social education or social pedagogy. However, it was criticised because it led to delinquent teenagers receiving free leisure and self-development opportunities that more 'deserving' youngsters did not receive. Perhaps young people would commit crime to get these benefits; why should 'undeserving' criminals get them? Being aware of consistent social attitudes to providing services for the 'undeserving' might have made practice more careful to avoid this criticism, or social workers might have had their defences ready. Seeing these continuities can help us to decide on ways to practise that avoid some of the social pitfalls that may damage social work and the people we serve.

Things do not change completely and all at once. Therefore, to understand what they are doing, to practise confidently and work within change as it occurs, social workers need to understand the continuities in their work, alongside change. Working with change involves being able to analyse three things: continuities, what is unchanging; evolutions, what develops slowly; and change, what shifts abruptly.

This is important for three main reasons. First, the social work task usually includes helping people who are experiencing continuities, evolutions and changes and having difficulties about it, so understanding the changes and continuities that are affecting them is an important feature of social work practice. Second, social workers operate in a complex social environment, which also changes, evolves and continues, so they need to be able to analyse what is going on in their social, political and organisational environment. This helps to use resources effectively. For example, care management, used in British social services mainly to organise packages of care for adults in need of long-term help and support, has its origins in social work practices such as a cycle of assessment, planning, implementation and evaluation, and an American technique originated to deal with certain problems in the American social care system. It also incorporates certain major changes, such as the idea of creating a package of care services (Payne, 1995, 2000b). By understanding both the origins and the changes, we can see better how they offer possibilities for effective practice and how the changes might hinder practice. The third reason for understanding continuities and changes in social work is to secure confidence in what we are doing. Social work often seems to be in constant change, even crisis, outside our control. Clarity about what is significant, about continuities and changes in their economic, historical, political and social context can help us to welcome appropriate change and recognise continuing values and practices. At the same time, we can avoid cynical sayings like: 'We're doing what we always did with a new word to describe it.' Some change is genuine innovation, some is manipulation and spin. Looking at continuities and change helps to identify which is which and maintain a positive but critical reaction to forces for change and continuity.

Social works and their histories

Change and continuity, then, are a matter of political, social and historical judgement and interpretation. Most histories of social work are written by people from the West: the USA, Europe and Australia (for example Woodroofe, 1962; Leighninger, 1987; Satka, 1995). Countries elsewhere are less considered, although I have included some examples in Further reading and drawn from them where there is an interaction with Western social work. Histories have a particular perspective that comes from their authors. Social work histories usually assume an *internationalist view*, the centrality of Western social work with a chronology of events leading to it. Also, they assume that a narrative account of *what* happened explains *why* social work is as it is. The narrative assumes a single sequence in which one thing leads to another.

This book questions the internationalist perspective in three ways. First, it points to how in different places and welfare regimes differing 'social works' have interacted with Western social work. At present, it would be fair to say that Western social work maintains its cultural dominance. But alternatives exist, they are important in the relevant welfare regimes and at times they increase their international impact.

The second question about the internationalist view is that histories often neglect particular aspects of social work. An American journal and later book (Carlton-LaNey, 1994, 2001) focused on 'African American history' in social work, arguing that black contributions had been suppressed in wider American histories. Moreover, some histories assume that a Western, Judeo-Christian (from the Jewish and Christian historical tradition) democratic framework is essential to practising social work, or understanding its origins. This neglects traditions of charity and mutual support in Muslim and Hindu religions and different forms of social organisation.

Women are not excluded from social work histories, because much of at least the early history of social work is partly formed by great women leaders. However, conventional histories focus on the heroines and exclude the women who endure the daily grind. American social work's Nobel prizewinner Jane Addams and, in Britain, the people who have achieved titles and honours, such as Geraldine Aves and Eileen Younghusband, receive tributes, rather than the women who make things work at ground level, like social workers or home helps. Also, the social work that women dominate is of a particular kind, and the people who take on everyday state power within the social services, Poor Law guardians and masters, administrators, directors of social services, bureaucrats and civil servants, have usually been overwhelmingly male.

The third question about the internationalist perspective is its focus on the heroic progress of the social work profession. The worlds of the people social workers serve are also excluded from social work histories, the failings of the profession receive less attention and the interaction of social work with policy and services is unclear. The focus is on heroes and heroines, innovations in law, organisation or service provision, trends, theories and ideas. Ordinary people's tribulations seem in histories to be merely background to social work affrays. This book tries to incorporate a picture of the social background and ideas that affected social work's progress. Histories of social care or welfare covering services that offer personal help are different from histories of the social services, which may cover the welfare functions of government, including education, health, housing and social security or may refer only to the personal social services. Histories of social work, the profession, are connected to these, but are different. This book gives priority to social work but emphasises how it is embedded in and interacts with histories of welfare and the social services, broadly defined.

This book interprets, comments on and assesses social work as a product of Western societies in the early twenty-first century. Social work as a form of personal, family and community assistance was formed during the two previous centuries and, because of the global influence of Western culture, it has had an impact on welfare and social provision in other societies. This book traces some aspects of that interaction, in particular through its connections with social development and social education, while focusing mainly on Western social work. Narratives, not *a* narrative, of social work interconnect, but not necessarily in a linear way. For example, in Chapter 10, I argue that social work education did not develop in one form from a series of events in the early twentieth century, but a number of different 'social work educations' developed at different times and places, becoming interconnected at various points. I use this information then as part of an explanation. First, it is part of my overall thesis that we must identify and study a number of social works rather than one. Second, explanations are assumed by a 'simple' story of events, hiding a set of assumptions that Western social work is the main valid link. One of my purposes is to draw out and validate a range of social works. These may not have had the historical sway of Western social work, but I expect and hope that in another century, the historian will see how Western social work has been adapted and displaced by alternative social works that we may now see in embryo drawn from different imaginations and historical traditions.

Problems with a single historical narrative

Because histories are usually presented, like stories, as narratives, they often assume that whatever is being chronicled, in this case social work, has a continuous identity and nature and that continuity can be understood and explained. Within that identity, the story is of changes. Moreover, since at least the Enlightenment, histories often assume that changes represent development. One of the characteristics of modernity, the way of thinking which characterises the West since the Enlightenment, is that human civilisation progresses, the progress can be identified and studied and history represents that progress. Indeed, progressivism, an American political movement of the late nineteenth and early twentieth century, is a landmark phase in the development of American social work (Chapter 2).

However, there are alternative assumptions. Perhaps things do not progress: they might disappear. Things once regarded as part of social work have become no longer relevant. For example, when I became a social worker in Britain in the 1960s, prison governors and health visitors were regarded in some respects as part of social work. Over time, their roles have diverged from how we now usually understand social work. This has come from changes in public and political conceptions of the pattern of services and the links between them and the organisation and education of the relevant occupational groups. The process by which some activities became 'not social work' is relevant to the process by which social work is formed. Even though the short compass here is not able to cover all the possible byways, we should be aware of their possible impact.

Activities and occupational groups are formed both by what they are and also by what they are not. In a more recent change, the probation service, once clearly a social work occupation in England and Wales, has been defined by the British government as a criminal justice occupation akin to police and prison work, whereas in Ireland and Scotland it is still integral to social work.

Narrative involves selection from a wider story. Merely selecting some rather than other elements of the story implies our own explanation. A different person might select differently, create a different story and imply a different explanation. The theory and assumptions behind selection may form an explanation, but they may be merely taken for granted within the story, rather than being brought out. Germain's (1970) brief history of social work theory, for example, analyses developments in social work theory as a search for theories that more effectively guide social workers in acting. She assumes that greater effectiveness means using increasingly scientific theories. However, alternative views of the development of social work theory see it as the product of other political processes within and outside social work (Payne, 1997b). Alternative understandings exist of what is 'scientific' or alternative views about whether pursuing the scientific is 'effective' and what kinds of effectiveness might be relevant (Hämäläinen and Vornanen, 1996). Therefore, an apparently simple narrative history hides some important factors in explaining why events took place, even though the significant events and trends might have been identified. The explanation lies in Germain's partly assumed analysis rather than in the events of the story recounted.

One of the problems of the idea of continuity is that history sometimes seems to have parallels with the present. People say 'history repeats itself'. But events are a creation of their time and the patterns of circumstances that create them. When we see patterns in the past, we are creating them with our hindsight, affected by our current concerns and our contemporary understandings and interests.

Another point is that change and continuity partly depend on the level of analysis. Jones's (1993) history of the mental health services in Britain identifies and tells the stories of many changes. But she subjects these changes to a broader analysis. She argues that there is a discourse going on all the time between medical and legal influences on the understanding of mental illness. So, in one sense, there is much change, yet in another, the underlying stream is of continuity.

Some sets of social ideas would reject this point of view. Marxism, for example, is based on historical materialism. That is, in summary, social structures and experiences are formed from the historical experience of how people provide for themselves materially, within the economy. So Marxist readers will want to say that history is always important because social work's interaction with the economic and political structures of particular countries at particular times must inevitably be the crucial determinant of how it was and what it becomes.

In historical analyses, therefore, we must consider what factors are being repeated or changing, so that we may interpret change and continuity, and we must be cautious of our own political and ideological position and how it affects our analysis.

There is also the problem of how chronological to be. In the detail and flow of the story, it is easy to lose the substantial explanatory and analytical points that historians are making. This also makes them easy to believe, instead of keeping the critical faculties alert. However, to pursue and understand analyses, I find it useful to have a chronological context. Therefore, the next three chapters of the book offer a brief chronological account of social work in three periods, while the remainder of the book sets out an analysis of particular areas of social work. However, it also tries to identify the dominant themes of these very broad periods.

To sum up the criticisms of social work history, it is, very often:

- *Celebratory.* It tends to be concerned to make social workers feel committed to their heritage; to honour the great and good.
- *Hindsight-biased.* It looks backwards from where social work is now. Aspects of life that went in other directions formed social work as much as the things we are now.
- *Euro- and ethnocentric, and gender-biased.*
- *Neglectful of the peoples served.*
- *Institutionally constrained.* It is about a social institution, a profession, and it is primarily a history of institutions, organisations and agencies. So, therefore, social work's historical assumptions are of the existence of the institution, social work, and much of the evidence is garnered from the records

and memories of particular institutions. Of course, those records have been constructed for the purposes of those institutions, and not for the independent analysis of the history of the wider social form, social work. Therefore, they will be biased and biasing.

Inevitably, reviewing accounts of histories of social work, my perspective will reflect many of these failings too. However, I have tried to use a wide range of sources, from different countries, acknowledging different theoretical perspectives and including some economic, political and sociological perspectives as well as narrative histories. Also, I have tried to be critical of the interpretations given to conventional narratives and invite you to be so too.

The book's framework

The basis of history is in its detail, because this forms the evidence for interpretations of events. Since the focus here is on interpretation and analysis with a broad focus, rather than an accumulation of local minutiae, I rely on existing accounts of social work histories. Graham (1996) cites hundreds of studies on Canadian social welfare history (globally, a relatively minor field) and this suggests that global welfare history includes millions of detailed historical issues and facts that a short book cannot cover. My purpose is to set a context for understanding change and continuities in social work histories that I hope will stimulate readers to work on local and particular histories and examine, question and develop possible historical interpretations.

Chapters 2–4 contain a summary of the development of social work, mainly in the nineteenth and twentieth centuries, which I hope might be helpful to readers who do not have a grasp of the sequence of events. Some of the discussion in the latter part of the book relies on this narrative account of the development of social work. Each chapter contains a brief general commentary and conclusion to provide some overview. Each describes developments in Western social work as it emerged in the UK, and identifying influences from and upon Europe, the USA and in some other countries. There is some information about personalities, where they are important. I also include some information about broader trends in international social work to show how Western social work had a broad impact on social work globally, through colonial and postcolonial cultural influences. I question the postcolonial ethnocentricity of the internationalist perspective on social work history. I want to show, on the one hand, that countries learned from each other and that international trends affected many countries. On the other hand, social work responds to local conditions and culture and in particular welfare regimes created by each country's social policies and political structures. These in turn construct different kinds of social work in different countries. Social work elsewhere has its impact but it is important neither to minimise the differences by claiming that there is one social work nor to deny the influences and, perhaps, excessive impact of Western social work.

After the chronological account of social work's histories, I look at particular factors in the construction of social work in Chapters 5–10. These areas of social work have been selected to reflect my analysis of the factors that contribute to the construction of a profession within its social networks and the availability of research.

I identify six aspects of the construction of social work, arguing that these factors allow us to identify the construction of any profession. They are:

- The social issues that were important in the creation of social work (Chapter 5). The character of a profession is partly created by the nature of the people served, the problems that they present to their society and how that society responds to them.
- Values and philosophies central to practice (Chapter 6). Professional and political values underlie how social work is practised and how it fits within social care systems.
- Agency, legal and organisational contexts for practice and sources of authority for practice (Chapter 7). Social work combines elements of caring and the management of social order. Both elements are expressed in its organisational and legal structures.
- Occupational groupings and professions (Chapter 8). Since social work is an occupational group, occupational and professional organisation are relevant to understanding its histories.

■ Knowledge and research (Chapter 9). What knowledge professions use and how it is developed is important for how they work
■ Education for the profession (Chapter 10). Education is a crucial element in understanding any distinctive occupational group.

Each chapter focuses in turn on each of these different components in the historical formation of social work, with a final chapter to draw together some overall points to help social workers to think about the continuities and changes they experience. I have drawn some connections between the chapters, but there are other links to find. In doing so, you will be engaging in the process of understanding social works as historical entities and their development within wider social contexts. There will be much more to do, since a short book such as this can only introduce in outline some of the important trends and connections. But I hope it will stimulate you to go into the detail, which will allow histories of social work to be developed and reconstructed to offer new interpretations and understandings in the future.

CHAPTER 2

Before Social Work: to 1945

Social work's cultural context

All societies have ways of helping individuals, families and communities in difficulties. Welfare has its particular form of organisation and social purposes at any time. Day (2000: 55–81) describes many societies over thousands of years, some primitive, some great civilisations, in which helping activities, philanthropy and charitable help were available from private individuals, the state and religious organisations. Our hindsight sees ideas that connect current Western ideas about social work described in Chapter 1 back to organised helping in the ancient Mediterranean world of Greece and Rome. There were Greek and Roman traditions of charity and philanthropy (Hands, 1968), there was divorce, child abuse, abortion, prostitution in Rome (Gardner, 1986) and ways of dealing with these and other social issues. Heasman (1965: 21), concerned to draw a link between early Christianity and Christian social work in the 1900s, discussed Christian, Greek, Jewish and Roman societies as concerned with 'social work'. However, these societies did not have social work as we conceive it because they did not have a society in which such a conception could emerge. We see similarities because all societies have to tackle helping people, not because their experience directly influenced the development of current Western social work.

Until the European Renaissance in the 1700s, when scientific and cultural ideas were renewed, religion was an important form of authority, balancing states, which were led by monarchs and princes. Buddhism was an important carrier and motivator of social development throughout East Asia and Judaism and Islam were important philosophies that valued mutual social support in the Middle East. Powerful African and Islamic civilisations grew up and had long periods of success, including welfare provision (Day, 2000: 82–5).

The way the Christian Church provided organised help in the European Middle Ages alongside and sometimes in competition

Table 2.1 Summary of historical trends in social work

Charity and help for the poor is a characteristic of all societies, including ancient civilisations

In many civilisations, with the important civilisations of China and Japan being good examples, there was a strong emphasis on authority and social order attained through loyalty to family, community and other traditional structures.

In medieval Europe, grinding poverty in most of the population, together with its consequences, was met by Christian charity, but this was increasingly seen as inadequate and unpredictable.

During the 1600s and 1700s, stimulated by the Renaissance in and Reformation of the Catholic Church and the emergence of Protestantism, provision shifted towards state assistance, mainly to maintain economic development and prevent disorder, particularly during economic and social crises.

During the later 1700s and early 1800s, growing industrialisation in agriculture and manufacturing placed strains on traditional forms of welfare and social supports, but the laissez-faire ideas of liberal economics promoted individualistic self-help. Social assistance developed, emphasising institutional care and efforts at reducing dependence on welfare help.

In the late 1800s and early 1900s, developing states increasingly accepted responsibility for social help, and better communication and organisation led to the development and spread of ideas for organising social welfare services and, within them, social work, social pedagogy and related professions.

In the mid-1900s, the development of welfare states in many Western countries led social welfare services to become widespread, and social work developed as a profession, becoming an institutionalised part of public services in many developed countries. Social development and community work methods directed at social change were widely used in developing countries and areas, since individualistic social work seemed inappropriate.

In the late 1900s, economic growth became more variable, and concerns that welfare states could not be supported led to a retrenchment in social services, including social work, and a wider range of welfare regimes. There was a greater concern for critical analysis of and accountability for social work within a managerialist framework. With the collapse of Communist regimes in many parts of the world, social work was initiated for the first time or renewed in many countries. Social development continued its influence in developing countries and other social professions influenced particular countries.

with the role of monarchs and princes in providing for the welfare of their peoples are a backdrop for later developments in social work to react against. As organisational responses to social changes arose around industrialisation in the late 1800s, organised welfare developed in and then separated from the churches throughout the 1900s, becoming a recognisable social work, and this influenced other cultures and social systems. Social work became incorporated within established social welfare systems with the emergence in the mid-1900s of welfare states. Table 2.1 summarises these historical trends as a background to this and the next two chapters.

Understanding social work as it is today requires a focus on recent history, rather than the distant past. Therefore, in this book, I treat the most important origins of social work as lying within the fifty years up to 2000, when it became established in welfare states (Chapters 3 and 4). In this chapter, I deal with some forerunners to the recent development of Western social work.

Churches, charity, dependence and public disorder

European context

Towards the end of the Roman Empire up to AD500, great movements of peoples across the world created social change. However, the period from the fall of Rome until the Industrial Revolution in Europe heralded social work was not a time of barbarism followed by medieval stagnation. Many achievements demonstrate social progress and change. It is a vast and variable canvas. Social work emerged in Western European Christian societies, dominated in the medieval period by the Roman Catholic Church. Understanding some major ideas in play during this time helps to understand how social work as it emerged in the 1800s was different, but also points to debates that still arise today. Organised religion, local communities and monarchs and princes all made contributions in dealing with many social problems during medieval (up to perhaps 1600) and early modern (to 1900) periods of welfare provision. Debates arose about whether civilised religious society imposed a duty to provide care or whether the responsibility was to provide services that were effective in meeting social objectives, particularly in preventing disorder. Shifts of policy occurred between 'outdoor relief', as social security doles and community care in response to poverty were called, and institutional provision. There were also concerns to maintain local provision and influence as against central state or religious responsibilities, especially where it was in the interests of and engaged the involvement of local elites. The situations and issues were different, but many of these issues are familiar to social workers today.

Most of the population in medieval times experienced grinding, miserable poverty. The Christian churches were significant poor relief and social care providers in Europe until at least the late 1700s, and this pattern also influenced the New World, the Americas, as it began to open up from the 1600s onwards. In medieval Christian religion, interpreted through Catholicism in most of Europe, there were two paths to salvation: contemplation in monasteries or convents, or *vita activa*, the active life of charitable works in the community. Brandon (1998) argues that the monasteries, the contemplative side of this, provided little external charitable support. Charity was not valuable in itself, but as a sign of spiritual order in the world. Augustine thought that giving alms atoned for sin and listed suitable acts, such as feeding the poor, taking in pilgrims and visiting sick and imprisoned people. According to Aquinas, abstract religious ideas could take hold among people through rituals incorporating practical charity.

Throughout Catholic Europe, therefore, charitable acts became standardised and confraternities (religious communities with diverse roles often including charity) organised charitable acts as practical rituals so that religion 'ritualized relief to the poor, creating a welfare system with its own distinct organization and rhythms' (Flynn, 1989: 48–9). Many developments were stimulated by disaster, such as the impact of bubonic plague, the Black Death (Slack, 1985), and war, since mortality affected living standards (Hatcher, 1977). Hospitals and infirmaries cared for homeless and sick people.

Private donations were supplemented by public alms giving. For example, furriers in one confraternity in Spain gave each patient a goat's hair cape, a fur robe and shoes as part of a ritual of clothing the poor. To improve the safety of travel, confraternities also maintained bridges, often with chapels and shrines. Unwanted children were cared for and dowries were provided to enable needy women to marry. Imprisoned people were helped with food, drink and heating if they could not provide it themselves, and debtors had their debts paid off and were re-established in the community. Experience and systems of provision were written into church statutes and these transmitted ideas and influenced other parishes and communities. Thus, the Catholic Church created a relatively non-bureaucratic system of welfare, which engaged popular support through religious ritual, and which, once established, became part of unquestioned tradition. In trading and commercial social groups, organisations of craftsmen (in Germany Zünfte) and merchants' guilds (Gilden) provided welfare for members who fell on hard times and their widows and orphans (Otte, 1997).

There were critics and attempts at reform (Flynn, 1989: Ch. 3). People expressed concerns that charity created dependence, perhaps exploitation, by indigent classes (that is, poor people who failed to provide for themselves). There were moves among confraternities in Spain, for instance, to judge whether young women's reputations justified providing dowries for their weddings, although theologians also defended the natural law against people who, because they 'ascertained that the pauper behaves wrongly, do not want to ascertain his misery, nor take care of his need' (Friar Tomás de Trujillo, 1563, quoted by Flynn, 1989: 79). Charity was also unreliable and inconsistent, varying from time to time and place to place and inadequate in a crisis.

Public authorities sometimes became involved when a crisis occurred because of these problems of charity; public involvement in welfare is not wholly a product of the 1900s. Famine in the 1530s, for example, led to private charity being seen to be inadequate, in Zamora, Spain, and the city council became involved. Under pressure from peasant migration to the cities, German states such as Nuremberg (1522), Strasbourg (1523), Mons and Ypres (1525) began to centralise poor relief. In this way, poorhouses began to emerge in the 1700s in Germany and elsewhere (Otte, 1997). Efforts to control begging and institute poor relief swept Europe. This may be because of the Reformation, with Protestant churches replacing Catholic influence and leading to greater use of civil powers, as Catholic associations were closed down and had to be replaced. Mutual influence between Catholic and Reformation administrations may have existed. However, Catholic administrations, such as that in Venice, followed judgmental policies, refusing alms to 'sturdy rogues', that is, destitute adults capable of work. They focused on beggar children, promoting rescue work among what would now be called 'street children', aiming to make them self-sufficient adults. Public authorities also became involved where ideas and values changed. For example, Cavallo's (1995) detailed study of Turin in Italy shows how there was a move from 'community' to institutional care in the 1700s and 1800s. At the outset, charity was seen as a civic responsibility, which led to organised outdoor relief. Then there was a shift towards a view that it was a personal responsibility, which led to hospitals gaining importance as symbols of the prestige of donors. In the late 1600s, concern rose about marital violence, desertion and widows and young women unable to marry. This was because in elite families there was gender conflict and this made women benefactors more aware of female vulnerability and opposed to marriage.

Institutional arrangements in particular countries rather than widespread religious change also led to variation. For example, Italy had a strong tradition of communal government in some urban areas – almost city states. Some had very advanced civic provision. Examples are Venice's public health provisions against bubonic plague, the charitable activity of confraternities and occasionally large hospitals with hundreds of medical patients (Cavallo, 1995: 6). Although other cities were more under the thumb of feudal elites, there was nonetheless considerable development. Cavallo (1995) identifies active work on poor relief in Turin, where a comprehensive municipal plan in 1541 led to long-standing and thriving charitable services that powerfully maintained the role of the city in conflicts with central government as it became more powerful in the 1700s.

Although I am focusing on Europe as the source of current Western social work, many of these patterns were worldwide. Both China and Japan, for example, have long histories of state provision by lords and emperors, mainly in the big population centres and at times of famine or disaster. The role of Buddhism throughout East Asia has been disputed (Goodman, 1998: 152). Since it encourages adherents to accept the status quo fatalistically and discourages the idea of responsibility for those outside a personal circle, it seems to set its face against more general welfare, and this has led some to the view that the ideology of Christianity was crucial to the development of social work. Two points may be made against such a view: first, the considerable evidence of welfare provision through religion and the state in the ancient East and second, many aspects of Eastern religion impose requirements to help others. Brandon (1998) argues, however, that, unlike some Christian forms of monastic spirituality, Buddhism encourages a concern for the existing and public world, rather than mystical retreat, since Buddhist monks must interact with the lay world of peasants, offering them spiritual guidance in return for food and shelter. Kumar (1994: 6) argues that Indian philosophy contains many confused and opposing views.

As an example of practical welfare, in Japan Buddhism developed a focus on group loyalties, rather than seeking transcendental attitudes. Thus, social welfare is traced to welfare institutions set up by Prince Shotoko, who introduced Buddhism to Japan, as well as the Taihō Code of 702, the first public assistance programme. Its policy was based on a subsidiarity principle like that of modern European policy: responsibility for people in need lay first with their family, then with other relatives and then the local community. Subsequently, Buddhism became separated from the feudal state and became a belief of individuals. Charity was a religious practice, for example, in Eison relieving *hinin* (non-persons) in the Tanakura period (1400–1500s). In the oppressive, conservative, feudal Tokugawa period (1603–1868), welfare was devolved to family and local community in the 'five-family-unit' system, providing the mutual assistance necessary to facilitate subsistence agriculture. This forbade, at least initially, social mobility and maintained strict local social control of behaviour, while also providing for local welfare from the local lord, substituting for the emperor (Ikeda and Takashima, 1997). Hard work and frugal provisions were the main ways of dealing with poverty, in a mirror image of European Poor Law policies; possibly the only practical policy in a largely subsistence economy. These local units subsequently developed, particularly in wartime during the 1900s, to form neighbourhood associations, which are still important aspects of the Japanese welfare system.

Returning to medieval Europe, in addition to practical reasons for a public role in welfare, there were theoretical debates. For example, the widely translated *De subventione pauperum* (1526) of Juan Luis Vives (1492–1540) proposed that the state should act against poverty, using employment schemes for jobless people, centres for practical help for needy people and help for poor families in their homes (cited in Flynn, 1989: 87), and many cities, for example Lyons in France (Michielse, 1990), adopted such policies. The focus of concern for many public authorities in the 1600s was tension between the economic burden and risks of public disorder if some provision was not made for the poor (Fairchilds, 1976). This is typical of the variation of provision and its response to public concerns about disorder.

The French policy of *renfermement,* whereby elderly people, children and families in difficulties who were begging were placed in institutions, had widespread influence, but it remained part of a system of charitable help in the community. By the late 1700s, this residential provision became more significant, part of a shift to institutional provision, which began in the 1500s culminating in the late 1800s (Porter, 1987). Even when, during the French Revolution at the end of the 1700s, a national system of welfare was proposed, this was variable in its application, and much less was attempted in the Napoleonic period (1800–15) (Jones, 1982). Consequently, many Catholic areas retained traditional religious charity well into the modern era. This is evident in provision for children and families.

After the Protestant Reformation (when Protestant churches broke away from the Roman Catholic Church) and the Renaissance and the Enlightenment, which emphasised rational planning and social thought, the churches' influence was progressively displaced by municipal and organised local charitable provision, often motivated by religious impulses and social prestige. Municipal and local charity were increasingly interwoven with provision deriving from central government, as greater centralisation developed and the state became a more important force in all societies and came to take up responsibility for many areas of social life, including welfare. As the churches withdrew from welfare and the states took over, the scene was set for social work.

British developments

Britain reflected many of these European trends, although because it became Protestant in the Reformation, the Catholic

Church had less influence. Charity emerged from both religious and social responsibility in the medieval period: the two were closely related. Jordan (1960) shows that from the 1400s to the 1800s there was a substantial growth in philanthropic activity. Leading members of society saw it as important to undertake charitable works and accept social responsibilities for less fortunate people. Early state involvement came about when labour shortages in the 1300s, allied to a period of state paternalism, led to attempts to control wages (through the Statute of Labourers 1351) and labour mobility (through the Poor Law Act 1388). Vagrancy was a problem because of the fear of disorder. Unemployed and poor people would migrate around the country in search of work or financial support and this was difficult to cope with because social control relied on local knowledge and relationships. The problem worsened in the 1400s because land enclosures to create private farms led to depopulation in many rural areas, and because of rapid price inflation (Fraser, 2003). A period of bad harvests prompted increased fears of disorder and a series of Elizabethan Poor Laws to respond to this culminated in the Poor Law Act 1601 and the beginnings of a shift towards institutional care (Chapter 8). The English approach was of 'classification': aged, sick, disabled and mentally ill poor people needed institutional relief in almshouses and workhouses, able-bodied people were set to work in a house of correction (not at the outset residential) and children apprenticed to a trade. Able-bodied people who became vagrants or refused to work were punished in the house of correction. Local justices of the peace became responsible for the Act's administration: this emphasised the local roots of responsibility for poor people, but led to wide variation of provision. England was unusual compared with most European countries in having extensive state provision, even if it was local and variable. The development of legislation from these times is summarised in Table 2.2, to give a picture of the legal and administrative development relevant to current social work.

The Scottish system remained separate, drawing much more heavily on charitable donations and organisation by the church (Mitchison, 2000). This was important, because one of the earliest experiments in organised visiting of the poor in Glasgow, by Chalmers (see below), developed this approach in the direction of social work method.

Table 2.2 British legislation and reports important for social care to 1945

Date	Title	Comment
1351	Statute of Labourers	Controlled workmen's wages
1388	Poor Law Act 1388	Parishes to provide for residents, whose mobility was thereby controlled
1388	Statute of Cambridge	Manors responsible for destitute children
1601	Poor Law Act 1601	Instituted a pioneering, locally administered system for helping poor people
1744	Act for Regulating Private Madhouses 1744	First regulatory provision for madhouses
1808	County Asylums Act 1808 (amended 1811, 1815, 1819)	Provided for public asylums for mentally ill people
1834	Poor Law Amendment Act 1834	Introduced the new, more centralised and oppressive Poor Law system
1854	Reformatory Schools (Youthful Offenders) Act 1854	Support for a system of schools to reform young offenders (later 'approved schools' – 'list D' schools in Scotland)
1887	Probation of First Offenders Act 1887	Initial, unsuccessful, attempt at developing probation
1891	Lunacy Act 1891	Legal controls on incarceration of mentally ill people
1891	Custody of Children Act 1891	Permitted any person or institution to take on the custody of children, shifting total responsibility from the Poor Law
1908	Old Age Pensions Act 1908	Established insured old age pensions
1909	Royal Commission on the Reform of the Poor Laws	Landmark review of the conflict between socialists and 'social workers'
1911	National Insurance Act 1911	Established insured social security for employees
1925	Widows, Orphans and Old Age Pensions Act 1925	Further social security provision for non-employees; established the contributory principle
1929	Local Government Act 1929	Poor Law responsibilities transferred to local authorities
1930	Mental Treatment Act 1930	Began the move away from legally based incarceration for mentally ill people
1933	Children and Young Persons Act 1933	Consolidation of welfare provision for children; allowed for supervision in cases of neglect, delinquency and truancy; approved schools for offenders developed out of reformatory and industrial schools

Sources: Gilbert, 1970; Parker, 1988; Jones, 2000; Corby et al., 2001

The state begins to supplant the church

Overall trends

Five interrelated factors influenced how social work emerged during the 1800s and 1900s. This section examines these factors more closely.

1. In the 1700s, agriculture, and then the manufacture of goods, were industrialised. This led to underemployment in rural areas, people wandered the country looking for work and began to accumulate in cities as industrial employment emerged.
2. In the industrial towns, a middle class emerged to take local responsibility, and the municipalisation of local government in the 1800s was an impetus for local commitment and activity.
3. The churches' power and religious belief declined and their welfare work was transformed into a more secularised form of caring, through the Reformation, (Sipilä et al., 1997: 28) and, in the 1800s, when evangelical Christianity contested established religion.
4. Charity and women's welfare work became organised and, as social work developed, it became the site for a form of 'caring power' (van Drenth and de Haan, 1999), in which women enhanced their education, participation and freedom from patriarchy (social domination by men)
5. State responsibility for social intervention broadened, because people felt a need to maintain social order in more complex and tumultuous societies.

The following account traces many of these factors in Britain and the USA, where a particular Western form of social work emerged, making links to other countries where they had influence on Anglo-American social work, or developed major differences.

Industrialisation and urbanisation in Britain

Until the late 1800s, Britain, like the rest of Europe, was largely an agricultural country. In the early 1800s, for example, the largest employment groups were agricultural work, domestic service and hand-loom weaving, all interrelated as domestic, family-based occupations (Burnett, 1994: 42). Major changes occurred as agricultural work became mechanised, and hand loom weaving carried out in rural cottages developed as outwork and then declined as, particularly in northern England, work was centralised and mechanised in 'manufactories' (later abbreviated to 'factories'). Moreover, after the French Revolution (1789–99) and the Napoleonic Wars (1799–1815), agricultural work went through a series of crises and depressions. This led to the migration of marginal workers around the country and eventually to cities, providing an unskilled labour force for factories. However, the French Revolution and the Napoleonic Wars stimulated anxieties about social order for middle- and upper-class people (Young and Ashton, 1956: 9). Defences against 'the mob', through both armed force against riots and social amelioration, were politically important in the first third of the 1800s.

Many revolutionary and radical movements grew up among working people, including revolts against the social changes provoked by industrialisation and oppressive employment conditions. Important social movements such as Chartism, which sought political reform to gain the vote for working men, and trade unionism laid the basis for a labour movement, which grew to power in the early 1900s. This created a tradition in Britain for general reform along collective and socialist lines that counterpoints, entwines and disputes with the development of social reforms and welfare in the latter part of the century. Seed (1973) usefully distinguishes the movement for social work as a method and form of practice, with the broader development of public administration of social affairs and the increasing responsibility of the state for social matters. He also identifies a tradition of 'romantic individualism', related to social pacifism, often associated with the Quakers, a nonconformist religious group, which often produced influential social action, such as that by Elizabeth Fry (1780–1845) for welfare in prisons. Her example also had a European influence (Rose, 1980), as later did the work of Josephine Butler.

The greater social responsibility of the state provided a supportive context for welfare provision in which social work as an activity gained a greater influence and impact, and the two came together after the Second World War (1939–45), but these two movements were largely separate at the outset. The Edwardian period, the first decade of the 1900s, saw charitable and individualistic help challenged by socialists for the first time (Jones, 1979; Thane, 1982). The Fabians, a radical middle-class society, argued for universal welfare measures such as social insurance in conflict with supporters of charity, for example on the Royal Commission on the Reform of the Poor Laws (1909). The development of the Labour Party also raised the stakes in social reform, as the Liberal Party sought to maintain their pre-eminence in social reform less allied to working-class movements (see also Chapter 6).

As large towns and cities grew up, through hurried and speculative building of poor quality homes, people moved away from traditional social restraints and tight rural social networks. Concerns about moral responsibility among people in cities and crime, health and other social problems led to increasing interventions and attempts at social restraint. There were campaigns to develop preventive public health, particularly as a result of epidemics of cholera, typhus and typhoid fever in the first half of the 1800s (Jones, 2000: 14 ff.).

While these urban changes were universal, some places suffered more than others. Simey (1992), for example, makes a good case for the particular problems of Liverpool, because its geographical isolation meant that there were no administrative structures based on parishes at the beginning of the 1800s. Also, its rapid growth as a port in the American trade meant that labour was casual and insecure, workers being more affected than elsewhere by economic cycles of growth and depression. Traditional structures were inadequate in many towns, and the 1800s marked a succession of organisational and democratic reforms.

An important forerunner to social work was Thomas Chalmers (1780–1847), who carried out surveys of the poor in Glasgow and created an early form of community social work (Young and Ashton, 1956: Ch. 4). His surveys found, to the concern of others, that many parishioners in a poor area had no involvement in religion or the church. His scheme for relieving poverty in another poor parish of Glasgow, St John's, divided it into districts of about 50 families, each supervised by a deacon, who could call on a small fund subscribed to by members of the parish. The deacon investigated people who came for help, and encouraged family members to work, before using the fund by applying to the Court of Deacons: it was a performance indicator of the deacon's failure to have to do so. The deacon was also to encourage mutual help and support. The meeting of deacons acted as a kind of case conference, and incorrigible cases were stigmatised by being listed on a 'pauper's roll'.

Chalmers's career demonstrates forerunners of social work's emphasis on local organisation, detailed assessment, basing work on the evidence of individual circumstances gained through local visiting and knowledge. There was also the concern, important to the later charity organisation movement, to avoid promiscuous alms-giving.

Municipalisation and the local bureaucratic elite

An important structural reform was the creation of a consistent system of local government, which, particularly in the cities, heralded local loyalties and a commitment to public service development. In Britain, national Poor Law, public health and other administrative structures were brought together in the Local Government Act 1871, and a consistent system of local government was established by the County Councils Act 1888 (Jones, 2000: 61). As similar developments appeared in Europe, a municipalisation movement gathered pace, and innovations were shared internationally (Hietala, 1987).

Germany was important because of its tradition of local administration in which local state responsibility was controlled by the local bourgeois elite, as in Britain. Important associations responsible for major services were led there by these elites. Education was seen as a basis for dealing with social problems, leading to the emergence of social pedagogy, a practice allied to social work that seeks social improvement by informal education (Lorenz, 1994a).

Where did this local tradition come from? German-speaking countries were, by the 1700s, small absolutist states, as rulers struggled to gain power from the local nobility and did so by assuming responsibilities for state provision. Political and social stability in pursuit of economic and commercial success was important. A middle-class elite concerned with developing trade and industry emerged, with the state taking responsibility for the stability that would support them. This elite was excluded from national political life, which was dominated by aristocratic and military power. Instead, the local elite sought influence in the devolved regional and municipal government and on private and voluntary organisations, which became important social care providers. Racial and reproductive policies have also been important. People felt the need to establish national identity in the late 1800s, when in Germany 'nation' was becoming associated with the idea of 'race', which was emerging internationally for the first time. This provided a fertile context for the impact of national socialism (Naziism) in the 1930s.

Paupers increased in the early 1800s, as war and industrialisation affected Germany in the same way as it affected Britain. The poor had traditionally been the responsibility of municipalities. In 1853, the town of Elberfeld developed a system of neighbourhood visiting by volunteers, much like that of Chalmers. The Elberfeld system was the forerunner of developments throughout the world, and particularly influenced Japan. It was designed to deal with the social problems of a rapidly industrialising town in the Rhineland. Poor families were allocated in groups of four to volunteer visitors, who checked on their efforts at self-improvement fortnightly (Rosenhaft, 1994: 26).

In the late 1800s, bourgeois control of local government was ceded to professionals and experts. A corporatist approach to organising welfare developed, in which important welfare organisations and trade unions representing workers were incor porated formally into policy-making and service provision, with the state taking a supportive role. This meant that welfare was undertaken by independent organisations dominated by professionals rather than by state bodies under political control. Women's growing participation in local politics led to municipal activity being seen as a feminine area, local government being the only place where women of property had a vote. Public insurance for workers was pioneered in St Gallen, Switzerland, during the 1890s. Local government sought to incorporate workers' movements into local government through local social commissions and the provision of social insurance, for example under the Ghent (Belgium) system, whereby municipalities provided subsidies to trade unions that paid unemployment benefit to their members.

However, Germany was not alone. Associated with a growing concern for understanding and reconstructing social order, a 'bureaucratic elite' (Donajgrodski, 1977) also emerged in Britain, concerned with managing social issues at a local level and coordinating responses at a national level in a range of areas of social life, such as crime, education, housing, poverty and, especially, public health. The churches lost influence in the more complex and alienating social relations of the cities, so that moral influence declined as a form of social control and the medieval helping structures of the churches became less effective. Trying to reclaim the cities where traditional parish religious structures were less influential than in rural areas, Christian charitable activity associated with evangelical work (that is, Christianity that seeks to develop faith among uncommitted people) increased. Many evangelical charity workers of the early and mid-1800s 'saw themselves as primarily evangelists and ... they would only claim a case as a success if the client "embraced Christ"' (Stroud, 1970).

The USA presented a similar picture. It grew out of colonies set up by Britain and other European countries. As the colonies grew, most states in the USA provided welfare through a combination of church welfare, outdoor relief and the workhouse (Green, 1999). Colonial communities often coped by boarding poor people and new immigrants in local households (Guest, 1989). Attitudes varied: whereas northern states, mainly occupied by Quakers, saw poverty as a slur on their colony, to be eradicated, southerners treated it as a natural part of life, and an opportunity to be charitable (Bernhard, cited by Green, 1999: x). Something of this difference was equally apparent in Europe, as we have seen. The War of American Independence (1775–83), when the USA became independent from Britain, led to a lack of trust in the church, which was associated with the British crown, and responsibility was passed to local public officials. A lot of relief was provided: in 1691, Boston had four full-time officers to deal with the poor (Trattner, 1999: 30).

The early 1800s saw a flowering of organised welfare work, particularly by and for women, in the 'women's benevolence movement' (Treudly, 1940; Melder, 1967; Chambers, 1986). It was focused on widows, orphans and employment, particularly in times where epidemics or economic depression affected the capacity of women to survive. Benevolent work shifted charitable activity towards organisation and an institutional base for helping; welfare homes, both controlling and enabling, were established. An influential early development in 1843 was the New York Association for Improving the Condition of the Poor (AICP), which used local organisation and friendly visitors (Becker, 1961; Lubove, 1965). In the south, black slaves and free blacks did not receive welfare help, even after emancipation from slavery, partly because the southern economy was weaker (Trattner, 1999: 219). However, in the later 1800s they developed mutual help in unemployment and burial insurance (Green, 1999: xi). Mutual aid, for example in child welfare, led to segregated services. Peebles-Wilkins (1996) describes the development of industrial schools for black dependent children in the south.

Most poor relief continued to be the responsibility of local and state governments and so there was wide variation, although the federal government channelled some help through states and voluntary organisations, but federal assistance was granted to the special categories of veterans (former servicemen) and former sailors (Loewenberg, 1992). However, the overall trend of the 1800s was towards charitable help increasingly organised away from the churches rather than state assistance. Germany, with many emigrants to the USA, and the Jewish communities of Eastern Europe and their traditions also had an influence in the USA, particularly through interest in the Elberfeld system. Towards the end of the century, fund-raising became organised through federations of local organisations with shared interests. Eventually, wider federations grew up, creating 'community chests' for fund-raising, the first appearing in Cleveland in 1913 (Lurie, 1959) and being taken up as 'war chests' during the First World War.

Reform, rescue and the beginning of secularisation

Forsythe (1995), referring to Britain, describes the approach to general social reform in the 1800s as 'reveal and appeal', that is, to publicise social failings through publications and meetings and appeal for charitable help and legal reform in response. Much Christian charitable work was focused on families, in particular child rescue and moral welfare work. Thomas Barnardo (1845–1905) started in the mid-1860s as a mission preacher and ragged school teacher, hoping to become a missionary overseas (Wagner, 1979). However, experience of the appalling conditions of London's East End, now devoid of a middle-class elite, led him to provide a refuge for orphaned and abandoned boys. This rapidly blossomed, with his skill in publicity and commercial acumen, into a nationwide organisation, eventually also helping young people to emigrate overseas to the countries of the British Empire (Chapter 7). Edward Rudolf, a London clerk active in the Anglican Church, founded the Church of England Central Home for Waifs and Strays, eventually to become the (Church of England) Children's Society (Stroud, 1971). Thomas Bowman Stevenson, a Methodist preacher, similarly founded the National Children's Homes. All of these organisations survive. There were similar social entrepreneurs in many regions: examples are Bristol's Müller's homes (Tayler, 1860) and Liverpool's Nugent Care Society, eventually to become Catholic Social Services (Bennett, 1949).

Moral welfare work emerged particularly from the work of Josephine Butler (1828–1906), the Salvation Army and 'purity' campaigners (Young and Ashton, 1956: 207–22), although homes for 'fallen women' and 'penitent prostitutes' originated with Robert Dingley's Magdalen Hospital in 1758, named after the prostitute who was an associate of Jesus Christ. Butler's campaigns focused on the Contagious Diseases Acts of 1866–9 (Bell, 1962; Petrie, 1971; McHugh, 1980; Walkowitz, 1980; Boyd, 1982; Bland, 1995; van Drenth and de Haan, 1999; Jordan, 2001). These public health measures required women within a 15-mile radius of garrison towns who were designated by the police as prostitutes to submit to a fortnightly medical examination, often brutally carried out. This became one of the first feminist issues, because of the double standard that lies behind oppressive control of women's behaviour, while ignoring the responsibility of the servicemen. However, male campaigners from evangelical, temperance and socialist movements were also active (Taithe, 1997). The Acts were repealed in 1886.

The campaign gave greater prominence to matters of sexual morality. Other campaigns were also influential. For example, Ellice Hopkins' White Cross League campaigned for moral purity, getting people to sign pledges to treat women respectfully and avoid using bad language. Campaigning led on to rescue work, drawing on the experience of the temperance societies, which tried to reclaim men and women alcoholics, and were important in the foundation of the probation service.

Catherine Booth, the wife of William Booth, the founder in the 1870s of the Salvation Army, and Wilson Carlile's lay mission workers of the Church Army, many of them female, went out onto the streets to find women prepared to give up prostitution, and training and written guidance developed around the skills of doing so (Young and Ashton, 1956: 212–16). Homes and refuges grew up to accommodate the rescued women, and Butler's innovation, in her Liverpool home, was to link rescue with longer term training for independence. Homes were also needed that would accommodate the, often illegitimate, children of the women, and this led to the growth of mother and baby homes, and the later association of the moral welfare movement with the adoption of children, which was becoming its major role by the 1930s.

All these activities, while strongly associated with Christian endeavour, moved welfare work away from the direct management of churches, thus beginning the shift towards the secularisation of welfare.

Social work emerges

Overall trends

Social work emerged in Britain in this social context from three different sources: the Poor Law, charity organisation and the settlement movement. Charity organisation developed 'social casework,' a method that eventually combined with Poor Law welfare to become local government social work. Settlement work drew on movements for social reform to develop more radical social action in a move towards community and groupwork, especially for young people. Each of these sources influenced each other. Working-class mutual help has some connections with these sources, but has had less attention as an element of social work.

The Poor Law

Unlike most of the rest of Europe, England's Elizabethan Poor Laws of the early 1600s had stimulated a reasonably generous, uniform system of poverty relief, administered by unpaid local officials and financed by a specific local property tax, the poor rate (Kidd, 1999: 13). However, the Poor Law Amendment Act

1834 introduced the 'new Poor Law', influenced by a growing acceptance of versions of the economic views of the classic liberal economists of the 1700s (Chapter 6). These ideas promoted individual personal responsibility and self-help. The economist Malthus (1766–1834) added to this a concern for the economic burden of growing population, proposing that relief should be limited because it would otherwise encourage a higher birth rate among working people. This was an important ideological basis for the rigours of the new Poor Law (Winch, 1987). Another factor was the growing costs for a purely local tax, particularly in the south-east, of a relatively generous system of support, epitomised by a system of subsidy to agricultural employers devised in Speenhamland, a village in Hampshire.

The 1834 Act replaced this with a more centralised system of control and finance based on workhouses, managed by the local bureaucratic elite, supervised and regulated by a national board, but only variably implemented. The intention was that poor relief would be 'less eligible', that is, made less attractive than self-help, and the workhouses were a crucial aspect of this approach. Instead of remaining in the community and being paid poor relief, people would have to accept living in the oppressive and controlled conditions of the workhouses, where the sexes were segregated and conditions bleak. Inmates would have to work for the assistance they received. This latter condition was similar to previous schemes involving subsidy of employment. There was resistance to the oppressive character of these regimes, particularly in the north (Cole, 1984) and in Wales, where poverty was more extensive. The system was imposed in Ireland but mitigated in Scotland, where a different tradition and legal system prevailed. Many areas continued to make money payments through 'outdoor relief'. As with all controlling social regimes, workhouses were assailed by various scandals, which also stimulated resistance. For example, at Andover, inmates grinding old bones were found to be so starved that they were eating marrow and scraps of meat from the bones they were working on, illegitimate children and unmarried mothers were marked out, the master inflicted physical and sexual abuse on the inmates, and harsh conditions were rigorously imposed (Anstruther, 1973).

The new Poor Law is important for the development of social work in Britain for four reasons. First, since most unemployed people were orphaned, elderly, disabled or sick, workhouses developed as caring and hospital institutions. Care, particularly for elderly and some disabled people, was humane and of high quality in many areas, particularly compared with the quality of life of many poor people at the time (Parker, 1988: 16). Institutional care became an important basis for social provision, and the reaction against institutional care was an important driver for developments in the mid to late 1900s. Workhouses also pioneered developments replacing large institutions, such as small-scale scattered homes (Birkenhead County Borough, 1974), and 'boarding out' (foster care), through systems that provided apprentices to local employers (Kidd, 1999: 55–8).

Another important factor was that workhouses were grouped into 'unions', which were large enough to employ people, to provide a large workforce with a 'social control through caring' role. These employees became the basis of a paid social work profession. At the end of the Poor Law in 1948 they transferred into local government social work agencies and their role formed elements of the British social work approach. As municipalisation developed, the local bureaucratic elite managing workhouses participated in local government, and the Poor Law was merged with local government in 1930 as a result of the Local Government Act 1929, forming the basis for a local government social work service. Growing criticism of the Poor Law eventually led to a demand for a new approach to practice in dealing with the poor. The new practice created a new system of social provision through social reform and new ways of helping people personally influenced by developments in charitable work. Finally, movements for social reform, such as the Royal Commission on the Poor Law (1909), focused on improving or displacing this comprehensive system of welfare, rather than the development of individualised systems of care such as those promoted by early social workers associated with charity organisation.

Insurance and working-class mutual help

Important alternative forms of welfare in the 1800s originated from mutual help movements such as friendly societies, building societies and cooperative movements. These all concerned groups of working-class people pooling resources through subscriptions, to make payments in times of sickness and unemployment, gain control of their own housing and the distribution of food and household goods. The development of the friendly societies, their stabilisation and final public acceptance, with registration under the Friendly Societies Act 1875, made them an important resource for working men in difficulties (Gosden, 1961). These developments became associated with other working-class movements, particularly the trade union movement, and its political outgrowth, first in influencing the social policies of the Liberal Party and then in the formation of the Labour Party, which still incorporates Co-operative Party MPs. Mutual help movements became associated with working-class endeavours and the development of social insurance, and in the early 1900s with the Liberal Party social reforms, which brought old age pensions and unemployment insurance into being. Thus, mutual help became allied to efforts at social reform with broad application for the benefit of working people, rather than systems of individualised personal help.

Germany was again influential. Bismarck, the first chancellor of the united German state, introduced legislation providing insurance for health (1883), accidents (1884) and invalidity and old age (1889), mainly to combat potential unrest among industrial workers (Otte, 1997). Interest in the German social insurance system grew in the UK after the 1890s, when the British concern was mainly with poverty in old age. The German insurance system was only incorporated in the Liberal reform process in Britain in the 1906–08 period (Hennock, 1987).

Charity and social work

Concern about charity grew in the 1800s, leading to a method that became social work emerging within 'scientific charity'. During the 1800s, charitable responses to suffering in the great cities proliferated throughout the world, and this eventually led to the charity organisation movement. 'Organisers' were concerned that too much alms-giving for short-term relief created dependence among working-class families, a continuation of medieval concerns, mentioned above, but reinforced by the ideas of the liberal economists (Chapter 6). The moral basis for the charity organisation movement was thus similar to that of the Poor Law: that welfare should not inhibit work and self-help. There was a practical basis for organising, since the chaotic plethora of private charities in London often did not investigate need (Woodroofe, 1962: 26). However, the 'organisers' are a classic example of 'blaming the victim' in claiming that the apparatus of charity caused the 'pauperisation' of the poor, that is, forcing them to make a career of being poor. This debate was also similar to that in Catholic medieval Europe: does charity dignify the giver, or should it contribute to the moral and social improvement of the receiver?

Beatrice Webb (1926: 209), a Fabian, comments: 'To the unsophisticated Christian of the 1800s, almsgiving was essentially a religious exercise, a manifestation of his love of God.' The COS subverted this view. Webb (1926: 208–9) quotes an incident from Henrietta Barnett's life of her husband, the founder of the settlement movement (below) as typical of the COS approach:

> One old gentleman [on a committee] ... slipped a sixpence ... into a poor woman's hand, as Miss [Octavia] Hill was pointing out to her the reasons why we could not give her money, and offering her the soundest advice. The old gentleman was afterwards called to account ... and melted into tears for his own delinquency.

The London Charity Organisation Society (COS) was established as the Society for the Organisation of Charitable Relief and Repressing Mendicity (mendicity means idleness, *not* mendacity, which means deviousness) in March 1870 with the aim of providing principles to guide charitable giving and co-ordinating charitable organisations (Woodroofe, 1962). District organisations were established, bringing together local charities. The methods used were to investigate and assess whether applicants for assistance were deserving of help: being deserving, their moral stature would be enhanced, and they would not be demoralised by not being careful with their money and dependent upon others. Loch (1883: 11), the influential COS secretary, argued that:

> inquiry throws into prominence the imperative necessity for ... all the finer elements of charity – personal influence, a long-suffering patience, a quick sympathy, the setting aside of social prejudice and patronage for charity's sake. It shows that material help, if these things are lacking, is but as husks, flung before the poor as if they were without common humanity.

Ideas such as these also developed in the housing movement, where attempts were being made to provide better housing for working-class people and improve housing conditions. A method of 'friendly visiting' evolved from the work of Octavia Hill in the London housing movement, where female visitors would assist women in organising and planning their family life and budgets more effectively. Both assessment and help revolved around the idea of 'character' (Fido, 1977), embodied in applicants' past histories, kept in careful records (Chapter 9). This was the beginning of 'assessment' as a bedrock of social work practice.

The COS was not an alternative to the Poor Law, but rather the other side of the coin. COS workers saw the Poor Law as appropriate for the undeserving poor, who did not make enough effort towards self-dependence, and their own work as complementary to it. Moreover, in each locality they were largely run by the same people: the local bureaucratic elite (Parry and Parry, 1979: 23). Similar organisations developed throughout the country. Miller (1988) provides an account of the ideals represented in the Liverpool Central Relief Society. As this secular charity grew up, it began to oppose the Christian idea of charity as dignifying the giver, seeing it as incontinent alms-giving. The Liverpool CRS was at odds with the Christian churches and the London COS opposed Barnardo (Wagner, 1979).

These ideas rapidly spread to America and, in the absence of the extensive state provision of the British Poor Law, strongly influenced the development of social work there. In turn, because the professional and academic strength of the American social work profession was a dominant force internationally until the 1950s, conceptions of Western social work were strongly influenced by this tradition, rather than the official public services of Britain and European countries. The American Civil War (1861–5) created poverty and dislocation, temporarily reversing the American emphasis on charitable giving, and both Confederate and Federal governments provided considerable direct relief. Much of this assistance in the south was characterised by racial segregation, blacks being excluded (Green, 1999). After the war, public and charitable assistance and institutions continued to develop, particularly with industrialisation and urbanisation, becoming a fertile ground for the development of charity organisation movements, as in England. Eventually, this led to movements for training and, in the early 1900s, the development of a career for women in social work. Between 1890 and 1910 the number of American social workers grew from 1,000 to 30,000, of whom 80 per cent were women (Abrams, 2000). Involvement in social work became an acceptable substitute for domestic life for middle-class women. Women's colleges established employment bureaux, and one of these, the National Social Worker's Exchange, developed into the American Association of Social Workers, the first comprehensive professional association (DuBois and Miley, 1999). Here, it is possible to see how the creation of a paid job led directly to professional organisation.

Another important organisational forerunner of British social work, in the first decade of the 1900s, were the guilds of help, inaugurated in Bradford in 1904 following some of the principles of the German Elberfeld system (Lewis, 1995; Cushlow, 1997; Laybourn, 1997). These sought to build on a more inclusive form of help, emphasising civic responsibility, connected to and supported by municipal endeavour to deal with the problems of unemployment and poverty in particular localities, and covered sixty or more local and Poor Law authority areas across the country, unlike the London-based COS and its counterparts in major cities. They focused on issues such as high infant mortality and tuberculosis. However, although more committed to community endeavour, they mainly used middle-class female volunteers.

Settlements

Settlements were founded as a movement for working-class education and the maintenance of moral Christian social behaviour in poor neighbourhoods in the new cities. The first settlement was Toynbee Hall, founded by Canon Samuel Barnett in 1884 in the East End of London, a poor dockland area. The idea was that public school (that is, fee-charging, elite schools) and university students would live in houses in poor areas and use their education and moral example to assist in social development. Early activities included personal development education through activities such as children's country and seaside holidays, art exhibitions, literary and dramatic societies and youth clubs (Knapp, [1895]1985; Matthews and Kemmis, 2001). Relief of poverty and debate and campaigning on social policy also emerged as part of the education activities.

As with the charity organisation movement, the settlement idea was rapidly imported by the USA, settlements being founded in New York in 1886 and 1889, and Boston in 1891 and 1892. In Chicago, the famous Hull House was also formed in 1889, developing an association with the University of Chicago that was important in the academic development of social work. Jane Addams (1860–1935), one of Hull House's leaders, was an important influence on the nature of social work. While the Christian motivation and concern about the dismal social life of big city slums in the newly industrialising eastern and mid-western cities were the same as in Britain, American cities were also melting pots for migrants from many European countries (Addams, [1910]1999; Brown, 1999; Carson, 2001). Settlements were among the first institutions in the USA to value and involve immigrants and racial minorities in social life, recognising some of the social issues raised by migration for the first time (White, 1959). However, they could also be sources of social control, through the impact of local politics on very local organisations needing to raise money, which imposed an emphasis on social conformity (Karger, 1987). An important role was moral guardianship by reforming 'wayward girls' in the big city (Abrams, 2000).

From social casework to social work

The crucial innovation that created social work from all these movements was the development of social casework as a method. The absence of consistent state responsibility for poverty in the USA gave a stronger influence to the charity organisation movement. Therefore, it was in the USA that, in the late 1890s and early 1900s, social casework developed from friendly visiting by charity organisation workers to undertake a thorough assessment of need for charitable help and improve the morality of poor people of the immigrant slums of the USA. It was just as relevant to the working-class slums of Britain. In particular, the influence of psychology and psychoanalysis in the USA from the 1920s emphasised the psychological origins of family problems that seemed to require the individualised help of social casework. The method of detailed home assessment and personal influence by a professional allied to practical help became social casework with the addition of psychological techniques for influencing behaviour.

The focus of the British guilds of help on infant mortality and tuberculosis emphasises the importance of responding to health problems in the origins of social work. Health-related, or medical, social work (Willmott, 1996) developed from the appointment in 1895 of Mary Stewart, a COS worker, as almoner to the Royal Free Hospital in London, with the aim of reducing the abuse of charitable funding in the overcrowding of the outpatients' department. She and other early appointments were regarded with suspicion and resentment by medical and nursing staff. An aftercare service for tuberculous patients was established at St Thomas's Hospital, London in 1909, and its success was such that this became a statutory service in 1919. Subsequently, as local authorities took over responsibility for the Poor Law, they extended the use of almoners to municipal hospitals, first in London and then elsewhere. This is another instance where municipal power spread the impact of social work.

In the USA, hospital and medical social work also emerged from the COS and settlement movements. Health issues concerned community workers in the settlement movement, and there were campaigns on the diseases of poverty, particularly tuberculosis. Hull House, followed by others, opened a free medical dispensary. Dr Richard Cabot introduced the first social worker in an American outpatient clinic in Massachusetts in 1903, and the first experimental social work department in 1905 (Dhooper, 1997: 132, 172). Social work was officially recognised there in 1914. Social workers were used as 'friendly visitors' and for social investigations (Auslander, 2001). Within a decade, more than 100 hospitals had social work departments. The American Association of Hospital Social Workers formed in 1918, pursuing functions similar to the British organisations.

The guilds were also a sign, among many others, of growing concern from the 1890s onwards about the British system for dealing with poverty. As ideas of unemployment emerged (Chapter 5), and socialist thinking (Chapter 6) became more politically influential and drew attention to the inadequacies of existing provision (Brown, 1971), state responsibility for poverty and unemployment became a logical outcome and the Poor Law was increasingly seen as an inadequate expression of it. The period of 1900–14, therefore, became one of substantial social reform, particularly during the Liberal administrations of 1905–14. Following the German example, insurance against unemployment and old age pensions were introduced. A Royal Commission on the Reform of the Poor Law (1909) became the focus of a conflict between COS views on the importance of charity organisation, represented by Octavia Hill, and the Fabian priority for more collective social provision, represented by Sidney and Beatrice Webb.

The USA also saw developments in the range of welfare institutions between 1880 and 1920 during the 'progressive era', as part of movements for social reform associated with President Theodore Roosevelt. A loose alliance of intellectuals, professionals, labour unions and small businesspeople worked against excessive profits in big business and public corruption, which had begun to raise concern as industrialisation increased. Their beliefs included assumptions that there would be an orderly progression of humanity (Lasch, 1997). Progressive policies focused on welfare capitalism, whereby economic progress would lead to social developments that would meet the needs of the poor, even though they were not to blame for their condition (Guy, 1995). The economist Simon Patten (1852–1922) is said to have coined the term 'social work' or influenced it through his economic theory (Mitchell, 1934). Both the charity organisation movement and settlements had a major influence on the development of American social work during the early 1900s, but the concern to professionalise led to considerable developments in theory and practice techniques, particularly calling on psychology and psychoanalysis (Borenzweig, 1971; Chapter 10). After the First World War (1914–18), progressive era reforms declined, and settlements were criticised as Communist hotbeds in scares about Bolshevism in the 1920s as other countries came to terms with the Communist regime established in Russia from 1917. What Andrews (1992) describes as 'second generation' settlements (between the 1930s and 50s) often became local sites of social welfare provision, moving towards casework and especially groupwork with young offenders and neighbourhood grassroots organisations (Coyle, 1961).

Thus, the more radical political impact of settlement work, which gave rise to a generation of Labour politicians in Britain, was less significant in the USA, although it was always present (Chambers, 1963). Jane Addams was, thus, an exceptional figure, the only social worker to receive a Nobel prize for her peace campaigning in the 1920s. She saw her pacifism as a logical extension of her community practice (Farrell, 1967). In British settlements, by contrast, important social thinkers, reformers and politicians had early formative experiences. Attlee (later Labour prime minister), Beveridge (the writer of the report that influenced the founding of the welfare state in the UK) and Tawney (an important social democratic theorist) all worked at Toynbee Hall (Briggs and MacCartney, 1986; Meacham, 1987). Before the First World War, 46 settlements were formed, 25 for women, 11 for men and 10 mixed. Many had a Christian foundation, and were similar to Christian missions. By 1922, more than 60 were in existence. Many cities developed settlements for a variety of reasons, and they came into and out of being during the 1900s. For example, a university settlement in Cardiff was a response to professorial enthusiasm leading to a Cardiff branch of a Welsh University Association for the furtherance of social work in 1902. This founded a settlement in the deprived area of Splott in 1904, which lasted until 1924 (Walker and Jones, 1984).

The British approach to probation (Bochel, 1976) developed from the work of police court missionaries employed by the Church of England Temperance Society from 1875 onwards in London, among the groups that grew up to combat widespread heavy drinking. Magistrates would release offenders to their informal supervision. An Act of 1887, building on American experience to allow probation for first offenders, failed because no formal supervision was provided; this was remedied in the reforming Liberal administration by an Act in 1907. The service was set up locally, with magistrates in control, but after the First World War greater central direction developed. The Temperance Society and the remains of Anglican Church involvement disappeared during the 1920s and 30s, as a Home Office grant was provided for local services. This was a period of growth and formalisation of responsibilities, with probation becoming less of a part-time occupation, and officers providing reports for courts, undertaking matrimonial conciliation and aftercare work with young offenders from approved schools. The Children and Young Persons Act 1933 reinforced developments, consolidating previous legislation. It gave local authorities (mainly education departments through their school attendance officers) and the probation service dual responsibilities for young offenders. The

Act cemented a move from a rescue model of practice towards a greater emphasis on treatment, which emerged from the development of ideas about delinquency and child guidance.

The early 1900s also saw important developments in child welfare in the USA (Trattner, 1999: Ch. 10). A campaign developed from a White House conference on dependent children in 1909, leading to the establishment in 1912 of a Children's Bureau, headed first by Julia Lathrop, a leading charity worker. The Bureau identified a high infant and maternal mortality rate and pressed for services to combat this. The Sheppard–Towner Bill, introduced by Jeanette Rankin, the first woman member of Congress, in 1918, was finally passed as the Infancy and Maternity Act 1921 against the vociferous opposition of the medical profession, concerned about the introduction of 'state medicine'. Following this success, child welfare became an important part of federal services until 1929, when the Congress removed its funds, due to economic recession, medical and political opposition and weakened female support. It continued, with varying influence, and was important as a source of women's leadership and influence within government (Parker, 1994). However, Machtinger (1999) argues that its support for casework and the criteria for maternal fitness limited it in achieving broad social security provision for families. It also sought unsuccessfully to shift the juvenile court system towards a welfare role, creating instead a separate child welfare system focused on treatment, an early example of clashes between welfare and criminal justice systems (Rosenthal, 1986). As in Britain and France (Chapter 5), a system of indentured labour for poor youths developed into fostering (Hacsi, 1996).

The 1909 conference also led to campaigns for relief for children at home, rather than them being placed in institutions. This was sometimes opposed by grant-giving charities, but, over the next two decades, most states enacted some provision for widows' pensions and assistance to families with dependent children.

British education welfare (known internationally as 'school social work') was another sign of a move from child rescue to support of children's development. It emerged from the enforcement of school attendance by attendance officers or 'the truancy man' after elementary schooling became compulsory in the 1870s. Usually employed by the education departments of local authorities, and in London supported by a famous service of volunteer helpers, the School Care Committees, these formed a separate group of welfare workers. As other local education services for children with problems grew up, a stronger welfare element emerged from the enforcement role (Blyth and Cooper, 2002).

An early concern for child delinquency was one factor leading to psychiatric social work in Britain. The British Child Study Association, from 1893, had encouraged teachers to study individual children, rather than focus on class teaching, and psychological work on childhood grew up in local government education authorities. There were eugenic concerns to improve the health and social abilities of the population 'stock' (Chapter 5), and in the American mental hygiene movement (Chapter 9). Psychiatric social work came from a history in the later 1800s of aftercare provision for people discharged from asylums, emerging in the state hospitals of Boston and New York. By the end of the war in 1918, it was already established widely in major cities in the east and mid-west. Training started at Smith College, an elite women's college in Boston, which developed a six-month course for psychiatric aides to the US army medical service in 1919 (Grinker et al., 1961). The American Association of Psychiatric Social Workers was set up in 1920. A focus on mental hygiene and concern for responding to juvenile crime led to child guidance clinics becoming a movement in the 1920s (French, 1940).

Similar concerns about crime and health in Britain influ enced a range of mental health and crime charities. English social workers went to the USA for training; the mental health course at the LSE started in 1929. Its graduates formed the Association of Psychiatric Social Workers in 1930, which became influential in the development of social work in Britain. The Mental Treatment Act 1930 began to shift mental health legislation away from a legalistic emphasis on compulsion and restraint, providing extra impetus (Timms, 1964).

Japan: Western influences on traditional welfare cultures

Japan's welfare originated, as we have seen, from a different cultural background of an authoritarian state and Buddhist religious philosophy. Nevertheless, there were interactions with

Western developments, as contact with the West was extended during the 1800s. While the inflexible administration of the Tokugawa period broke down in the mid-1800s, the Confucian moral teaching on the responsibility of family and local community for the relief of distress was maintained (Goodman, 1998). As capitalism and industrialisation developed during the early 1900s, this meant that much provision of welfare and general social support for employees and their families in the locality devolved onto individual companies. Companies still provide extensive health and social services today.

State responses, for example in the Poor Relief Ordinance 1874 which remained in force until 1929 (Takahashi, 1997), were mainly, as in Bismarckian Germany, concerned with managing social unrest. In Japan state policies were affected by Malthusian Poor Law views about the need to limit benefits, and relied mainly on moral persuasion and compassion rather than rights. Social policy theory developed the idea that social provision was a way of mitigating social tension. Building up the army and navy was also important, so retirement and disability allowances were reserved for or gave priority to the forces, as in the USA of the 1800s and some modern countries, for example Communist China. Extensive modernisation during the late 1800s, based mainly on German, British and American models, was pursued explicitly to stave off the colonisation by European powers that China had experienced. This led to private, religious-based charities, mainly providing residential care for orphans, handicapped and elderly people, being grafted onto indigenous family and community systems. The examples developed by Christian missionaries were copied by Buddhist organisations. A society for social policy influenced by Fabian policies developed around the turn of the century. Social work was seen as being for the relief of hardship, while social policy was concerned with workers' protection from the impact of industrialisation. A central relief charity was established in Tokyo in 1908, but unlike the London and American COSs was under the control of the Ministry of the Interior. Eventually, in 1937, it merged with the Health Ministry to form a Ministry of Health and Welfare.

These trends were criticised, however, and Japanese thinkers and administrators sought indigenous models of provision. The civil servant Ogawa Shigejiro argued the importance of the local community and the family, especially the mother handling the family budget (Tamai, 2000). Moving in 1913 to Osaka, which was struggling with a large influx of migrant workers from Korea and the countryside, he set up a study group on social work. From the idea of Chinese household mutual support, the five-family-unit system, the German Elberfeld system and British COS models, they developed a locally based volunteer visiting scheme, the *hōmeniin* (*hōmeni:* a city area designated as poor; *iin:* supervisor). The Elberfeld system had more influence than the COS, since it used male, rather than female, workers. However, subsidised by the public purse and donations, the volunteer could pay outdoor relief and, pursuing a policy that it was better for the poor to be independent of the state, mainly advised families on the management of their budget, as in the COS system. The *hōmeniin* system was reinforced by 'rice riots' in 1918, and became a widespread practice, incorporating Western ideas about social work. Relief developed to include child welfare and casework, there was talk about 'social solidarity' from French writings and debates about its relationship with social reform took place, only to disappear in 1929 as more repressive policies were introduced (Takahashi, 1997). At the same time, social control functions were taken over by local neighbourhood associations. These two systems became tightly interwoven as part of securing civil participation in the war effort during the 1940s. Several welfare laws passed during the 1930s were an explicit preparation for war, particularly promoting motherhood: 'A mother who does not give birth to more than five children does not fulfil her duty' was a slogan of the time (Takahashi, 1997: 45). The system was reformed after the American occupation of 1945, because of its association with the militarist administration.

Groupwork and community work

Groupwork and community work emerged from mainly Christian social responses to urbanisation in Europe. The initial concern, as with casework, was the moral reform and protection of the new urban working class, especially children and women. Migration from rural to urban areas led to populations cut off from family and village sources of leisure, protection and family life. Organisations such as the YMCA and YWCA (Young Men's and Young Women's Christian Associations) in Britain and the

USA provided cheap accommodation, food and leisure facilities for migrants and others (Reid, 1981; Andrews, 2001).

Important sources of community work include:

- The settlement movement
- The movement for informal and working-class education, which in Germany and Nordic countries became associated with social pedagogy
- Christian and non-denominational youth work, such as the boys and girls brigades and scout and guide movement
- Work with children in ragged schools and Sunday schools, which were the first opportunities for education in many industrial cities
- Radical and socialist political action, encouraging working-class people to meet in groups for education, especially men through cooperative and trade union movements, and women in a range of community associations
- Trade unionism
- Social development in developing countries.

Many of these developments were linked, for example education, political action and youth work were important aspects of settlements. Similarly, education and socialist political action are linked with trade unionism. As with casework, a practice method emerged during the 1920s and 30s in the USA (Reid, 1981: Ch. 4). Ideas in radical education, which sought to replace rote learning with helping children learn how to solve problems, led to a concern for how to structure and plan groups. Later work focused on how to provide leadership. Groupwork also developed in working with mentally ill people and delinquent children in the 1930s, as part of movements to provide treatment rather than just incarceration. Coordination of voluntary effort in Britain came out of the Royal Commission on the Poor Laws, which encouraged the development of alternatives to Poor Law provision; what are now councils for voluntary service began to form during the period 1909–14. Community organisation emerged as a concept during the First World War in the USA as part of the process of resettling servicemen returning from the war, using community chests (originally 'war chests'), a local organisation for collecting donations. As the Great Depression of the 1930s in Britain and the New Deal in the USA had to deal with economic dislocation, poverty and unemployment, general welfare provision began to shift to public agencies. Community development work began to form a separate stream of activity focused on community organisations (Kramer and Specht, 1969).

The Depression in the 1930s

The whole world was affected by the economic Depression in the late 1920s and early 1930s, starting in the USA. State provision for unemployment and social security continued to be residual and permissive in the USA, until the Depression led to the election of Franklin Delano Roosevelt's Democratic government. This implemented a programme of public employment to combat severe poverty, the New Deal, through the Federal Emergency Relief Act 1933 (FERA), and with Aid to Families with Dependent Children (AFDC) incorporated in the federal Social Security Act 1935. Social workers, pre-eminently Harry Hopkins (1890–1946) and Frances Perkins (1880–1965 – the first woman member of a president's cabinet) – were influential in policy and practice (DuBois and Miley, 1999: 39–40). Many social workers were heavily involved in these initiatives, particularly in rural areas, and they radicalised social work for a period. In the UK, the Depression revealed the inadequacies and oppression of the Poor Law in meeting social security needs, and laid the basis of political support for the development of the welfare state reforms in the 1940s. However, although there were many local and charitable responses to the extremes of poverty experienced during the Depression, social work as a method was not well-enough established to seek to make a contribution. Many people most concerned with the experience of the working class during the Depression were, as in the USA, radicalised and became more committed to more general social responses to poverty, rather than the individualised help of social work. It was not by any means clear, therefore, that social work was going to be the way forward.

Conclusion

This chapter examined developments leading to social work during the period before the institutionalisation of welfare states in Western countries after the Second World War. Welfare services are present in all societies of any complexity, and they have taken the characteristics required by the needs and social expectations of the time and place. The early historics of social work in the UK reflect the development of an important organisational structure for state social work in the latter part of the 1900s through the growth of the Poor Law, its paid welfare workforce and the ideological structure of institutional and financial control, responding to liberal economic philosophies. This inheritance often shows through in ideological debate and organisational responses to social problems in the UK. However, as we have seen, it is but another example of similar debates and responses that affected British and European social welfare provision previously.

An activity that came to be social work developed in Western countries at the time of industrialisation and urbanisation as the churches lost influence and non-church Christian organisations began to give way to the state. Chalmers, the COS, the evangelical child rescuers, moral welfare and guilds of help are all examples of the development of methods, which grew into social work practice. Localised organisation, provision of residential care to enable rescue and a practice of home visiting to give advice and provide personal support in difficult times for poor families are the crucial elements. The importance of local middle-class bureaucratic elites to Poor Law, municipal and charitable organisation, together with the use of 'caring power' to enhance the social and economic position of women through involvement in welfare work, brought these elements together to form a new profession. The importance of these aspects of the local state provide a contrast with the situation in the USA, where government was less actively involved in welfare. There, the local elite became involved in charitable works.

The settlement movement, the charity organisation movement, working-class mutual aid and guilds of help were all secular organisations that contributed directly, in a ferment of demand for social progress, to the creation of social work. The crucial element that defined social work from other forms of welfare was its developing method and its policy and theoretical ambitions and distinctiveness. This distinguished it both from similar activities in the past and other related activities that grew alongside it.

The method devised in Western industrialising nations interacted with the traditions and cultures of other parts of the world, making connections with modes of welfare elsewhere, and being incorporated into and adapted for the values and aims of those societies, as in Japan. It became something different, responding to the different needs and social expectations of those countries. Other activities akin to social work, like social pedagogy, began their own development and began to establish their own different role and theoretical position.

Before social work, charity had been personal and occasional, mainly provided by benevolence, a volunteer activity, a matter of alms for the poor and the sick or *noblesse oblige* (a responsibility of being rich). As it became a paid occupation, identifying the distinctiveness and validity of the work became important, endowing it with theory and the motivation for the development of a professional group. Where charity had been inadequate or its purposes controversial, or where social order had been at risk, responsibilities for welfare had been taken up by the local or nation state, as it always had been. With industrialisation and urbanisation, maintaining social order became more complex and the needs and possibilities for welfare action became more extensive as social knowledge and understanding developed. The occasional acceptance of responsibility by the state became a consistent and recognised role. Consequently, the paid occupation had opportunities to seize and knowledge to encompass and develop. Moreover, it provided an acknowledged role for middle-class women, always influential in social caring, but now to create profession to enable them to gain employment as part of a move towards using 'caring power' to gain political and social influence.

There had been some progress, but for the paid occupation of social work to become a secure profession, it needed to build on this platform of possibilities. The opportunity arose after the Second World War created the need for widespread social reconstruction, and the international economic organisation to make that reconstruction possible. A new focus on social solidarity and social policy created the context in which the method and values of social work, as with other social interventions, could gain an institutionalised position in Britain and many other societies. This phase of social work is the focus of the next chapter.

CHAPTER 3

Social Work and Welfare States: 1945–1970s

Is the development of social work and the welfare state intertwined? Between 1945 and the 1970s, it was a common assumption that societies had made progress so that the organised provision for people's personal welfare was part of the role of the state and the most economically advanced states were welfare states, providing universal welfare for citizens. During this period, in many Western countries, it looked as though social work was becoming an accepted part of such universal welfare provision, in the same way as health care, housing and social security.

These social developments took place within a new international economic framework. In the industrialised world, exchange rates and economic development were managed by institutions such as the World Bank and the International Monetary Fund (IMF) set up by the 1944 Bretton Woods agreement. In effect, the USA agreed to support the re-establishment of the war-devastated economies of Western Europe. In return, it would gain industrial and commercial influence and all countries would benefit from the consequent economic stability and growth. The apparent success of welfare states, therefore, depended on maintaining this policy of managed economic growth in developed economies.

Four types of economy formed different contexts for the development of social work: the rich Western states, the Communist regimes of the 'second world', the developing economies of the 'third world' and rapidly developing economies typified by the 'tiger' economies of the Far East. Social work developed differently in each, but, as in the period up to 1945, there were mutual interactions and influences. Some of these influences were largely colonial and postcolonial. As the European empires broke up, their welfare traditions retained influence. Equally colonial, but in a different way, the USA gained influence for its developing social work method, particularly through the economic and social development activities of the United Nations (UN), strongly funded and influenced by the USA.

But is social work essential to the welfare state? If they are to be comprehensive and universal, is social work a crucial aspect of that comprehensiveness, or would a truly comprehensive welfare state find personal help unnecessary? The nature of welfare states is contested, and a critical understanding of both welfare states and the role of social work within them is an important aspect of understanding social work. Particularly since Esping-Andersen's (1990) work on welfare regimes, we must ask what kind of welfare state we are discussing.

Social work in Western welfare states

Welfare states developed in European countries, and elsewhere, after 1945 partly as a response to the experience of war (Digby, 1989: Ch. 2). Populations had been mobilised in mass participation, at least partly in hopes of better times, reflected, for example, in the public support in Britain for the Beveridge Report (1942). Many countries had been occupied, devastated by fighting and destabilised by having their political institutions displaced. Consequently, welfare provision was necessary as part of restructuring, redevelopment and stabilisation. Social work in Western welfare states and societies reflects four traditions:

- Social work in Britain, America and other English-speaking countries is part of state provision that is more strongly contested than in European countries
- The Nordic or Scandinavian countries are important examples of universal public welfare states
- Germany's different 'corporatist' tradition (see Chapter 2) reflects the integration of decentralised social welfare supported by the state

■ Southern European states are typical of states often dominated by the Catholic Church and conservative political traditions, with less well-developed provision.

However, there are differences in time frame and priority. For example, among Nordic countries, Finland's welfare state developed later than those in Denmark, Norway and Sweden. Also, some Western European countries are outside these groups. An example is Ireland, where the UK welfare state was seen especially by the Catholic Church as a socialist attack on the role of the family (Ferguson and Powell, 2002).

In Britain, the period of the post-war Labour governments (1945–51) led by Attlee, the former social work lecturer and writer, is when the British welfare state was formed and social work was incorporated into it, and grew from a not very significant role into an established position. Substantial social legislation was partly based on the ideas of the wartime Beveridge Report (1942) that five social evils should be vanquished: sloth (unemployment), ignorance (education), sickness, squalor (housing) and want (poverty). However, Beveridge was primarily concerned with social security provision, and pre-existing Labour policies, including more socialist ideas for a national health service, also influenced developments (Laybourn, 1995: 209–36). Titmuss (1951: 508) argued that the experience of war created a social consensus that accepted more radical, universal policies than previously. Others have suggested that the reforms of this period built upon and extended previous policy trends (Laybourn, 1995: 209–10). None of Beveridge's evils was specifically concerned with welfare, and the focus of developments was in collective social provision, such as social security, health care and universal education. Moreover, these came to be seen as a comprehensive system of social provision, a welfare state. There is debate about what a welfare state comprises, but important elements of the Beveridge vision were:

■ Comprehensiveness, 'from the cradle to the grave'
■ Universality, available to all without charge
■ Full male employment policies as an underlying base, with an assumption that women would, post-war, have a mainly domestic role.

Comprehensiveness almost excludes the idea of social work, and this is what led eventually to questioning of its role from the 1980s onwards. Cradle to grave provision of education, health, housing and social security might mean that interpersonal help is unnecessary. However, these changes also led to developments in social work services, as part of the general movement to improve welfare, which, in taking up the social casework method, sought to demonstrate the value of interpersonal help as part of a universal welfare state. The arguments for this include a social democratic view, espoused by writers such as Wootton (1958), that people need help to find their way around the complexities of a welfare state, to a more liberal view that individuals often need help with personal difficulties, whatever general provision is available.

One reason for the development of social work alongside other welfare provision was the formation of the National Health Service (NHS), by the National Health Service Act 1946, implemented in 1948, and the new social security system, by the National Assistance Act 1948. These developments grew out of the winding up of the Poor Law, by this time part of local authority services. The rump of other Poor Law welfare services had also, therefore, to be reorganised. This was achieved through Part 3 of the National Assistance Act 1948, by local authorities providing accommodation for people in need. During the Second World War, the poor level of provision for elders in the UK and inconsistencies caused by localised responsibilities was revealed by evacuation, in the same way as it had been for children (Means and Smith, 1998). A number of voluntary organisations grew up to support the civilian population, and in particular to assist women to work for the war effort. Elderly dependents thus had to be cared for, and home helps and the meals on wheels service were developed through the Women's (later Women's Royal) Voluntary Service (WVS, now WRVS), which, in an attempt to survive as an organisation, continued them after the war. Concern about the cost of pensions in the UK led to attempts to reduce the level of provision for elders, and welfare provision for home care and mobile meals remained in the voluntary sector.

Converted Poor Law accommodation was the main source of old people's homes and provision for homeless families. Associated with this, a welfare service was established in each local authority. This was sometimes part of the local authority public health department and sometimes managed separately. Homeless single people were dealt with by the National Assistance Board, which had responsibility for discretionary social security, through reception centres. In this division, within the same Act, between local authority welfare and national social security provision, the social work tradition from the Poor Law was incorporated into local authority welfare and separated from income maintenance.

Another important change for the development of social work in the UK came out of separate but related developments. Late in the wartime period, there was a child care scandal in which the O'Neill children were found to have been ill-treated in foster care. The Monckton Report (1946) found that coordination and communication were poor and the supervision of children inadequate and by untrained people. The Curtis Report (1946) on the general position of services for children found no consistent pattern of child care provision, no authority had overall responsibility for children with social needs and Poor Law authorities, education and local health services all played a part. Allied with a campaign led by Lady Allen of Hurtwood, the scandal led to pressure for a coherent child care service, whose focus would be on foster care, rather than, as in the Poor Law and education services, on institutional provision. After a debate about professional control in which both local education and health services sought dominance, a separate children's service was established in each local authority by the Children Act 1948.

These moves, arising from the formation of the broader welfare state, permitted the creation of two welfare agencies within local government. They incorporated the caring traditions of the Poor Law, cutting off the authoritarian, stigmatising history of 'less eligibility' and the medical dominance found in the Poor Law hospitals. These welfare services were separate from the administrative requirements of income maintenance, so that they were able to focus on social work responsibilities, as in Germany since social insurance schemes had been established there. In this way, the organisational context was established that enabled the incorporation of the social work method and values from the voluntary sector and from developments in the USA into local authority provision as part of welfare state social services.

The establishment of a reasonably comprehensive welfare state weakened the voluntary sector. A major aspect of charitable endeavour had been the voluntary sector hospitals. These now disappeared as charities. Major charities such as Dr Barnardo's, the Royal National Institutes for the Blind and the Deaf, the (Church of England) Children's Society and the (Methodist) National Children's Homes all found it difficult to identify a role, when the public focus was on comprehensive and developing public services. The London Charity Organisation Society (COS), able to claim an important influence on the development of social work practice, found a new and more limited regional role as the Family Welfare Association. Other similar bodies around the country also changed or passed into history. However, those that remained became the largest charities of the new era: thus, voluntary sector activity shifted from a focus on health, to a focus on social care. New organisations grew up with a focus on the new social casework and work with families, for example the Family Service Units that emerged from pacifist work in the Second World War (Starkey, 2000; Chapter 5).

The professional focus of social work shifted from the voluntary sector to the public services. Size, budgets and public responsibility lent influence to the local authority welfare and children's departments, strengthened by moves to develop professional training. The foundation of the NHS removed the 'almoner' role, which had been a major factor in the development of medical social work. The comprehensive nature of the NHS reinforced the professional acceptance and standing of medical and psychiatric social workers. The Mackintosh Report (1951) on social workers in mental health services was particularly influential, recommending a professional register of psychiatric social workers.

British social work during the welfare state period

British social work was becoming state social work and, at least for a time, it was a '*welfare* state'. Many aspects of British social work developed during this period and Table 3.1 lists some policy and legal developments and their importance. However, these were partial and fragmented until a movement during the 1960s towards unification of personal social services. The major local government services in child care, welfare for elders and people

Table 3.1 British legislation and reports important for social care 1945–70

Date	Title	Comment
1945	*London County Council Remand Homes* (Vick Report, Cmd 6594)	Report of residential care scandal; created impetus for child care reform
1946	The Boarding Out of Dennis and Terence O'Neill (Monckton Report, Cmd 6636)	Report on foster care scandal; created impetus for child care reform
1946	*Report of the Care of Children Committee* (Curtis Report, Cmd 6922)	Report on inadequate child care services, recommended reform by creating a coordinated local government child care service
1947	*Report on the Employment and Training of Social Workers* (1st Younghusband Report)	Reviewed need for training in social work – Training Council in Child Care established in the same year
1948	Children Act 1948	Created local authority children's departments, with trained children's officer
1948	Criminal Justice Act 1948	Strengthened and formalised probation
1948	National Assistance Act 1948	Established post-Poor Law social security system, welfare of elders and people with handicaps
1951	*Social Work in Britain* (2nd Younghusband Report)	Emphasised need for high-level training provision, eventually leading to the foundation of the National Institute for Social Work (Training)
1952	Children and Young Persons (Amendment) Act 1952	Imposed a duty on children's departments to investigate reports of children at risk; acceptance of a preventive role for social work
1957	*Royal Commission on the Law relating to Mental Illness and Mental Deficiency* (Percy Report, Cmnd 169)	Recommended community care and treatment of mentally ill people without compulsion
1958	Adoption Act 1958	Consolidated the main provisions for adoption
1959	*Report of the Working Party on Social Workers in the Local Authority Health and Welfare Services (3rd Younghusband Report)*	Recommended training course for staff in local authority welfare departments (mainly working with elders and people with handicaps); led to the Certificate in Social Work.
1959	Mental Health Act 1959	Established local authority mental health service; focus on community care and treatment rather than incarceration; included provision for people with learning disabilities; social workers as mental welfare officers, with a role in compulsory admission of mentally ill people to hospital

cont'd

Table 3.1 cont'd

Date	Title	Comment
1961	*Report of the Committee on Children and Young Persons* (Ingleby Report, Cmnd 1191)	Recommended coordination of local authority provision for young offenders
1961	*Report of the Inter-departmental Committee on the Business of the Criminal Courts* (Streatfeild Committee, Cmnd 1289)	Institutionalised the provision of social inquiry reports (pre-sentence reports) as part of sentencing in the criminal courts
1963	Children and Young Persons Act 1963	Permitted local authorities to make grants and act to prevent reception of children into care
1964	*Children and Young Persons in Scotland* (Kilbrandon Report, Cmnd 2306)	Recommended reporter and children's hearing system for dealing with young offenders and child care
1965 (Home Office)	*The Child, the Family and the Young Offender* (White Paper, Cmnd 2742)	Recommended preventive and treatment work to respond to deprivation of young offenders
1968	Health Services and Public Health Act 1968	Developed a range of local authority health services, including making home help services mandatory
1968	*Report of the Committee on Local Authority and Allied Personal Social Services* (Seebohm Report, Cmnd 3703)	Recommended single local government social work service for families, with a qualified director of social services
1968	Social Work (Scotland) Act 1968	Established local authority social work departments (including probation) in Scotland, with a duty to promote social welfare
1969	Children and Young Persons Act 1969	Intended to provide for young offenders to receive appropriate treatment as the main focus of provision; established 'intermediate treatment'; not fully implemented by the incoming Conservative government in 1970
1970	Local Authority Personal Social Services Act 1970	Established local authority social services departments in England and Wales, implemented April 1971
1970	Chronically Sick and Disabled Persons Act 1970	Duty on local authorities to identify disabled people and provide appropriate services
1971 (DHSS)	*Better Services for the Mentally Handicapped* (Cmnd 4683)	First major planning document for an important 'cinderella' group
1972	Houghton Report on the Adoption of Children	Recommended a stronger role for local authorities in adoption and a reduction of influence of religious organisations

cont'd

Table 3.1 cont'd

Date	Title	Comment
1974 (DHSS)	*Report of the Committee of Inquiry into the Care and Treatment Provided in relation to Maria Colwell*	First modern child abuse inquiry, led to the establishment of local coordination and registers of children at risk
1974	Otten Report on social work in the health service	Identified a significant role of social workers in the health service
1975	Children Act 1975	Implemented Houghton Report and a more focused and assertive child protection system
1975	Ralphs Report on education welfare officers	Recommended a social work focus and training for education welfare officers
1976	Race Relations Act 1976	First effective anti-discrimination legislation
1976 (DHSS)	*Priorities in Health and Personal Social Services in England*	Priorities to 'cinderella' services, for elders, mentally ill and learning disabled
1977 (DHSS)	*Priorities in Health and Social Services: The Way Ahead*	Implementation strategy on priorities
1979	Jay Report on mental handicap nursing and care	Recommended ending long-stay hospitals for learning disabled people and the development of housing-based services in the community

with disabilities expanded and training was introduced. The same is true of the other local service, probation. Inspectorates and development services were set up in the main ministries, the Home Office for probation and children's departments, and the Health Ministry for welfare departments, where the powerful Chief Welfare Officer Geraldine (later Dame Geraldine) Aves (1898–1986) achieved considerable development (Willmott, 1992). The Conservative administrations of the 1950s did not substantially question the welfare state, but there was still a preference for the market rather than state provision, welfare departments of government were understaffed and underfinanced and Treasury concern over expenditure remained high (Bridgen and Lowe, 1998). The legislation of the 1940s was mainly permissive and divided responsibility at central government level meant that there was no ministry to take overall strategic direction. However, in the early 1960s, concern about some social issues, particularly juvenile delinquency, did lead to pressure for development and eventually to the Seebohm reforms.

Local authority services became the base for improvements in provision in a number of areas. The Children and Young Persons (Amendment) Act 1952, for example, required children's departments, originally set up to coordinate care for orphans and deprived children, to investigate reports of children at risk. The Children and Young Persons Act 1963 further extended their role by permitting them to spend money and effort on preventing admission to care. National coordination also developed with the foundation of the National Bureau for Co-operation in Child Care (1963 – later National Children's Bureau), with local authorities and most large children's charities in membership (Pugh, 1993). This became an important force for development. Slowly expanding mental health provision was reformed by the Mental Health Act 1959, arising from the Percy Report (1957), which picked up a trend towards community treatment and proposed a legislative framework that removed compulsion and reduced stigma. 'Duly authorised officers', who could sign orders committing people to asylums under the Lunacy Act 1890, were transmuted into mental welfare officers and incorporated into local authority health departments. These became responsible for community provision, aftercare for patients discharged from or not admitted to hospitals under the new legal regime and support services such as hostels and daycare. Psychiatry became more integrated into medicine, as it increasingly became part of general hospitals, provided more medical treatments (Ramon, 1996: 24) and psychiatrists formed a Royal College on the pattern of more established medical specialties. Psychiatric social workers extended their influence from the teaching centres into community roles in adult community psychiatric services.

Social work education also developed, encouraged by government bodies. An important influence during this period was Eileen (later Dame Eileen) Younghusband (1902–81), the only daughter of Sir Francis Younghusband (1863–1942), one of the last British imperial explorers of Asia, a writer and a mystic (French, 1994). She had been brought up to an upper-class life but, influenced by the inspirational preaching of Dick Sheppard, a fashionable Christian missionary:

> was more interested in social justice than social propriety, and moved out to a Settlement in Bermondsey [a working-class area of

London]. She patrolled the tenements of Stepney and ran a play-group – to the distress of her mother, who saw such activities as most improper.

(French, 1994: 316)

A bout of poliomyelitis delayed her attendance at the LSE for a certificate in social studies, followed by a diploma in sociology and then a tutor's post (Jones, 1984). By the 1930s, a family friend recalled, 'Eileen went off slumming it in the East End, doing good works and so on with some *vivid* Socialists' (French, 1994: 372). She was a magistrate from the 1930s to 1967 and a leader in juvenile justice. Sharing a home with Helen Roberts, a part-Jewish worker with refugees from Hitler's Germany, she became involved in this work, too. Later, 'the outbreak of war saw her desperately busy setting up a Citizens Advice Bureau in Kensington' (French, 1994: 376); later she worked in wartime food and rest centres (Jones, 1984: 45). Then, towards the end of the war, she became a civil servant to write a report on social security, moving away from voluntary work, and became involved in the Carnegie UK Trust reports on, first, youth leaders then social work, as an aspect of post-war reconstruction (Jones, 1984: 49). The famous report on social work (Younghusband, 1947) was written on unpaid leave from the LSE, for a small honorarium and expenses. It defined a field of social work and a central core of a curriculum, much as the Hollis–Taylor Report (1951) (Chapter 10) was soon to do in the USA.

With the success of this initiative, she was commissioned to write a further report, which, published in 1951, focused on the disadvantages of the specialised organisation of social work that was emerging. The case conference 'movement' (Jones, 1984: 53) in which Kay McDougall, now in charge of the LSE mental health course for psychiatric social workers, was active promoted regular coordinating meetings of all workers involved in a case (hence the title of McDougall's privately published professional journal, *Case Conference*). Younghusband's report recommended an integrated school of social work as part of a process of confirming the role of universities in professional training, as opposed to academic preparation and professional supervision (Hartshorn, 1982). The subsequent Carnegie grant to establish an educational experiment was not enough for this, but allowed the LSE to run a 'generic' social work course in which all specialisations would be taught together. This course used the term 'applied social studies' to distinguish it from non-professional social studies courses at the LSE, and was explicitly intended to conceal its training element from those concerned about the academic standing of university courses. Many professional bodies saw this as the beginning of training in American 'casework', and although there was some opposition from supporters of practical experience, this was seen as the way forward by many leaders in different professional groups (Hartshorn, 1982). The experiment became controversial and a raging battle followed (Donnison, 1975; Hartshorn, 1982: Ch. 7; Jones, 1984: Ch. 8) between Younghusband (who was not a professionally qualified social worker) and the leaders of the developing professional organisations and the specialised LSE courses, McDougall and Clare Britton (later Winnicott following her marriage to the eminent psychoanalyst Donald W. Winnicott). Although the initiative was supported by the profes sional associations at the outset, and the model was taken up at other universities, clashes over the need to merge the courses, because the Carnegie grant could not sustain separate provision, led to Younghusband leaving the LSE, when McDougall was appointed to lead the merger. This conflict over 'profes sional qualification' was again to confound the formation of the British Association of Social Workers (Payne, 2002; Chapter 8). Younghusband was employed during the 1960s as a consultant in the National Institute for Social Work Training, created as a 'staff college' for leaders and trainers for the newly emerging profession and became a leading figure in international social work education (Chapter 10).

At the same time as the Carnegie experiment, Younghusband chaired a report on training for social workers published in 1959, which encouraged the development of training for officers in welfare departments of local authorities, who were dealing with elders and disabled people. These were to be provided, under powers granted by the Health Visiting and Social Work (Training) Act 1962, in local technical colleges (later mainly polytechnics, which were established 1969–71). There were fears that this would create a lower tier qualification from the university-based professional courses. However, when the qualifications were merged in the early 1970s, this anxiety proved unfounded.

Eventually, a new kind of voluntary agency emerged, of which the Child Poverty Action Group was the ideal type. Founded in the mid-1960s, it identified failings in policy for a particular group, people in poverty, and campaigned for administrative and legal changes to improve their position, focusing on the politically attractive category of children and their families. It and research associated with the Institute of Community Studies in east London identified continuing problems caused by poverty. Similar movements arose elsewhere. For example, France experienced an awakening to problems of poverty similar to that in Britain, influenced at the outset by Lenoir's ([1974]1989) book *Les Exclus* (The Excluded/Marginalised). Another example is the influence in the USA of works such as Harrington's (1962) *The Other America.*

Probation was another area of substantial development during the welfare state period (Bochel, 1976). It was strengthened by the Criminal Justice Act 1948, which renewed and strengthened the legal basis for probation and made provision for the service to take on voluntary aftercare for ex-prisoners, in addition to the small number of serious offenders receiving statutory aftercare. Aftercare for ex-prisoners was taken more seriously during the 1950s, usually being undertaken by a local discharged prisoners aid society, coordinated by the national Central After-Care Association. Also, in this period, American 'social casework' had a considerable impact on both training and the development of staff supervision. The Streatfeild Committee on the Business of the Criminal Courts (1961) recommended that social inquiry reports (now called pre-sentence reports) by probation officers should be a regular aspect of the sentencing process. This was the culmination of decades of attempts by the National Association of Probation Officers to gain formal recognition of this role. The Morison Report (1962) recommended that community provision for offenders should be integrated with the probation service and the service took over the aftercare of prisoners, and eventually the prison welfare service as well in 1966, incorporating borstals and detention centres (prisons for young offenders) in 1969. Following the White Paper *The Adult Offender* (Home Office, 1965a), which proposed a parole scheme whereby prisoners were released under statutory supervision before the end of their sentence, responsibility for this was also given to the probation service by the Criminal Justice

Act 1967. Under the Children and Young Persons Act 1969, responsibility for supervision of young offenders in the community was shifted during a transitional period to the new social services departments.

It was, therefore, possible to see the development of probation as a wholly positive upward path, but the shift of work with children to social services departments meant that its focus bore more tightly on work with adult offenders. This prepared the way for it later to become a penal rather than social work service.

British social work and social services departments

The growth of local government social services, and the acceptance that the voluntary sector should not be at the centre of provision, led to a perception that the increasing range of provision needed to be coordinated and developed consistently. This feeling gathered force around concern about 'juvenile delinquency' in the late 1950s, the time when teenagers first became an identifiable cultural phenomenon. The first developments were in Scotland (Cooper, 1983), where juvenile courts were rare. Set up in 1961 to review the situation, the Kilbrandon Committee (1964) decided that delinquent children and those in need of care and protection were largely the same population. It proposed a radical solution based in the separate Scottish legal administrative tradition of a 'reporter' working out which children should be referred to hearings for compulsory care and which should receive a range of voluntary support measures. The Kilbrandon Report proposed a 'social education service', which would support the hearings system. These arrangements were implemented by the Social Work (Scotland) Act 1968, notable also for its Section 12, which imposed a duty on local authorities to promote social welfare. This was a significant advance on the responsibility on children's departments in England and Wales merely to prevent admission to care.

The Labour government of 1963, gaining power after a long period of Conservative administration, took these ideas up. Policy statements and speeches announced a drive to deal with delinquency and support family life in both Scotland and the UK Westminster Parliament. A Labour Party study group (Longford Report, 1964) pointed to the need to deal with child and family deprivation as part of dealing with delinquency. A subsequent White Paper (Home Office, 1965b) applied this policy, proposing, following Longford, the need for a comprehensive family service.

In 1965, the Seebohm Committee (1968) was established to study ways of reforming local authority personal social services, as it described them, to this end. It recommended merger of the main local authority social services into a social services department, together with domiciliary health services, such as home helps and meals on wheels, which had been made mandatory by the Health Services and Public Health Act 1968. The Seebohm Report was strongly supported by social workers, who campaigned for its implementation against ministerial indifference and some opposition, as with the Children Act 1948, from public health doctors. However, the strength of social work support, and the distraction of medical and local government interests with the impending local government and health service reorganisations, enabled the report to be largely implemented in the dying days of the Labour government, through the Local Authority Social Services Act 1970 (Hall, 1976). This Act was more administrative than the Scottish Act, and did not contain the duty to promote welfare, Section 1 of the Children and Young Persons Act 1963 being considered sufficient.

The Act came into force, and social services departments (SSDs) were established in 1971. At the same time Alf Morris's private member's measure, the Chronically Sick and Disabled Persons Act 1970, imposed a duty on local authorities to identify, register and provide services to disabled people and the Children and Young Persons Act 1969 established a more therapeutic range of services for young offenders, including 'intermediate treatment'. Northern Ireland followed suit through the Health and Personal Social Service (Northern Ireland) Order 1972. This incorporated social services into joint health and social services boards, since, because of Republican and Loyalist conflict, significant at the time, there was some distrust of local authorities.

The USA: welfare society?

The USA is sometimes regarded as the classic liberal state, with a residual welfare system. After the Second World War, rather than develop the progress of welfare through the state that arose from responses to the Depression of the 1930s, social work in the USA focused on the development of method, extending the psychodynamic model of casework used in elite voluntary agencies, mainly for families. This was to have an important, although increasingly controversial, influence on the rest of the world, since during the 1960s and 70s, this method became a widely accepted model of social work practice. So, while the USA did not develop European-style state-organised services, its economic and political influence led to increasing cultural and academic influence. As the European welfare states developed, the question was raised: Was this a 'welfare society', whose economic power provided welfare without the need for significant state involvement?

Aid to Families with Dependent Children (AFDC; Chapter 2) continued through this period as the main provision for families. Day (2000) suggests that because the Social Security Act 1935 shifted funding from private to public agencies and most social workers worked in private agencies, there was a split between social work and public welfare. Trattner (1999: 305) argues that the availability of, even inadequate, social security and improvement in employment and income for most people in the USA led to a flight from reform to casework in the 1950s. Helping military families in the 1940s also provided the basis for fee-paying private practice. The emphasis of social work in the 1950s on psychodynamic and other psychological theories led to a separation of emotional and personal problems from material needs, which were seen as 'presenting problems' concealing psychological needs. Another factor was the post-war 'baby boom', associated with the domestication of women's lives as men returned to take up the wage-earning role in families. Urban expansion led to extensive suburban development and an increase of depression and isolation among women. Thus, dealing with 'family problems' focusing on women's feelings seemed an appropriate response (Day, 2000: 289).

However, during the 1950s, urban change led to substantial immigration of new Spanish-speaking ethnic groups from the Caribbean and Latin America, and visible urban decline. Efforts to intervene in urban decline and juvenile delinquency and the social consequences of teenage gangs were reflected in the popular musical *West Side Story*, which contained one of the first (ironic) references to social workers in popular culture: 'Dear kindly, social worker …'. The social worker in this case turns out to be authoritarian and oppressive in the perception of the teenage gang. In the south, significant tensions arose, as Supreme Court decisions outlawed intentional racial segregation, and campaigns for civil rights for black African-Americans developed (Katz, 1996: 260). Settlements after the war often became local community centres, but lost their influence as leaders and innovators in their area, sometimes as the area they worked in declined in importance in a city, and often because of the increasing importance of public services (Peterson, 1965).

During the 1960s, however, the casework model began to fade in importance, partly allied to a resurgence of interest in social reform. The reasons for this were partly political, as in Britain: the 1950s was a period of conservative Republican government, replaced throughout the 1960s by more socially concerned Democratic governments. Industrial change and growth had also led to inner city problems, and anxiety about the emergence of alienated young people, also as in Britain.

The Kennedy administration of 1961–3 established a committee on public welfare, which accepted the claims of social workers that psychoanalytic casework could motivate families towards improvement. Consequently, social services were incorporated into social security provision for families (AFDC) but separated from payment administration. Payment was extended to two-parent families without unemployment benefits, having previously been limited to households headed by women (Day, 2000: 316). The administration also focused on youth offending, and mental health. The Juvenile Delinquency and Youth Offenses Control Act 1961 developed community preventive projects in inner cities, notably Mobilization for Youth, originally started by the National Institute for Mental Health in 1958 (Trattner, 1999: 130), which was important for the development of community work. Another key development of the 1950s and 60s was the running down and closure of county asylums (Brown, 1985). The Mental Retardation and Community Mental Health Centers Act 1963 encouraged the development of community mental health centres, which became an important base for innovative social work. Legislation for medical care (Medicaid and Medicare) for poor and elderly people encouraged social work in health care, in both hospitals and a variety of community settings, such as neighbourhood health centres, outreach programmes for poor people and community mental health centres (Dhooper, 1997: 173). Assistance with nutrition was introduced by the Food Stamp Act 1964, by which surplus agricultural produce was made available to poor people.

In the mid-1960s, urban rioting and active civil rights campaigning raised the need to do something about increasing inner city problems. Among the explanations for these problems were the deteriorating economic position of blacks (African-Americans) in the south, leading to migration to northern cities and pressure on resources in inner cities (Higgins, 1978). American Indians (now often called 'native Americans') and Mexican and Spanish migrants also suffered significant poverty (Trattner, 1999: 317–18). There were threats of violent disorder and a need to woo voters in the cities, leading to political pressure on Johnson, president after Kennedy's assassination, to create what became known as the 'great society' programme.

The legislative basis for the Johnson's 'war on poverty' was Title II (s. 202) Equal Opportunity Act 1964, which mobilised federal resources to provide services and assistance to eliminate poverty, coordinated by a public or not-for-profit agency and with the 'maximum feasible participation' of residents and members of the public. A new federal department, the Office of Economic Opportunity, was set up to administer the service, organising local 'community action programs'. An important element of this, the New Careers programme, sought to employ local indigenous workers as paraprofessionals in the new public and voluntary social services. Mirroring the Peace Corps, an international project, a volunteer programme, VISTA (Volunteers in Service to America) also encouraged participation. The civil rights movement also engaged social workers. For example, Whitney Young (1921–71), a black social worker, worked in social work education and the urban league movement, receiving presidential awards for his civil rights work, while also being president of the professional association of social workers (DuBois and Miley, 1999). Formed in 1966, the National Welfare Rights Organization held mass demonstrations to improve rights in the administration of social security (Trattner, 1999: 344).

However, progress in many of these developments proved illusory (Trattner, 1999: 324–5). Bureaucratic organisation, fragmentation in complex local administrations and political delay and obstruction meant that there was a gap between promise and delivery, and this contributed to further unrest. Moreover, the failure contributed to doubts about the capacity of social science-based interventions, including social work, to deliver social change, and encouraged a conservative backlash. The legislation of the 1960s increased the number of people receiving social security benefits and reawakened concern about fraud and dependence, leading to a concern about a 'culture of poverty'. Later, the Social Security Act 1967 focused on concrete social provision, such as daycare, drug treatment, housing and help with work rather than casework services.

Thus, in the USA, the culmination of campaigning, radical social change through community interventions and attempts at welfare reform meant that, although there were improvements, the seeds of a period of questioning were also sown here.

European developments in the welfare state period

The developments in Britain were largely insular: the British welfare state was highly regarded, and the UK was not, until the early 1960s, a member of what became the European Union (EU). The American development of social casework, watched across the world, was influential. Many of the same trends were apparent in other developed Western economies.

The Nordic countries, for example, shifted towards a universal model of a welfare state, following Sweden's example in the 1930s. While this demonstrated similar trends to those in Britain, in this more propitious political environment, the different Nordic traditions created a welfare state with different emphases. Sipilä et al. (1997) argue that political agreement on the post-war need for reconstruction and development of social services as part of it, led to social democratic governments favouring public provision, supported, however, by conservative oppositions. Services expanded, they became professionalised through training developments, and controlling, compulsory provision was marginalised in favour of supportive welfare provision. They came to be seen in a more complex way. For example, daycare was seen less as a service for working women and more as a provision for remedying a lack of care and providing good early developmental opportunities. State responsibility was emphasised by the withdrawal of a legal duty on children to maintain their parents in old age by Sweden (1956), Norway (1964), Finland (1970) and Iceland (1991). Denmark never had such a requirement.

How did this political and social movement affect developments in social services and social work? Sweden developed a post-war policy of close cooperation between trade unions and employers on employment and workforce policy-making. Extensive public housing, social security and education reforms built on the stability and social democratic policy base of the 1930s (Hort and McMurphy, 1997). The poor law was finally repealed in 1956, being replaced by public assistance, child welfare and temperance acts. From the early 1960s, county council or municipal provision of medical and social care for elders, children and others was universal.

In Norway, the Common Platform agreed by political parties was substantially based on the British Beveridge Report and a series of long-term plans led to growth in a range of public social services (Hildeng, 1995). More effective welfare administration in local authorities was considered necessary, and a plan to create a social work school came to fruition in 1950, with the foundation of the Norwegian College of Local Government Administration and Social Work (NKSH), which developed strongly in subsequent years (Chapter 10). However, this initiative, as is typical in many European countries, tied social work closely to local government administration.

Finland, like Norway a dispersed rural country, began to build on interrupted reforms of the 1930s (Satka, 1995). When Russia had taken over the country from Swedish rule in 1809, to maintain the loyalty of the administration local aristocrats had become civil servants, and efficiency and high social status was assured for them by making legal training compulsory. Finland became independent in 1917, and a civil war between conservative White and socialist Red groups ensued, with the Whites winning and reinforcing the conservative and legalistic character of the public administration. When poorhouses were replaced in the 1930s by a system of locally administered welfare benefits and services, the system was based on a highly developed regulatory system, which neglected the interpersonal elements of delivering welfare services. Welfare workers were trained in a largely legal administration of services, but informally gained skills in managing the delivery of services, even though a 'Finnish peculiarity is the almost untouchable status of jurisprudence and lawyers in state administration and in the Finnish relations of ruling in general' (Satka, 1995: 191). After the Second World War, in which the country had been devastated by different invading armies, industrialisation began partly to pay war reparations, and gathered pace during the 1950s. Several, mainly female, welfare workers trained abroad and brought back social casework techniques focusing on psychological problems, supported by a UN consultant. However, this was resisted by the mainly male, legally and administratively trained, welfare workers. Urbanisation occurred in the 1960s, and substantial expansion in the social services took place at that point.

Nygren et al. (1997) trace the explicit use of social service terminology by reviewing the official use of the concept of the social services in Nordic countries. In doing so, they identify the early 1970s as the point at which traditional concerns for poor relief shift into a wider concern for social care. They identify six factors:

- A general aim in the early 1970s to create new universal services
- Incorporating social services into an overall social policy
- Coordinating social and other services, particularly with health
- Ideological aims to remove the stigma of poor relief
- Consequent aims to develop a service ideology, regarding people as consumers of services rather than clients of treatment and seeking to provide services as of right, rather than support on definition of need.

Elder care and to some extent daycare for children were regarded as needing this kind of service ideology, while compulsory services for offenders and drug abusers were often seen differently. Norway and Denmark, with stronger traditions of social pedagogy, offered separated pedagogical services, mainly in daycare for children and young people, associated with the education system and paid for substantially by user charges.

In Sweden during the 1970s, there was an attempt to move away from concepts of 'treatment' towards adaptation and service provision, particularly in the work of the Social Care

Committee 1974. Rather than acting as 'guardians', the aim was to have rehabilitative relationships between worker and client. These optimistic aims were enacted in the Social Service Act 1982, which in particular removed the compulsory elements of previous legislation, although new compulsory legislation was enacted to provide for young offenders and drug abusers. Most local authorities divided their activity into care for elders and disabled people, child care and individual and family care. The latter did not wholly become the desired universal service, and still retains stigmatising elements.

In Germany, after the disruption of the Nazi period, the war and its devastation, the pre-existing corporatist approach (Chapter 2) developed and local organisations were re-established in a close relationship with the state, in much the same way that trade union, local government and central government relationships were the bedrock of the Swedish welfare state. German local government services were organised into three offices for youth, social assistance and health, reproduced at local, regional and national levels, but the high degree of local autonomy and inter action with welfare organisations means that there is considerable variation in structure (Lorenz, 1994a). The Federal Social Welfare Act 1961 enacted a right to public welfare support if someone suffers material deprivation. A landmark legal challenge in 1962 tested whether the constitutional right to welfare was negated by the emphasis in the Act on voluntary organisations' major role; this confirmed the partnership principle. A social code was enacted in 1976, and subsequent legislation is incorporated into it. The Youth Welfare Act 1951, followed by the Child and Youth Welfare Act 1991, renewed child care and protection provision and local youth services, with, in the latter legislation, greater emphasis on parental responsibility and participation with public services by service users.

Southern European states had little development in social work, mainly because of the influence of conservative Catholic regimes, including the Spanish and Portuguese dictatorships. Leibfried (2000) argued that their system was rudimentary, offering little more than 'an institutional promise of welfare', referring only to social security. However, like Germany, the social security elements of welfare are employment-related, whereas welfare services, including social work, are mainly publicly funded and directly provided by the public sector.

Nevertheless, they are still less well developed than in Northern Europe (Guillén and Álvarez, 2001). Part of the reason for this was the reliance of the Iberian dictatorships until 1974 (Portugal) and 1978 (Spain) on the Catholic Church and charitable effort. Social provision was reformed to provide more extensive social help and began to catch up with broad-based European provision at that point (Rodrigues and Monteiro, 1998; Rossell and Fernández, 1998).

Social work's 'period of silence' in the 'second world'

In the vast area controlled by the Soviet Union and in China, Communist parties had or gained power and these countries formed a political bloc, which came to be described as the 'second world'. Here, there was 'the period of silence in social work' (Bagdonas, 2001), and social work was displaced by an emphasis on employment- and trade union-related welfare, and a denial of the existence of many social problems, which were supposed to be dealt with by the adoption of socialist policies. Universal, but poor quality, housing and good health care and social security services were provided in the public sector. Extensive social expenditure, for example on children's daycare, permitted high female participation in the workforce. A few countries, including Poland and Yugoslavia, retained some social work education capacity and provision; some like Bulgaria shifted in its policy towards social work (see Table 3.1). Southern Europe slowly began to develop social work services, but the big expansion was to be in the 1980s and 90s. Although the social context was very different from the position in Western countries, the same development of more comprehensive state social provision took place in Soviet Russia. Harwin (1996: 24–31) shows that Khrushchev, in power from 1953–64, needed to re-establish humanitarian and social justice purposes after the oppression of the Stalin years, and did so partly through social and humanitarian policies and services for children and families.

The need for individualistic welfare such as social work was denied, and social work often did not exist, although training with an academic emphasis and general family services were sometimes available, for example in Czechoslovakia, where social workers also organised welfare in the work unit (Harris,

1997), and in Romania and Yugoslavia (Ramon, 1995). Where long-term care was needed, institutions such as orphanages, homes for mentally ill and physically and learning disabled people were the norm (Ramon, 1995). Personal welfare was provided through education, public health and workers' benefits systems, whereas institutional forms of social provision provided support through state ownership of the means of production and policies of social equality (Inkeles and Bauer, 1959). Well-established social work professions withered away. Examples in Table 3.1 show changes in the role and organisation of and education for social work during this period.

Simpura (1995) argues that in the Baltic Communist states' welfare systems, welfare was characterised by:

■ Denial of social problems
■ State-centred management of social welfare
■ Strong workplace and trade union roles in providing social benefits, rewarding political loyalty and labour
■ Favouritism in providing social benefits.

The meaning of favouritism may be made clearer by an example from a statement by the Chinese Ministry of Civil Affairs (that is, social welfare):

there are 24 major tasks of the civil affairs work:

■ Supporting the army and giving preferential treatment to families of revolutionary armymen and martyrs
(China Civil Affairs, 1995: 8)

A similar pattern to Simpura's analysis is demonstrated in relation to China by Chan and Chow (1992) and it was characteristic of most Communist countries. In 1987, street offices were given directives to set up 'the four ones' by 1990: a home for elders, a welfare factory, a welfare fund and a social centre for elders (Chan, 1993: 106). Services for disabled people, allowances for families suffering from hardship and youth facilities to prevent offending have also been established through street offices. Pollis (1981) also draws attention to a repressive administrative style and the priority given to the economic development of the state, over the political and individual rights of individuals. The origins of

Table 3.2 Social work in three Communist countries, before, during and after Communism

Country	Pre-Communist development	Communist period	Post-reform	Studies
Bulgaria	Two-year education established, 1912, based on German and Swiss models. Social workers worked in municipal social relief services, factories employing women, schools, with police on 'morally endangered women'. Emphasis on work with women and children and young people.	Social work education ceased, 1944. Socialist state took on the task of providing for people's prosperity and social progress, through many agencies and practices, diluting the expertise of social work. Denial of social problems. Priority to employment as solution to social problems. State provides social care and social insurance. Department of Public Health and Social Care reintroduced training for specialists in social relief, through two Colleges of Medicine, 1973. Social workers became investigators/directors in relationships with people needing relief. Focus on getting people re-employed after ill-health.	Social work education re-established in state and 'free' (private) universities, 1991. Social work provision minimal, but an emphasis in medical, disability and learning disability issues. Rejection of social science emphasis.	Vladinska (1994)
China	Residual welfare system, relying on family and kinship support. Historical tradition of meagre, stigmatised state relief, but heavy reliance on private charitable organisations. Minimal number of agencies. Acceptance of fate and 'reliance of the heavens'. Social work education at Yangshin (now Beijing) University from 1925: at least 10 other universities also had social work education.	From 1949, public welfare, state disaster relief and social insurance through state and local government, occupational welfare through work units, welfare services through social organisations and community care through street offices. Priority to providing employment and welfare through employment. State socialism enables all to participate in achieving equality and justice; self-reliance and self-help; emphasis on family help. State economic development more important than welfare; repressive administrative style.	From 1978, economic reform policy to create an enterprise economy. Lack of employment opportunities created a 'welfare gap'. Denial of social problems created by economic reform led to discontent. Ministry of Civil Affairs expanded social programmes in recognition of this need to respond to disability, increasing numbers of elderly people, with reduction in potential caring population due to 'one-child' policy aimed at reducing population. Sociology with some welfare elements developed in 1980s. Social work education reintroduced during 1990s.	Chan and Chow (1992); Ngai, (1996)
Estonia	Independent republic from 1918; Ministry of Work and Social Care, 1918–29, focused on care of mother and child; orphanages created. 1925 and 1935, Social Care Acts. Ministry for Education and Social Care, 1929 responsible for health, children's, social care and pensions. 1930–40: various social and health care charities established. 1935: Social work and household economics educational institute established by Estonian Women's League.	Training of social assistants ceased, 1950. Social Insurance Commissar (1940–6) and Ministry (1946–79) responsible for disabled and retired, especially soldiers and military families. Ministry of Social Care (1979–91) responsible mainly for pensions to mainly veterans and war disabled. Homes for elderly people increased from Retirement Act 1956. From 1987, organisations for elderly and handicapped. Denial of social problems, state-centred management of social work, priority to work and trade union for social support, political supporters favoured.	Period of national awakening, 1985–91; independence 1991. Ministry of Social Affairs reorganised, 1992, to unite social and health care and labour. Priority given to child protection and responding to crime. Social work education refounded, Tallinn 1991; Tartu, 1992. Social workers employed in all local authority areas (but with wider administrative responsibilities).	Tulva (1997)

such policies were primarily political, derived from a belief that a just and equal socialist society would meet personal needs by participation in working for a socialist future. Claims that mutual help extends from family to wider neighbourhood assistance may reflect a political imposition, rather than a preferred way of living (Chan, 1993). As in other Communist countries, local residents' committees and street offices provided the organisational base for local welfare work. Chan and Chow (1992: 39) also report that Chinese officials argue that the Chinese people are accustomed to authoritarian and patriarchal rule, treasuring 'collective well-being' rather than individualistic values. Such explanations propose that cultural differences explain the greater emphasis on collective welfare and authoritarian social control in these countries as compared with Western societies.

Another point is that welfare services in some of these countries were poorly developed before Communist regimes gained power. Chan and Chow (1992: 12–13) show that in 1933 only 834 welfare institutions existed in the whole of China, with non-governmental agencies providing 85 per cent of the services. China was rent by civil conflicts for much of the century. The Baltic (in Northern Europe, near Scandinavia) and Balkan (in southeastern Europe, between Austria and Turkey) countries were new states created in the aftermath of the First World War. The example of Estonia in Table 3.1 illustrates this. Such societies had had many other issues to deal with in founding their social and state identity in the relatively brief period before they were assailed by the Second World War.

Developing countries and social development

In Africa and Asia, many countries were colonies of the European powers, mainly Britain and France. Social work development in this group of countries only began during the 1950s and 60s. Colonies had largely been territories exploited economically and socially by the colonial powers. Social work provision was limited to occasional welfare services relevant to changes created by colonial development. In Singapore, for example, social work first emerged as a few almoners were appointed to local hospitals as part of an effort to deal with the social disruption caused by the Second World War. Social work was remedial and most help was given through informal social networks (Ow, 1996).

An important characteristic of social work developments in the 1950s and 60s in these countries reflected other global political and social movements. This was a long period of optimistic economic development and political conflict between Western and Soviet political blocs. Many of these conflicts were played out in developing countries. Part of these movements was a substantial decolonisation in African and East Asian countries. Most economic and political effort was poured into economic and infrastructural development projects (mainly civil engineering projects on which private industry depends), but some was employed in social development. This was for five reasons:

1. Many new governments in newly independent colonies were at first socialist in approach and placed some importance on social aspects of development.
2. Social stability was deemed important for political stability.
3. Industrialisation created migration to newly developing urban areas, a degree of breakdown in traditional social supports for families and individuals and a need for responses to urban problems of delinquency and social dislocation.
4. For little expenditure, a good deal of impact could be achieved on locally important problems.
5. Growing awareness of poverty in many developing countries raised concern about population growth and led to substantial activity in the area of family planning, which engaged the efforts of international social work agencies during this period.

Post-war, the intention of the colonial powers shifted to development, economically and socially, eventually as a preparation for independence. The British grant of independence for India and Pakistan in 1947 and Israel (technically a United Nations – UN – protectorate) in 1948, after long-standing campaigns, was the forerunner and an example to many other colonies. The British Welfare Advisory Committee was joined by a Community Development Committee in 1948. In 1954, the British Colonial Office originated the term 'social development' at a conference at Ashridge (Yimam, 1990: 42; Midgley, 1997: 185) to describe a combination of remedial social services and community development. This was later taken up by the UN, focusing on national, rather than local development. This trend strengthened as local politicians saw the success of centralised economic planning in Communist countries; however, some UN officials sought to integrate social interventions with economic planning (Midgley, 1997: Ch. 9). A UN survey of African social welfare in 1964 (Social Development Section, 1964) indicated mainly religious provision such as orphanages, youth work, some mother and child welfare, but a growing interest in social development. In Zimbabwe, social work focused on delinquency and problems with young people arising from the loss of family and tribal support when urbanisation developed (Gargett, 1977).

A significant element of this social infrastructure, however, was a movement for community development. This harnessed ideas about community work and developed them out of all recognition. Poole (1970) describes, for example, being seconded to Rhodesia (the colonial Zimbabwe) from his job as secretary of the Liverpool Council of Social Service in Britain to set up a coordinating body for the voluntary sector in this African colony. Batten's (for example 1967) work was particularly influential. Many colonial administrators returned to Britain after independence and found jobs in the voluntary sector. They applied this experience in community development to strengthen and promote community work in Britain. Poole, for example, returned from Rhodesia with ideas that he applied in the flowering of community organisations during the 1960s in Liverpool.

In a small number of countries, especially Japan, Korea and Taiwan, the Eastern 'tiger' economies, rapid economic development took place, unlike the second world and developing countries, where development was patchy. In the early stages, much of this was concerned with economic and social security development. In Taiwan, for example, a series of five-year plans focused on economic development. Lin (1991) showed that government expenditure on social welfare rose from 6 per cent of government spending in 1955 to about 15 per cent in the late 1980s, but social work services did not begin to emerge until laws on child welfare (1973) and welfare for elders and people with handicaps (1980). By 1991 only 1.4 per cent of the government's welfare budget was spent on such services. Restrictions on workers' freedom to organise and a large rural population with good family support meant that, unlike European countries, social work did not develop alongside industrialisation as a way of controlling working-class populations, but in response to international influences, particularly from UN development agencies. In Japan, social work moved from a more relief-based social work towards more welfare-oriented provision on a welfare state model, as high economic growth secured important benefits for its people. The Social Welfare Work Law 1951 conceived of social welfare as a state responsibility, devolved to regional administrations (Takahashi, 1997: 201). However, major companies continued to provide important social services to their employees, alongside health care. In Hong Kong, a social welfare office was set up in 1947 as part of the Secretariat for Chinese Affairs, the first time welfare was considered a government responsibility (Kwan, 1989). It became a full department in 1958. The 1950s and 60s saw initial rebuilding efforts focused on primary schooling and hospital provision after the impact of the Second World War, and the Communist takeover of mainland China, both of which produced a refugee problem. Social welfare was slow to develop, because of uncertainty about how to handle the refugee problem, cautious policy-makers, the lack of a lobby for social welfare and a lack of policy thinking (Kwan, 1989: 133). Most social welfare work was charitable, involving relief of the poor and residential provision for disabled people, until the development of government social work services in the 1960s (Chow, 1986). In the early 1970s, the emphasis shifted to housing and social welfare (Hui, 1989). Economic development led to social change and, as independence neared, moves were made to develop social infrastructure based on the model of the European nation state. By now, this model included welfare services. Therefore, social work agencies were introduced, although on a fairly small scale. Ow (1996: 239), in relation to Singapore, expresses the prevailing view as follows:

> After 1965 [independence], the need to survive as a nation made it imperative for the state to embark on a vigorous economic development programme. A systematic approach in which resources for social well-being was seen as linked to economic growth was accepted. Social work services expanded toward community development and self-help as another way of approaching the welfare of the individual, an approach perceived also as enhancing the cohesiveness of society.

As in Europe, some of the development in Japan and East Asian countries arose from American and, to a lesser extent, European efforts to re-establish economies and politically stable and congenial social structures in war-devastated countries.

In most colonies, economic exploitation had been the first priority until the Second World War, but as independence was either fought for or achieved by progression, greater attention was given to establishing an economic, political and social infrastructure to facilitate it. Development led to urbanisation and industrialisation, with its consequent social problems, as in Zimbabwe (Gargett, 1977; Hall, 1998). Yimam (1990: Ch. 2) suggests that in Africa missionaries' pioneering efforts were picked up after 1945 by colonial administrations and incorporated into government activity, in preparation for independence. Britain and France funded local social development, while Belgium, rather later in the 1950s, instituted a policy of promoting settled agricultural and urban communities. Africa saw social development programmes instituted through the activity of the UN during the 1960s as colonies became independent (Yimam, 1990: 54). Several colonies also set up ministries of social welfare or social development, supported from the previous colonial power, partly by voluntary organisations, soon to be called NGOs (non-governmental organisations), and partly copying the efforts of Western countries in community work and development during this period.

Many developments were a product of the activities of Christian philanthropic and missionary work, but this was sometimes inconsistent with the wishes and traditions of indigenous people, as in Korea (Whang, 1988), where even in the 1990s, half of Korean universities with a school of social work and 80 per cent of NGOs have Christian affiliations (Park, 1996). Kwon (1999) argues that the Korean welfare state developed in the 1960s at a time of economic growth, not caused by economic growth and class conflict but as the government's 'pre-emptive strike' (p. 132) against potential instability arising from social change. The government's main focus was on economic policy and development, and consequently social idealists' concern for social development was displaced by a pragmatic inclusion of a social element in economic policy, in a period when people were experiencing severe economic competition but democratisation was slow to develop.

The international economic and political situation continued to be important for the development of social work. Technical cooperation programmes, which led to important community development activities in Latin America, were intended to maintain political and social stability, for example. Sponsorship by the USA through the UN and the Organisation for American States suggests their importance to Western countries in maintaining bulwarks against political insecurity for the USA. Chapter 10 shows that developments in social work education in Latin America were strongly supported by the USA and UN agencies, even though often developed using established regional resources. Bastos et al. (1996) suggest that rural development efforts in Brazil, for example, during the early 1950s shifted to urban areas under the Juscelino Kubitischek government (1956–60), forming the basis for the growth of community development in the 1960s. This was the foundation for the radicalisation of Latin American social work through the reconceptualisation movement of the 1970s: radicalisation developed further into the 1980s (Jamur, 1996). In more conventional social work, Jamur (1996: 41) characterises this period as one of secularisation as the dominant influence of the Catholic Church was displaced by the development of a more professional discourse, claimed to be scientific in character. Westernised countries often reflected European and American developments. In South Australia, for example, Dickey (1986) describes a reorganisation of state services directed towards a developmental and community ideology; a substantial growth in the 1950s of voluntary organisations was increasingly incorporated into the state sector through grant aid. Federal social security became an important factor in welfare.

In India, a developing country, social work also expanded during this period in traditional Western-style services, although these were still not extensive. For example, until 1950 only two psychiatric social workers were employed in the whole country, whereas 37 were appointed between 1950 and 1970, constituting nearly 60 per cent of the first appointments to mental health services surveyed by Verma (1991) in the late 1970s. After independence in 1948, the constitution of India required the state to promote the welfare of the people, and in 1953 the Central Social Welfare Board was set up to assist voluntary organisations. The five-year plans also included provision for social welfare.

However, the main focus was not on Western social work, but on the Gandhian heritage of commitment to community welfare programmes, self-help, developing local resources, economic and cultural improvement (Kumar, 1994: 48).

In Japan, a social work profession modelled on the American system was developed during the post-war period of military occupation (Ito, 1995: 263–5), including professional organisation and social work education, but this was largely dismantled in a period in which the social services in local government were bureaucratised (Ito, 1995: 265–6). Deriving from the support of Christian missions and the occupation administration, some successful voluntary sector organisations developed a community role. Professional social workers worked in health and psychiatric care, child guidance and social work services provided by large industries for their employees.

Conclusion

Western social work emerged from the welfare state period, but this was not a universal development, as it appeared to be to social workers in Britain and some Western European states. The pre-1939 ideas about method and services became incorporated into the more comprehensive and better financed services of the Western welfare states. There was no one single tradition, although American casework influenced practice methods for a time. The Nordic countries, following Sweden's example, created a comprehensive welfare state model, but many Western countries developed little provision. Social work disappeared in the 'second world', developed an emphasis on social development in developing countries, and in the rapidly developing economies was incorporated into the state to reduce the social stresses of economic growth.

Chatterjee (1996) proposes that there are three competing accounts of the development of welfare states, none of them wholly satisfactory, that the welfare state is:

■ an ideological compromise between liberal individualism and socialist ideas (Chapter 6)
■ a camouflage for class, gender and interest group conflicts
■ a byproduct of industrialisation, seeking social stability at a time of extensive social change.

These issues are apparent in the development of social work. To achieve post-war reconstruction, most Western states arrived at a social settlement that accepted varying degrees of state welfare, supported by policies aiming towards high male employment balanced by continuing emphasis on individual responsibility through insurance and personal responsibility. Women resumed a domestic role supporting this social policy. Less industrialised Western states, particularly those affected by strong religious influences, and developing nations freeing themselves from colonial control began to develop elements of social welfare, but this was not yet strong. Communist nations provided state welfare through politically based work organisations, rather than social work. The impact of social work in the English-speaking tradition of Britain and American states, compared with the more socialist tradition of some European countries, suggests that it was one of the important individualist elements of the political settlement of this period, rather than being the product of the socialist aspect of the welfare state. It was always a discretionary rather than universal service. It compensated for inadequate general provision, rather than being central to the welfare states. Moreover, it supported the gender and class divides of the post-war welfare states, by its role in supporting family and community.

This ambiguous political position left social work less certain when it came under question in the last two decades of the twentieth century in the UK and USA than its success during the welfare state period might have suggested. Powell and Hewitt (2002) explore explanations for changes in the concept of the welfare state, including changes in economic systems, the political impact of ideas of social citizenship, the need for organisational forms to deal with more complex social requirements and changes in social attitudes. These changes have had their impact on social work as a variety of welfare regimes implies a variety of roles of social work. The next chapter examines this shift to greater questioning of social work as part of a questioning of the role of the state in welfare provision.

CHAPTER 4

Social Work in Question: 1970s–2001

In the last third of the twentieth century, political and social support for state welfare became more uncertain and social work's role and position more ambiguous. In countries with developed economies, social work came to be questioned, even attacked, in various ways. Yet the role of social services and the activities of social workers have, viewed internationally, continued to grow, because in many other countries where there has been little social provision, social professions made progress. Even where social work has been under attack, certain kinds of social work have continued to make progress. For example, Western-style social provision began to develop in Communist or formerly Communist states, social care remained strong in the Nordic countries, particularly child care support for female employment, social development became an important focus in developing countries, and there was interest in informal and social education in countries with a tradition of social pedagogy (Benelux, French, Germanic and Nordic countries) or radical informal education (South American countries).

The uncertainty arose more in English-speaking countries, therefore, even though there was retrenchment and questioning everywhere. This period, therefore, presents us with some of the conflicts and tensions in the role of social work in present-day societies, which help us to understand it better.

Crucial international trends during this period were the breakdown of the Bretton Woods post-war economic management system, in turn raising questions about whether universal social welfare was affordable. The globalisation of economies meant that companies were no longer economically dependent on a stable

83

local workforce, weakening political support for social provision and social reform and permitting the export of jobs to low-wage areas (Bujard, 1996). Consequently, the New Right, economic rationalist critique of the welfare state gained influence. Associated with this, managerialist approaches developed in the administration of public services such as social work (Pollitt, 1993), and attitudes to welfare and public services, such as social work, changed. In postindustrial, postmodern societies, containing a greater range and diversity and professional responses to that, social work seemed less important, and the professionalisation of services was questioned. During this period, the 'second world' of Communist societies, with their distinctive approach to welfare, broke down. In the Asia-Pacific region, new industrialised societies developed. However, many economies and political systems, particularly in Latin America and Africa, developed only slowly.

Chapter 3 discussed how the social developments of the 1960s had given impetus to social professions in many different welfare regimes. However, although social work seemed well established, except in Nordic countries its role in universal welfare provision was ambiguous. Therefore, when more conservative governments came to power during the last part of the twentieth century, its individualising rather than universal focus seemed appropriate to a New Right policy of selective social provision, but its flexible social attitudes and insecure establishment made it an easy symbol of the 'nanny state'. While the New Right critique attacked many aspects of social work and welfare, it was not one project with a focus on social welfare, but a range of movements, both responding to and initiating changes in views about citizenship and rights of the 'public' and the role of the public services (Hughes et al., 1998). Postmodernism implies a higher valuation of individual and small group development, pursuing sectional interests rather than the collective welfare that engaged support in the 'welfare state' era. This tendency towards extending variety in welfare structures and philosophies reduced the consensus about welfare. New social movements challenged the image that Britain contained a homogeneous social composition comprising mainly white families, with male 'breadwinners' and female wives and mothers. The New Right challenged the image of the state as a neutral interpreter of social expectations and social welfare as universal, benevolent and endless (Clarke et al., 1998).

Social work at its zenith

British social work reached its zenith with the implementation of the Social Work (Scotland) Act 1968 and the Local Authority Personal Social Services Act 1970; Table 4.1 summarises the legal and administrative developments since then. The British Association of Social Workers was created by a merger in April 1970 of eight specialist associations, mimicking the American merger of 1955 (Payne, 2002; Chapter 8). These developments united social workers' organisations and gave social work a professional leadership role within a local government department, buttressed by the legal requirement on local authorities to appoint a 'director of social services' (Scotland: 'social work'). The professional reorganisation identified social work as one generic activity, whereas previous specialist associations implied the independence of separate forms of practice, such as child care or psychiatric social work.

Considerable expansion of the services followed, during the Conservative administration of Edward Heath (1970–74), when Sir Keith Joseph was secretary of state for the social services, responsible for a central government ministry, the Department of Health and Social Security (DHSS), with social security and health as the main constituents. An important element of the expansion was a move to corporate management in local government This meant that separate professionally based departments were coordinated by a chief executive to pursue an overall strategy. The chief executive displaced the former town clerks, who had been the principal legal advisers to councils. This did not always work well, but where it did, social work gained from the Seebohm reorganisation by being, for the first time, at the top table in local government, providing a large and significant service. Local government reorganisation in 1974 created larger local authorities with considerable financial power and large workforces. Another reorganisation in 1974 created a single NHS from the previously existing three elements of the local authority health services, which had a public health remit, hospital services and family health services provided by general practitioners. As part of this reorganisation, health-related social work was, controversially, transferred from the NHS to SSD (social service department) management (Scotland: SWD – social work department). This made SSDs/SWDs the primary providers of all major social services in an influential local government department.

Table 4.1 British legislation and reports, important for social work 1981–2001

Date	Subject title	Comment
1982	Barclay Report on the role and tasks of social workers	Confirmed the role of social work as part of public services; emphasised community social work as a local generic response
1983	Mental Health Act 1983	Established 'approved social worker' with special qualifications to provide some civil rights protection on admission of mentally ill people to mental hospital
1984	Registered Homes Act 1984	Regulation and inspection of private and voluntary sector of residential care homes by local authorities
1985	House of Commons Select Committee (Report on Community Care)	Raised concerns about the effectiveness and coordination of community care policy in relation to at risk groups of mentally ill and mentally handicapped (learning disabled) people
1986	Disabled Persons (Services, Consultation and Representation) Act 1986	Local authorities required to provide an assessment of a disabled person's needs on request
1986	Audit Commission Report on community care	Confirmed the ineffectiveness and conflicting priorities of community care policies leading to 'perverse incentives' to continue institutional care
1987	Firth Report on financing of residential care	Confirmed financing and priority problems arising from the growth of private residential care
1987	Access to Personal Files Act 1987	Confirmed clients' rights to access to manual personal files
1988	Wagner Report on residential care	Recommended seeing residential care as part of a continuum of care services, extensive research reviews and support for case management
1988	Griffiths Report on community care	Recommended leading role in community care for local authority social services, a mixed economy of care and care management
1989 (DH)	White Paper: *Caring for People*	Government committed to Griffiths recommendations
1989	Children Act 1989	Revised the basis of child protection and child care work, with an emphasis on partnership between professionals and parents
1990	National Health Service and Community Care Act 1991	Implemented internal market in NHS and community care reforms

cont'd

Table 4.1 cont'd

Date	Subject title	Comment
1995	Disability Discrimination Act	First attempt at legislation in this field
1995	Carers (Recognition and Services) Act 1995	Required assessment of and provision for carers' needs separate from clients' needs
1996	Mental Health (Patients in the Community) Act	Confirmed Care Programme Approach to mentally disordered offenders and introduced supervision registers
1996	Community Care (Direct Payments) Act 1996	Permitted local authorities to make payments to clients to employ their own assistance
1998 (DH)	White Papers: *Modernising Social Services* and *Modernising Mental Health Services*	Introduced New Labour 'modernisation agenda', focusing on delivery of quality multi-agency services involving service users
1998	Crime and Disorder Act 1998	Introduced multi-agency youth offending teams
1998	Human Rights Act 1998	Incorporates the European Convention on Human Rights into British law
1999	Disability Rights Commission Act 1999	Established a Disability Rights Commission to pursue rights for disabled people
2001	Care Standards Act 2001	Established systematic regulation of social care services and social work profession

The following Labour government continued the expansion, until, in 1976, an economic crisis occurred and a rise in oil prices, the 'oil price shock', ended the stable period of economic expansion and led to expenditure constraints. These applied particularly to local authority staffing expenditures, and strains towards the end of the Labour government's second term of office led to a 'winter of discontent' (1979), in which many local authority services were affected by strikes. SSDs were also affected, particularly in major cities, and this episode was a factor in an emerging image of social work as radical and left-wing (Chapter 8).

The Kilbrandon (1964) and Seebohm (1968) Reports encouraged a focus on community and preventive work, which enjoyed a period of development. This connected with radical social work (Chapter 10; Bailey and Brake, 1975; Corrigan and Leonard, 1978). Many SSDs appointed community workers to stimulate local voluntary and community sector development.

The community development programmes of the Labour government focused on areas of urban decay (Loney, 1983). A range of initiatives such as Education Priority Areas and Britain's own poverty programme, the Urban Programme, sought to engage local community action in resolving the problems of localities where traditional industry was beginning to decline and with it employment and social support. Volunteering was also encouraged by the Aves Report (1969) on volunteering in the social services, and the Volunteer Centre (now Volunteering England) was set up as a result.

The Seebohm Report (1968) promoted a local focus for services, and the size of the new SSDs made it possible for the first time to create local 'area offices' displacing the town centre based offices of the former specialist departments. An unexpected inflow of work to more local provision, together with the idea of a 'single door' for people with problems and a more generic organisation of services, led area teams to organise 'intake' services (Buckle, 1981). The American innovation of task-centred work was tried out in an influential experiment and pronounced a success in enabling offices to focus and limit their involvement in complex cases (Goldberg et al., 1985). There was interest in workload management systems, such as Vickery's (1977), and priority systems (Hall, 1975).

Localisation stimulated interest in community relationships, and the idea of community social work emerged. The growing academic importance of sociology brought influences from structural-functional sociological ideas through systems theory in 'integrated' (Pincus and Minahan, 1973; Specht and Vickery, 1977) or 'unitary' (Goldstein, 1973) methods of practice. Community social work emerged in a number of experiments after the local government reorganisation, reducing the size of social services local offices, making them better informed and more proactive in local communities and connecting social work staff with the increasing number of paraprofessional staff in social services departments, who often came from the local community. Another factor was the incorporation of domiciliary care services, such as home helps and meals on wheels, into social services from their former position in health departments (Hadley and McGrath, 1980).

Child care services were affected by the implementation of parts of the Children and Young Persons Act 1969, the height of the movement to see offending as allied to deprivation. This led to a shift of the supervision of young offenders from probation to social services, the merger of the approved school system for young offenders into local authority children's homes and the development of 'intermediate treatment', promoting community leisure and education activities as a more acceptable substitute for offending. Concern was redirected towards cruelty to children by the importation, particularly by the social worker Joan Court (e.g. 1969), during the early 1970s from the USA of concern about 'battered baby syndrome', a medicalised description of physical abuse of children. Court's battered child research unit was an important factor in modernising and revivifying the work of the NSPCC. The concern about cruelty, not previously a big issue, was further stimulated by a series of scandals about poor child care provision and practice in the new social services departments (Chapter 7), the first being a foster child, Maria Colwell, who had been returned to and subsequently killed by her parents. Failures to listen to the concerns of foster carers and neighbours and other communication problems were publicised. Recommendations in a subsequent report (DHSS, 1974) began a process of setting up extensive administrative procedures. The minority report by a social work academic, Olive Stevenson, trenchantly set out the difficulties of the social work task. Local area child protection committees, representing local health and social care agencies, convened case conferences to investigate and make decisions about cases of suspected child abuse, and a register of cases where there was a fear of non-accidental injury to children was established in each area. Further cases, associated press criticism and high-profile inquiries led to defensive practice by social workers and increasingly high priority being given to child protection work over child care, allowing the Conservative government to retreat from a commitment to extensive child care provision to a more limited and authoritarian protective function (Parton, 1985).

The Chronically Sick and Disabled Persons Act 1970 began a phase of development of provision for disabled people. This also had a preventive and developmental element, because it encouraged local authorities to identify the extent of need. The research departments of the new SSDs carried out many community surveys, practical provision improved, but only slowly. A disabled people's movement was also fostered by the increased interest and commitment (Oliver, 1998).

In mental health, there was concern for the loss of specialism. Psychiatrists and GPs were concerned about the loss of the medically oriented male 'mental welfare officer', often with a mental health nursing background, from the health to social services department as they were replaced by younger social workers, more often female and with a more critical approach to psychiatry (Timmins, 1996).

The change in voluntary organisations towards a more campaigning and innovatory style continued. For example, the National Association for Mental Health was formed in the 1940s around the time of the creation of the NHS from a range of mental health interests, with a strong medical influence and the involvement of many social workers. It transmuted itself into a campaign for legal changes to the Mental Health Act 1959, improvements in care within the mental hospitals and the civil rights of patients.

Many of these developments were critical of the welfare state, both in the detail of how it treated individuals, but more generally in identifying how controlling welfare might be. The 'radical' social work view criticised how social work and welfare services became aligned with the interests of the rich and powerful, and how state services became bureaucratised and controlling. The professionalisation of social work was criticised as being potentially to the advantage of the professionals, but not to the people who use their services. They were seen as 'consumers' of services rather than clients for therapeutic help, and early consumer research (Mayer and Timms, 1970; Chapter 9) showed that they were often uncomprehending of what social workers were doing.

Similar experiences affected social work in Europe. In countries where social welfare was already well developed, progress continued. The development of the European Union also stimulated social provision. The objective of having a 'level playing field' in economic policy required social provision to be broadly equivalent in costs and extent. By the Treaty of Paris in 1972, by which the UK and other candidates joined the original six countries of what was to become the European Union, a Social Action Programme against poverty and homelessness was established (James, 1980). This developed into the Social Fund and a smaller anti-poverty programme, mainly focused on unemployment.

In Germany, where social work in health care had been confined to local public health offices and was underdeveloped, it spread for the first time in community services provided by health insurance organisations and in hospitals as a result of an enabling Act in 1972 (Göppner, 1998). Some *länder* (autonomous regions) passed legislation requiring social services in hospitals. Social work became more active in psychiatry, when this developed a more community focus in the 1970s and in the rehabilitation of drug addicts and alcoholics.

Nordic welfare states continued to develop. In Sweden, for example, social security entitlements were extended, and there was criticism of the discretionary focus of the existing social care legislation, which was the only element of the state that was not fully universal (Hort and McMurphy, 1997). A social investigation committee recommended coordinated legislation, enacted in the Social Services Act 1980, implemented in 1982. The approach was holistic, with the aim of taking people's full situation into account if they applied for help. Care and support was to be voluntary, based on democratic ideals of solidarity, promoting economic and social security, equality of living conditions and active participation in community life. There was a legal entitlement to care, if a person could not provide it in any other way, which must be designed to enhance the independent living resources of the individual. Legislation to provide for compulsory care of young people (1990) and substance abusers (1988) was only to be invoked if voluntary services were insufficient. Services were decentralised at the municipal level.

Where social welfare provision was less well developed, social work was slower to achieve new roles. López-Blasco (1998) argues that social work did not begin to develop in Spain until the effect of industrialisation and tourism led to substantial social change in the 1970s, and the second Vatican Council opened up the Catholic Church to greater social change. After the re-establishment of democratic government on the death of the dictator, Franco, social work began to develop, including social pedagogy (Chapter 2). The extent of social change encouraged the use of this model of informal social education.

Civil and welfare rights movements in the USA began to have an effect on social work (Trattner, 1999: 344–5). A newly formed Association of Black Social Workers demanded stronger roles for minority ethnic groups in the National Association for Social Work (NASW), and a greater concern for poverty and racism within social work and its agencies. A radical student Social Welfare Workers Movement rejected casework and argued for social work to promote social change. The Ad Hoc Committee on Advocacy (1969) recommended an advocacy role as essential to social work. The Council on Social Work Education (CSWE) included requirements to work for social change in the curriculum of social work education, and NASW changed its code of ethics to include a responsibility for social action. Similar radicalisation affected British social work, and community and radical trends drew interest at international conferences.

There was going to be much to fight for. The welfare reforms and attempts at social change of the 1960s began to dissipate in poor delivery and conservative backlash. One of the problems was a rising tide of economic difficulty. Inflation rose rapidly in the late 1960s and 70s. This had some benefits. The Republican president, Nixon, in power from 1968, although ideologically opposed to social welfare provision, inflation-proofed social security and food stamp benefits and this helped many poor people. Also administrative reforms produced substantial hidden improvements in benefits (Trattner, 1999: 351). However, rising welfare costs led to pressure for retrenchment especially through an austerity programme in the cities. The need for this was symbolised by New York City becoming bankrupt in 1975, mainly because of special features in its role in the state and the decline in its economic base, but with much of the blame attached to the rising costs of welfare (Katz, 1996: 290–1).

Japan's successful economy also led to substantial development of services, but in a rather bureaucratic pattern, with substantial state provision as well as large employers' services for their workers. Japan was seen to be developing a 'Japanese-model welfare society' (Takahashi, 1997: Ch. 8). Japan is dependent on oil imports and was profoundly affected by the oil price shock; welfare costs rose substantially. By the late 1970s, the policy was being criticised and the idea of a 'welfare society with vitality' developed, 'vitality' implying that provision should not be so extensive as to damage self-help and a sense of independence. Economic growth began to decline, and substantial retrenchment of expenditures began. Although Thatcherite and

Reaganomic policies were discussed, the emphasis was on strengthening Japanese family traditions.

In Hong Kong, another successful Far Eastern economy, the conceptualisation of social welfare as a concomitant of citizenship was beginning to emerge, partly as a result of rioting in 1966–67, after which the government realised that a more complex and strained urban society was developing than the previous small trading post. White Papers in 1965 and 1972 (Social Welfare Department, 1965, 1972) expressed a shift from a relief approach focused on refugees to a professionalised public service (Chow, 1982; Kwan, 1989). Liaison with local Kaifong community associations shifted towards community development policies to encourage self-help through mutual aid committees at the same time (Leung, 1982). These became radicalised by importing social action ideas in the 1970s and a number of neighbourhood-level community development associations played an important role in urban development in the 1970s, surviving into the 1980s. Such initiatives began to decline in importance as the colony approached incorporation into the People's Republic of China in 1997 (Leung, 1996).

British social work under attack: the 1980s and 90s

In the late 1970s, there was a perceived crisis in government, partly because of strains on the post-1945 economic order, given the push of the oil price shock. In Britain, there was conflict between trade unions and government in the 'winter of discontent', which led to a perception that the country was ungovernable. The incoming Thatcher government's response in 1979 to these issues was to increase control, particularly of expenditure, and this implied increased accountability, particularly through various performance measures and mechanisms. An important mechanism was the creation of the Audit Commission and the National Audit Office from pre-existing organisations, with the aim of evaluating not only financial probity but also effectiveness in achieving policy outcomes.

As soon as social work in Britain achieved being at the centre of a local government department with a more coordinated professional image, its position began to deteriorate. There were three elements to the questions about it:

- Service failures, particularly in child protection
- A professional attack on its 'therapeutic pretensions' (Nellis, 1989) and 'social policing' role
- A political attack on its role in the welfare state.

The professional attack came from both the Right and Left. The radical left-wing attack saw social work as a form of 'soft policing', pursuing the interests of capital operating through the state. Harris (1998) shows how this analysis relied on Braverman's (1974) thesis that scientific or rational management was encroaching on front-line workers' professional discretion through the development of large organisations similar to multinational companies. The right-wing attack was seen in a book by Brewer and Lait (1980), respectively a medical doctor and social policy lecturer. This criticised the inadequate evidence base of social work, drawing on behavioural psychology and the evidence of ineffectiveness that built up in the 1960s (Chapter 9). It also attacked the pretensions of training.

These two elements of attack led to concern within the profession, so that BASW promoted the idea of an enquiry into social work; this was eventually supported by the government as a way of defusing the growing scale of criticism. The Barclay Report (1982) on the role and tasks of social work encapsulated a political critique of the excessive pretensions of social work in a minority report by Pinker (1982), with the majority support for the idea of community social work. Research showed, eventually, that this technique did increase the responsiveness and community awareness of the social services, without necessarily making the outcomes for clients any more effective (Hadley and McGrath, 1984; Bayley et al., 1987).

Further child care scandals ensued (Chapter 7). Assessment and liaison procedures were steadily enhanced, leading to a defensive approach to practice. Reactions to these scandals in a Conservative political environment suggested that parental rights needed protection against professional overreaction, mainly by social workers. Research (Chapter 10) also showed the need for better planned services. Child care professionals supported a recasting of child care legislation in the Children

Act 1989, leading to a balancing of parental with children's interests. It also promoted concern for the child's 'wishes and feelings' by participation in decision-making as the consumer of services. Organisational change pushed forward better planned, long-term care for children, emphasising substitute care through adoption. In these services, there was evidence that decision-making was slow and children drifted in the system. The 1980s ideology of permanency planning (Morris, 1984; Maluccio, 1986) proposed that a decision about the best permanent placement for a child in care should be made quickly and implemented assertively. This was opposed by writers with a focus on poverty, who suggested that effective community support for families would resolve many of the difficulties that birth parents experienced (Holman, 1976, 1981, 2000; Henderson, 1995). A number of services offering family-based interventions grew up. An important development of family centres, based around care and parent education in the early years was a response to this trend (Stones, 1994). However, research and constant entreaties by the Department of Health suggested that agencies did not have enough resources to shift their work from crisis child protection services, where they were vulnerable to political and public criticism (Aldgate et al., 1994).

Implementation of the Act built on 1980s' anxieties about child protection scandals and produced a strong concern for effective assessment and multi-agency cooperation. These were enforced by a huge volume of Department of Health guidance and instructions. Social workers' acceptance of these reflected a covert bargain with government for support in the event of public criticism, provided that guidance had been followed, and encouraged the bureaucratisation of practice (Payne, 1997a). Garrett (1999: 42) suggests, in an analysis of the 'looking after children' provisions of the Children Act 1989, that technocratic devices to systematise and manage practice in the late twentieth century represent 'an extraordinary ambition, even conceit: an academic and technocratic project, according to the *Training Guide*, to codify and schematise "explicitly what good parenting means in practice"'.

The need to develop child care provision to meet the anxieties of this period tended to work against the generic practice of the 1970s. Among the most important areas where client group specialisation developed was in mental health work. The anxiety about the loss of social work expertise in this field, the slow pace of development in community provision in the 1970s from a low base together the Mind campaigns in mentally ill people's rights led to the reform of the mental health legislation in the Mental Health Act 1983. This formalised the role of social work as a defender of legal rights, by providing for an 'approved social worker' (Scotland: mental health officers), with special training and qualification to replace the mental welfare officers of the 1959 Act. The ASW would act as a counterbalance to medical opinion in the compulsory admission of mentally ill people to hospital.

Campaigns about what were then known as 'mentally handicapped people' also led to increasing recognition of their human rights; the hospitalisation of mentally handicapped children virtually ended. Increasingly, people with mental handicaps were seen as disabled, rather than as served by the mental health services, and the term 'learning disabilities' emerged. The Jay Report (1979) sought to promote the new policy of normalisation (Chapter 7), enabling people with learning disabilities to live with their families or in ordinary housing in the community and receive effective education. Material and educational resources were sought to realise normal lifestyles, and a change in people's attitudes was sought to avoid obstructing, by stigma and exclusion, how people with learning disabilities and mental illnesses want to live (Ramon, 1996: 52–4). Applied to mental illness services, this approach connected to the movement for dehospitalisation and deinstitutionalisation, so that people were moved out of hospitals and any institutions were made less forbidding and controlling. The idea of normalisation (Chapter 7) proposed that services should facilitate a life similar to non-disabled people. During the 1980s, the ordinary housing movement promoted living in small groups with community support (Bayliss, 1987). Moves to shift funding from hospital to community services gathered pace during the 1980s.

These changes began to raise questions about the long-standing policy of community care. A House of Commons Select Committee on the Social Services (1985) report on community care drew attention to the lack of progress in implementing community care, particularly for mentally ill and handicapped people. Shortly afterwards a study by the new Audit Commission (1986) showed that by reducing expenditure on local authority home care services and making social security grants available for admission to private and voluntary sector residential care, the government had created 'perverse incentives' that encouraged the use of costly residential rather than community care. This caused a huge increase in social security costs. Sir Roy Griffiths, a private sector consultant, investigated community care and recommended (Griffiths Report, 1988) continued local authority responsibility for it, as part of a quasi-market in which local authorities would add to their provision by contracting for services provided by a range of private and voluntary sector providers. Social workers would create 'packages of care' using care management (Payne, 1995). This practice reform was indistinct in government guidance, but was primarily intended to constrain cost pressures (Lewis and Glennerster, 1996). The proposals were enacted in the NHS and Community Care Act 1990 and implemented during the 1990s. They had a considerable impact on social work practice with adults, since in many areas it led to a largely managerial process, with many forms and tick-boxes to complete, reducing the interpersonal aspects of social work (Sheppard, 1995; Gorman and Postle, 2003).

At the same time, criticism of the fieldwork focus of the Barclay Report (1982) led the government to set up a review of residential care, eventually published as the Wagner Report (1988). Residential care was going through one of its crises. Part of the reason was the rapid expansion during the 1980s of a substantial private sector in residential care, mainly for elders. However, residential care for children was declining. One reason was that it was expensive and difficult to staff. Also, the style and role of residential care was changing, as the authoritarian emphasis of the old approved schools for offenders was rejected in favour of more treatment-oriented regimes, and more disturbed and difficult children needed more specialised care (Cliffe, 1991).

There was little direct political concern with the social services during the Conservative Thatcher administration (1979–90). They were not so large or costly as education and health care. Nellis (1989: 104) argues that the lack of political criticism was also because, as social services were low in public esteem, direct ideological criticism was not required. However, some Conservative political issues were pursued in a low-key way through political decision-making during the period. This included the Conservative emphasis on a traditional view of 'family', represented in the concern for parental as against children's rights in the Children Act 1989 and the development of a quasi-market in community care.

Harris (1999) argues that social work had been incorporated into state provision by developing a bureau-professional role in the welfare state period. However, Marshall's (1950) assumption, that social citizenship was derived from participation in and provision from the welfare state, meant that social work became the object of attack, in that it infringed clients' rights, making them passive and dependent. The New Right sought to define a consumer-citizen in a quasi-market as the appropriate understanding of the role of clients, rather than the 'social citizen'. This may be seen in a speech of Mrs Thatcher to the annual social services conference in 1976, where she argued that 'industry and trade are the basic social service because they provide a large number of jobs and without a job there is no way of looking after one's family' (Timmins, 1996: 359).

Lymbery (2001) summarises the consequences for the state social services (although he refers to social work) as:

- Becoming clearly non-universal, focused on statutory protective services for children and mentally ill people and on assessment for social provision for other adults with long-term care needs
- Continued cost-cutting leading to a process of constant change and uncertainty in agencies, increasing workers' stress and insecurity
- Growing emphasis on regulation and quality assurance
- Widening gaps between evident need and resources.

Pinker (1990) emphasised that the way in which the priority given to entrepreneurial provision by the Conservatives coloured attacks on the social services as part of public services. Harris (2002) shows how this criticism has introduced business terminology and procedures into social services, reorienting it from a welfare approach towards a service-providing organisation. More generally, the focus on government as a commissioner of services rather than a direct provider, the wider range of agencies providing social services and a stronger focus on effectiveness and financial management in service provision has strengthened the importance of management rather than professional work. Pollitt (1993) and Clarke and Newman (1997) show that managerialism is a new settlement of relationships between politics, economics and the professions, including local government professions such as social work. Professions organised through bureaucratic hierarchies (bureau-professionalism) are replaced by generalist management on behalf of consumers. Managers control professional decisions to meet the objectives of the organisation, and professionals' discretion is limited. These moves have had an international impact.

Another important development arose from the growth of user movements. Research into consumer views of social work (Chapter 10) during the 1970s drew attention to the difference in perspectives between professionals and clients of social work. One response to this was to seek greater participation by clients in social work decisions, for example, with a BASW report on client participation (BASW, 1980) and another encouraging access to case records (BASW, 1983). Subsequently, there was a movement to see clients as consumers of services and promote mechanisms for them to express their views. These initiatives initially connected to the emphasis on community organisation, but during the 1980s, the government's market approach to managing services suggested a greater emphasis on consumer opinion. Countering this, more radical views emphasised the rights of consumers as citizens to influence services and professional decisions (Beresford and Croft, 1993). Advocacy developed, involving volunteers and specialised organisations, to allow the views of people with learning disabilities unable to express their own opinions of services (Brandon et al., 1995). This progressed into movements to develop organisations of mental health services users and carers (Rogers et al., 1992) and more widely to promote partnerships between professionals, users and carers (Barnes, 1997). Advocacy for children and young people also grew up, particularly in care services during the 1990s, and then more widely (Dalrymple and Hough, 1995). A cadre of children's rights officers grew up to support this. Professional techniques developed to enable young people in care to contribute to decisions about them. One important example is family group conferences (Marsh and Crow, 1997), which emerged from New Zealand practice, trying to engage families in managing the behaviour of young offenders.

Important professional developments concerned the social responses to an increasingly diverse and fragmented society. This was most obviously an issue in relations between ethnic groups, although hostile relations between white British and ethnic minority groups stretch back into Roman or medieval times (Panayi, 1994). Many British people migrated to the colonies throughout the period of the empire; children in care were, for example, almost forced into emigration. Migration from European countries, particularly of Jews, and Ireland to the British mainland also took place in the 1800s, and this often led to discrimination and prejudice. However, legislation and administrative action on discrimination was limited and ineffective until the 1970s.

Growing migration from the new Commonwealth, that is, the Caribbean, African and Asian countries that were formerly part of the British Empire, occurred in the 1950s, and social conflict occurred. Legislation by the 1960s' Labour governments established institutions concerned with race relations and the legal control of discrimination. However, this had only minor effects on everyday practice in social work agencies, although during the 1970s it became increasingly evident that a high proportion of black people were being affected mainly by the disciplinary element of social services, for example children being taken into care, compared with the white population. Also, people from minority ethnic groups did not seem to receive caring social services in the same proportion as the white population. The Race Relations Act 1976 formed the first effective legislation attempting to deal with racial discrimination, indirect as well as direct (Solomos, 2003). It followed the similar Sex Discrimination Act 1975, which also formed the first effective legislation on discrimination against women. Both followed a movement building on American civil rights legislation.

The first response within social work to these changes was to try to identify particular services or issues that needed to be provided, for example the special needs of Asian women or Caribbean children. In particular, attempts were made to recruit foster carers and adopters from minority ethnic groups. However, during the 1980s, following concern about riots and civil disturbances in urban areas, social work agencies began to focus on ways in which their services discriminated against minority ethnic groups. This move responded to the growth of sociological analyses of racialised relationships (Macey and Moxon, 1996). It was also stimulated by a shift in radical social work from a class analysis towards focusing on the oppression of women and minority ethnic groups (Payne, 1997b). Some agencies attempted in-service race awareness training, but this was experienced by many white workers as blaming. Social work consequently also developed a literature on anti-racist practice (for example Dominelli, [1988] 1997). This focus broadened into anti-discriminatory practice, reflecting a concern about discrimination against a wide range of social work client groups, and anti-oppressive practice, reflecting a focus on ways in which services could be oppressive, rather than just discriminatory. Developments of these moves sought to promote diversity by responding to black perspectives (Ahmad, 1990), and promoting sensitivity to ethnic and cultural differences (O'Hagan, 2001).

During the late 1980s, CCETSW, the British social work training body, included training for anti-racist practice in its requirements, and established a project to produce guidance to include this in social work education programmes. There was an intellectual and political backlash against this in the early 1990s (for example Pinker, 1993), criticising the analysis that oppressive power is the major cause of discrimination and the tendency to zealous pursuit of anti-discriminatory behaviour. However, efforts to include anti-discriminatory perspectives in social work education continued (Penketh, 2000). A focus on empowerment practice, to assist minorities in overcoming discrimination, and attempts to value diverse cultures and identities in societies emerged from these controversies by the end of the 1990s.

Other aspects of anti-discriminatory practice important for social work derived from developing feminist ideas, which emphasised the oppression of women by social workers' decisions and practices and drew attention to the male domination of management and the high proportion of women in untrained domestic roles in social care (Dominelli, 2002). A disability movement campaigned successfully for increased rights for disabled people, and this led to legislation against discrimination and to enable them to receive payments to manage care for themselves (Table 4.1; Zarb, 1995; Oliver, 1996; Oliver and Barnes, 1998). A related carers movement, developing from research and feminist analysis of the effects of caring on women's lives (Finch and Groves, 1983; Qureshi and Walker, 1988; Morris, 1993), campaigned successfully for legislation to require social service assessments of carers' needs alongside the assessments of clients (Table 4 1). Such shifts in influence for service users and carers interacted with professional movements towards advocacy practice and client or consumer citizen participation discussed above.

Deprofessionalisation became an issue during the 1980s when Manpower Services Commission schemes for training and temporary employment of no more than a year supported expansion in voluntary organisations, especially in areas of higher unemployment. These gave a temporary and unskilled aspect to many services that were substituted for state services in the government's quasi-markets (Payne, 1986). This developed in a low-skilled and low-paid social care sector, employing women in home care and residential care. The quasi-market in community care encouraged these developments in the private sector, regulating them through a series of Acts, starting with the Registered Homes Act 1984. While the local state regulated private sector providers, resources to do so were limited, and constant attempts to support the market by reducing 'red tape', and bureaucratic controls on entrepreneurship limited the impact of local authority regulation. Thus, the growth of a private and voluntary social care sector added a new element to the local government social services of the 1970s. Dominelli (1996), in a feminist and radical critique, argues that a number of factors contributed to the deprofessionalisation of social work during the 1980s and 90s, alongside the social fragmentation of individualist and neoliberal social thought in a postmodernist society. The managerialist tendency produced by market difficulties in the globalised economy led to the development of a reductionist and technical competence-based training. It also led to practice innovations such as care management, where the concern was to tailor packages of care services to defined needs, rather than deliver a comprehensive social work service. The feminist critique challenged social work's management of problems and behaviours, rather than concern for the whole person and the social factors affecting their lives.

British social work under New Labour

After a long period of Conservative government, the UK shifted to a Labour government under Tony Blair in 1997, re-elected in

2001. While social care was not a major plank of policy, it was affected by general government policies and priorities, which focused on education and health. A 'modernisation agenda' focused on effective delivery of services, including multi-agency cooperation, and involving users' and carers' own priorities. The subtitle of the social services White Paper (DH, 1998b) stating government policy, *Promoting Independence, Improving Protection, Raising Standards*, reflected continuing concern about the quality and effectiveness of protection, especially for children and mentally ill people, where there were statutory responsibilities. However, developments were slowly building on past policies, rather than representing a new direction. For example, Hearn and Sinclair (1998) have shown that, in children's services, more effective planning and needs' assessment had developed, together with better consultation of service users and parents, but improvements in resources or major changes in services had not occurred. This was, however, early in the life of the government, when public funding was heavily constrained.

Although some improvements in child care provision took place, with better planning and shorter periods of children being looked after by local authorities, problems with the quality of care for children remained when the Labour government took power in 1997. A number of quality improvement projects developed, notably a Quality Protects project, aimed to improve the security of attachments to carers. It also sought to protect children from repeated harm; improve the education, health and social development of children in need and looked after; facilitate transition to adulthood; improve facilities for disabled children; improve referral and assessment and obtain good value for the resources used (Berridge, 1999).

Another feature of policy was increased regulation. The New Labour government was committed at election to regulation for the social work profession, but its focus on other priorities left legislating the Care Standards Act 2000 to late in the government's first term. A national Care Standards Council in each of the four UK countries was established to bring together regulation of residential and daycare, adding to a continuing process of 'joint review' of statutory social services by the Audit Commission, the central government agency for effective resource management, and the social services inspectorates of the four countries. Finally, after lobbying for half a century, social workers achieved the registration of social workers, the Act making provision for a differently named registration body in each of the four countries (the General Social Care Council – GSCC – in England), which also took over responsibility for social work education from a discredited and disbanded CCETSW in 2001.

An important political development was an emphasis on the European idea of 'social exclusion'. This is a broad concept, implying exclusion from or marginalisation in democratic and legal systems, economic and labour market participation, family and community involvement and from social integration through citizenship in a welfare state (Munday, 1997). For New Labour, these general elements of social exclusion were an important driver for the development of new services to promote, for example, single mothers' and disabled people's participation in the labour market rather than continuing reliance on social security. Such moves often rely on specifically focused services with personnel trained for the task. For example, a report of the Prime Minister's Social Exclusion Unit identified a gap in support between school and work as an important element excluding young people from the labour market. It merged elements of the youth and careers services in a new Connexions service, with specifically trained 'personal advisers', using social work and counselling techniques to deal with this issue. The Crime and Disorder Act 1998 was another multi-agency device, aiming to give priority to preventing and dealing effectively with youth offending, which was given a very high priority by the Blair government.

While, traditionally, responses to problems with excluded groups have often used generic social work with wide professional discretion within a system of bureaucratic control, New Labour policies use limited social work techniques within highly specified services, reducing the flexibility and range of the services in favour of the delivery of the specific political policy. An important general piece of legislation was the Human Rights Act 1998 (and similar Welsh and Scottish legislation), incorporating the European Convention on Human Rights into English legislation. It enables people to challenge gross abuses of civil liberties and requires legal and administrative action to take account of human rights (Adams, 2002: 170–1). Again, the focus here is on general social provision applying to all, rather than caring provision for groups with specific needs.

In summary, alongside deprofessionalisation in British social care, professional social work is increasingly restricted to a regulatory, service-organising and policing role. However, this new regime offers possibilities of developments in other respects. A number of specialised jobs picks up social work skills and incorporates them in multiprofessional services such as Connexions or drug rehabilitation teams, aimed at particular government priorities. These moves add to the development of specialised groups of social workers in health care, for example in forensic social work in secure units with mentally disordered offenders and in palliative care. The future of social work in Britain may be in a range of roles in services fragmented by quasi-markets, government initiatives and the development of multiprofessional work, where social work activity interacts with other professions' roles.

International trends

British developments during this period interacted with international trends. During the 1980s, the administrations of Margaret Thatcher in Britain and Ronald Reagan in the USA were an important international ideological influence. There was an international political movement towards economic rationalism responding to the deregulation of economic markets. As in the previous period, European experiences mirrored the British changes, but generally did not go so far. Even in Nordic countries, there was considerable retrenchment and overheating of economies. Political consensus on the value of social services was lost, with an increasing focus on incentives and services to increase economic activity. However, it is not yet clear that this is a fundamental reconsideration of the universal Nordic welfare state, rather than a readjustment of priorities within its fundamental approach (Kosonen, 2001). Sweden and Finland cut back on services (Sipilä et al., 1997) and, increasingly, the public provision of services was replaced by financial support for relatives. For example, in Finland, attempts were made in the 1980s to reduce demand for children's daycare, an important plank of Nordic welfare states, by promoting parents' allowances. In Sweden, the first non-Social Democratic government since the 1930s sought to reduce expenditure on social insurance during its periods in power from 1976–82, but these cuts were generally defeated or later repealed (Lundström, 1989). Denmark also launched a wage compensation scheme for 'housewives' in 1995. In Norway, economic growth could not be maintained as a goal of the welfare state, and there was a pause in reforms and a consolidation of the range of provision (Hildeng, 1995). Market mechanisms, promoted in place of the previous substantial reliance on the role of the public sector, and the introduction of income controls in the mid-1970s were signs of a struggle against price inflation. A feeling of crisis in the welfare state emerged, as Norway realised it could not rely on sustained growth in oil income to maintain public expenditure. A 'new moralism' of a communitarian style emerged, emphasising a degree of private responsibility for welfare, including an emphasis on voluntary organisations and a balance between social rights and duties (Hildeng, 1995: 193).

In Germany, the policy that matters of procedure had to be dealt with according to legal and statutory requirements led to bureaucratisation as services grew, which stifled creativity and led to criticism of social workers' practice, even though they gained official recognition and higher status. A financial crisis in 1975 led to cutbacks in state support and attacks on users of welfare services as 'scroungers'. Conflicts between voluntary providers and the state arose, as these organisations lost public support and came to be seen as bureaucratic dependents of the state. Self-help and more radical groups grew up, providing alternative services, particularly in the field of women's services and the environment (and, outside social care, peace protests). Conservative elements in the long period of Christian Democratic (conservative) government during the 1980s and 90s emphasised volunteering and dismantling state provision. Self-help and alternative provision interacted with these movements to destabilise the state sector. However, particularly in children and youth services, more flexible and involving provision emerged.

Development of social services continued, with the important Child and Youth Welfare Act 1989, enacted in the same period as the British Children Act, which renewed the work of a service that merged both child care and protection and youth leisure and informal education. These two aspects of service are seen as related, unlike the separation in Britain into child care within the social work profession and youth work associated with education and community development provision.

One of the reasons for this is the importance of the social pedagogy element of social care in Germany (Chapter 10), which involves a focus on learning and personal development, rather than a therapeutic role for social work. After unification with Communist East Germany, the West German model was spread across the country during the 1990s, conflicting with the extensive social care provision, but absence of social work, in the East. Thus, while social care and social work are well established, there are still many uncertainties about its contribution to the social fabric and state provision in Germany. Göppner (1998) argues that social work in Germany, while less influential organisationally than medicine, has a well-established legal position. It is more successful when it is able to demonstrate successful outcomes. Its role is seen as combining personal help with advocacy, consultation, social training and networking roles.

During the late 1980s and 1990s, considerable change took place in Eastern European countries, involving considerable social change from formerly Communist regimes. In many cases, a small part of this change was to re-establish or renew social work (see Table 3.1). It contributed a liberalising and pluralist element, especially where, as in the Czech Republic, there was a degree of suspicion of and disruption to state services (Harris, 1997). This and the involvement of international charitable development agencies and movements towards the marketisation of services led to a strengthening of voluntary, not-for-profit sectors. In some countries where there was conflict, welfare developments were promoted as a form of 'preventive peace-keeping'. For example, Macedonia in the southern Balkans was affected by war in neighbouring countries and had a UN 'preventive deployment force' pursuing three policies: troop deployment, 'good offices' in trying to reduce tension and a focus on the 'human dimension'. This included a range of welfare interventions, including, for example, community development work among the Romany ethnic minority community (Deacon et al., 1996).

A crucial development of the late twentieth century has been an increased level of migration between continents and countries, war and social disruption leading to increased refugees and ethnic conflict. Cannan et al. (1992: 90) identify three types of service widespread in Western Europe:

■ Emergency provision for refugees and asylum-seekers, often associated with immigration controls

- Services providing for long-established minorities, often focused on specific needs arising from ethnic difference with the majority population or cultural and social needs
- Services for travellers, including Romany peoples.

In the USA, dealing with inflation dominated the presidency of Ford, Nixon's replacement in 1974. Manufacturing jobs were lost. Unemployment rose markedly and so did the numbers of women receiving social security and trapped in poverty (Katz, 1996: 284–5). Oil price inflation, due to instabilities in the Middle East, also affected the USA, particularly in 1977, affecting the presidency (1976–80) of the Democrat, Carter. Building on Nixon's attempts to require male workers to take part in employment schemes as a condition of receiving unemployment assistance (workfare), Carter introduced employment assistance schemes, as the Callaghan government had with the Manpower Services Commission in the UK. However, the backlash against expensive state provision was signalled during 1978 by electoral support in California for its governor's tax-cutting policies. In 1981, Governor Reagan took office as president.

Reaganomics focused on restricting social expenditure at the federal level, pursuing the traditional position (Chapter 2) that such matters should be the responsibility of individual states. The New Federalism policy proposed delegating welfare policies back to the states from 1984 onwards, although this was not fully implemented, due to a deep recession, which necessitated a large relief package in 1983. Attempts to cut assistance for disabled people were successfully resisted, and this led to a widely supported refinancing of the insurance scheme, which had run into financial difficulties (Trattner, 1999: Ch. 16).

Reagan's policy was based on supply-side economics, that is, the assumption that controlling the supply of resources was a better way of managing the economy than controlling expenditure. This approach gave priority to individualistic enterprise, reducing the burden of taxation on business and increasing military expenditure in pursuit of foreign policy objectives. The assumption was that if industry and commerce were more successful and able to supply more wealth, the benefits of this would trickle down to others in the economy because it would be generally richer, a new interpretation of the USA's long-standing approach to welfare of promoting a generally wealthy society. There was no evidence that this worked during the Reagan administration. Several years of tax cuts were balanced by borrowing, and although there was some deterioration in services, a substantial reversal of welfare provision did not occur. This left Bush, his Republican successor, elected in 1998, to deal with serious debt problems and his administration took very little action on domestic issues. States affected by another serious depression reduced welfare expenditure and the AFDC benefits became increasingly insecure.

An important professional development of this period was 'managed care', arising from the private health insurance system for meeting individuals' health costs. Such costs are far more important for Americans than the publicly funded health services commonplace in Europe, which in the USA are reserved for poor people. Managed health care often includes payment for social work and this led to a strengthening of private practice in the medical model, building on the introduction of private social work practice in the 1950s (Chapter 3). Such arrangements encouraged time-limited and structured forms of intervention, where costs could be controlled. Problems also had to be defined in terms that allied them to health problems. Although this system could limit flexibility in social work intervention, it made social work as a form of individual counselling and sometimes groupwork available in an unstigmatising way to wider populations. Heinenon and Spearmen (2001: 27–8) suggest that this process has not developed to the same extent in the USA's neighbour Canada, which has a more public sector system and social work is usually excluded from health care insurance.

Clinton, the Democrat president elected in 1992, attempted unsuccessfully to reform health care by providing for a comprehensive state system of health care on Canadian or European lines. The Personal Responsibility and Work Opportunity Reconciliation Act 1996, a Republican measure eventually supported by Clinton, finally reformed AFDC by abolishing the federal administration, replacing it with grant aid to states, which would decline over the following six years. The Act sets a lifetime maximum period for social security assistance of five years, and requires states to provide assistance with finding work. Legal immigrants had restrictions on their eligibility for food stamps and Medicaid (Trattner, 1999: Ch. 17). These measures responded to the increasing perception that AFDC was a 'something for nothing' programme, and they reimpose moral and social ideas that require employment as a sign of social good standing, at least for the poor (Waddan, 2003).

During this long period of retrenchment in welfare provision, the social work profession took part in campaigning against the losses and continued to develop professional work to reflect advocacy, social action and empowerment as valued objectives. However, the pressures towards private practice (Chapter 3) continued, particularly since private practice social work, as a form of counselling, could be funded through many employees' medical insurance, although this encouraged service provision rather than casework (or clinical social work, as it became known) and brief rather than comprehensive interventions. This trend was roundly attacked as a betrayal of the values and objectives of social work by Specht and Courtney (1994).

As in Britain, child protection continued to be the major focus of child welfare services, particularly as concern about child abuse and sexual abuse developed, and many ideas flowed from the USA to Britain, in a shared conservative political climate. Family preservation also continued to be an important value. In the 1970s and 80s, the policy of permanency planning was also influential, promoting early decisions about arrangements for care, clarification of the child's legal status and attempts to maintain secure and continuous care (Maluccio et al., 1986). The Adoption Assistance and Child Welfare Act 1980, America's first specifically child welfare legislation, sought more adoptions, speedy family reunification if possible, and fewer out-of-home placements. As in Britain, concern about racial matching policies reducing the speed and use of adoption rose during the 1990s, and legislation was passed in 1994 and 1996 to prevent race and ethnicity being used to delay adoption placements. Clinton developed an initiative in 1997 designed to increase adoptions by providing a federal grant to adopters. During the late 1990s, emergency response services for the rapid assessment of children developed, family maintenance and family reunification policies built on a thirty-year tradition of services to support families of origin to care for their children. The Family Preservation and Family Support Act 1993 increased federal funding for such services and encouraged innovation, promoting effective assessment and planning for work with families. During the late 1990s, there were signs that managed care would be imported into child welfare provision from adult care services, where it is extensively used (Brooks and Webster, 1999).

The international move towards retrenchment in welfare affected other countries. Canada retained its commitment to extensive welfare state provision, until in the late 1980s and 90s, the federal government began to reduce its involvement, delegating provision to the provinces, where commitment to welfare provision was variable and in some cases residual in approach (Hofmeyer et al., 1995).

As in Britain, overcoming racism and oppression has been a constant struggle for people from many different minorities across the world; this is not solely an issue for Western societies receiving migration from poorer countries. Each struggle creates a small area of progress, but this may need to be replicated many times and in many different situations to lead to greater equality and justice. Examples are African-American social workers, employed by the YMCA, who worked to achieve provision of services for black servicemen in Europe (Chandler, 1995), and attempts to make New York City's charitable funding conditional upon the desegregation of organisations, which was resisted by Protestant but embraced by Catholic organisations (Smith, 1995). Peiris (1996) discusses ethnic conflict between minority Tamils and majority Sinhalese in Sri Lanka during the 1980s and 90s. This serious ethnic conflict led to a reliance for security on family and ethnic links in oppressed groups, rather than democratic and participative political structures, thus further isolating the oppressed group.

In New Zealand, there was little private philanthropy and the public sector took an increasing role in welfare from the 1890s, culminating in the Social Security Act 1930, which introduced a range of basic social security benefits. During the 1950s, a range of special benefits were introduced, and this increased contact with and knowledge of poorer people. As a result, and influenced by the UK Seebohm reorganisation, the Department of Social Welfare Act 1970 created a central role for government in providing direct services and support for other providers. This led to an increasing centralisation and bureaucratisation of social welfare and an emphasis on individual casework (Barretta-Herman, 1994). This was criticised as being inflexible and ultimately generating unsustainable, escalating demands on the resources on the state, particularly as referrals of abused and neglected children expanded during the 1960s and 70s.

Connolly (1994) shows how concern about overrepresentation of Maori peoples among welfare clients in New Zealand contributed to the reform of children's legislation. Campaigns by and on behalf of the Maori indigenous population for more flexible treatment of their cultural demands, particularly in the report *Puao-Te-Ata-Tu* (Ministerial Advisory Committee, 1986), had an impact on professional recognition of the need for more ethnically sensitive practice; there was a substantial review of attitudes. Restructuring followed, reducing the role of the central department. Authority for service provision and support was decentralised to districts through district executive committees and institutional management committees in 1986.

The emphasis on family involvement in provision for children in New Zealand responded to an inquiry into the death of a child under supervision and concerns that families from minorities were not adequately involved in responses to children's problems, and led to legislation in 1989 (Connolly, 1994). The Children, Young Persons and the Families Act 1989, again at much the same time as British and German legislation, promoted involvement of community resources, families and community groups into work with children in difficulties through family conferences. However, this was done at a time of budget and service cuts, leading to competition for resources and dissatisfaction with reductions in service. Therefore, although greater participation and community involvement were achieved and professional independence became much more responsive to community concerns, New Zealand is an example of a relatively extreme shift towards what McDonald (1996) calls 'residualism'. There was a substantial change in economic and political policies and structures. State guarantees of social rights were reinterpreted towards family and community responsibility. State provision of services was shifted to contracting with private and voluntary organisations.

Not all countries were fully affected by the international shift towards New Right ideology. During the 1980s, Japan still had a successful economy, even though growth was slowing. Therefore, the perceived financial insecurity of many Western countries was less of a problem. However, specifically Japanese concerns rose about the growing population of elders, and policies on family and community support were emphasised. This led to proposals for the local administration of welfare services and stronger 'care at home' policies, and 'diversification' of providers, that is, greater use of the private sector (Takahashi, 1997). Also, the post-war bureaucratisation of social welfare services came to be seen as stultifying. The pattern of bureaucratised public services, with professionalised provision on the American model in health and occupational services, began to change in the 1980s, associated with growing concern for the rising number of elders in the population. The Certified Social Workers and Certified Care Workers Act 1987 led to developments in training, a separate professional association and growing importance for the local government social welfare office, reinforced by eight pieces of legislation in 1990, particularly supporting domiciliary services. Child care and protection had languished, but also began to develop in the 1990s. The 1990s also saw internationally borrowed policies to develop voluntary activity and participation in the *komyuniti* using *kōdinētā* of *borantiu* in a *nettowāku* (Takahashi's, 1997: 196, transliteration of borrowed English words: community, coordinators, volunteers, network). However, these deal with the specific Japanese concern to promote family and community policies to deal with an ageing population in financially straitened times.

African countries continued to focus on social development, still seeking to establish social institutions and services similar to more developed countries. There was a tendency for approaches to divide between forms of development with a socialist (maintaining central control of economies with a commitment to social expenditure) or capitalist (trying to balance economic development and social support) emphasis. However, economic problems led to international economic agencies such as the World Bank imposing capitalist-style policies (structural adjustment policies) in many countries during the 1980s and 90s. However, in very poor countries, unacceptable social stresses resulted and, during the 1990s, some areas of social expenditure were maintained (Adepogu, 1993). An important movement was the pan-African movement, which claimed a shared consciousness and intellectual and cultural heritage among black peoples throughout Africa (Yimam, 1990: 77). This promoted ideas of social welfare based on family and tribal systems, rather than using Western individualist ideas and values, such as self-determination (Silavwe, 1995).

In South Africa, where the apartheid regime was displaced by a new democratic system, a rather traditional form of social work shifted towards a greater emphasis on social development, with the concept of 'developmental social welfare' (Rankin, 1996). In Brazil (Jamur, 1996), as in many South American countries, the period of the 1980s was one of democratisation in politics and radicalisation in social work.

Some countries, while not excluding social work, did not allow it to develop. Often this occurred in countries where Islamic thought, and to some degree other non-Christian and Jewish-based religions, were politically and socially dominant, leading to an emphasis on the family, community and temple as the basis for welfare and social care. An example is Turkey, where a system relying on major voluntary organisations was developed after the Second World War by legislation in 1948 giving welfare responsibilities for early years children to the Ministry of Health and Social Assistance and for older young people to the Ministry of Education (Atauz, 1999). From the 1960s, social welfare was included in the government's five-year plans, a general directorate of social services was set up in the Ministry in 1963 and in 1967 a school of social work was established. By legislation in 1983, the agency for child protection was incorporated into the general directorate. This has a central and many local offices; however, most provision for children is still in large institutions. Foster care was introduced in the 1960s to promote more family care, but was only successful as a step towards adoption. There are also voluntary organisations working with poor and handicapped children and street children. The general directorate provides residential and daycare centres for disabled people. Family care is the most significant provision for elders and institutional care is rare. However, advice and day centres are available. In the 1990s, a small number of refuges developed in big cities for physically and sexually abused women, operated by women's organisations or government agencies. Atauz's (1999) account shows a range of relatively unprofessionalised provision, mainly using residential and institutional care, with little training provision for such a large country.

One aspect of the rejection of social work in some countries is the influence of fundamentalism in religious beliefs. The idea of fundamentalism originates from pamphlets called *The Fundamentals: A Testimony to Truth* used in a Californian evangelical campaign of the period 1910–16 against liberal individualism (Midgley and Sanzenbach, 1989). Similar movements in favour of traditional moral values, and against cooperation among churches developed in many religions after 1980, but especially influenced Islam. Many of these movements, both in the West and elsewhere, criticise the liberal humanistic base and rationalist, tolerant views of social work and social welfare. Thus, the association of the rise of social work with increasing secularisation makes it a target for religious as well as political criticism.

One response to this has been an increasing focus on spiritual concerns in welfare provision. Examples of this include the international hospice and palliative care movement, where social work played an important contributory role in its development, concern for varying approaches to spiritual needs in different ethnic groups, and developing helping approaches from explicitly spiritual traditions, such as Eastern Zen and African Maat (Payne, 2005).

Conclusion

From 1970, social work achieved a significant role in many societies. Generally, it has maintained that role, but it has been challenged. Challenges have arisen from economic and political insecurity, a debate about the role of the state in relation to other providers of welfare and the contribution and value of social work as an activity and a profession.

In many rich Western countries, including Britain and the USA, economic insecurity led to a political move away from the role of the state in welfare associated with an attack on social work as part of a dependency-creating state. The globalisation of economies made it possible for multinational companies to place less importance on the benefits of social welfare as a contributor to social order, because they could export jobs to low-wage areas, rather than maintain a commitment to welfare in developed countries. Mechanisation and computerisation meant that they did not need to maintain large armies of low-paid workers. They could pay a relatively small number of highly paid professionals in knowledge-based industries. The economic cost of welfare states could be attacked because it was less important to powerful industrial and commercial interests. Thus, paying for welfare was less accepted and more an area of political conflict.

Associated with this, the consequences of the growth in social provision led to a concern about its economic cost to government, even though there is evidence of widespread support for social welfare. The institutionalisation of the social work profession, relatively recently achieved, made it a target in this conflict. It is important to identify two elements of the attack, since they have different origins. Often, these elements are associated with an attack from both the Right and the Left, but in many respects, the views expressed led to similar proposals. The Right was concerned about social work leading to dependence on the state rather than individualistic attempts to deal with problems. The Left was concerned about the individualistic character of social work and the way it compensated for gaps in universal services. Moreover, the institutionalisation of social work was not accountable to consumers and communities, and its disciplinary role clashed with its caring role in child protection and in managing the rationing of services where there were increasing concerns about cost. Both the British modernisation agenda and developments in New Zealand were attempts to struggle with the issue of professional accountability. Many countries developed regulation for social work during this period.

The shift away from social work was not a universal characteristic of developments during this period. Southern European states, the formerly Communist world, South America, South Africa and many Asian states re-established or substantially developed social work. Ideas about social development also made significant progress in developing countries.

This period, then, tells us something about the position of social work in political, social and economic debate. It is valued and possibly necessary as an element of development, particularly where social disorder or disruption is a recent experience. Its basic provisions in developing secure communities and responding to famine, poverty and conflict are significant. We can see this during this period in its development in Southern and Eastern Europe, Latin America, developing countries and Pacific rim states. However, in many of these states, it is not a particularly large-scale activity and, consequently, is not subjected to extensive critical oversight by powerful external stakeholders.

Its continued success has depended on dominant political views on the role of the state. Where these are predominantly social democratic, leading to support for a stable and progressive welfare state, as in many Nordic countries during this period, social work will be seen as a worthwhile part of this. Indeed, Sipilä et al. (1997) argue that social welfare provision is integral to a developed welfare state, although this argument applies mainly to widespread community child care to permit high female participation in the workforce in some Nordic countries. Where the dominant political perspective is of economic rationalism, a coherent system of social provision is less valued, and social work will stand or fall by its success in ameliorating social problems rather than being seen as an intrinsically worthwhile activity. Its regard will be affected by the extent to which it is an institutionalised occupation and its success in gaining acceptance for its knowledge base and social contribution. Thus, in many European countries and in Britain, where it is integral to many state services, it has often flourished while being despised or ignored. However, in the USA, with a strong integrated professional association and wide acceptance of social work's academic status, and in Nordic countries, such as Sweden where professional association roles are strongly associated with universal trade unionism and there is a strong academic social work profession, it maintains a fairly high regard.

An influence on the progress of social work will be its own success in the context of the services it offers and the welfare provision of which it is a part. Thus, the academic and professional success of social work in the universities in the USA, Britain and Sweden strengthened its general standing and acceptance, in spite of doubters. However, as with all professions, this partly depends on the credibility of its knowledge base, and the success with which practice achieves outcomes desired by the dominant political philosophy and policies at the time.

The picture in the UK over this period shows a shift from a high point of independence and development of the social services as part of government towards a more contested role. The period of the 1980s questioned the value of social work. One outcome has been a managerialist emphasis on quality assurance and regulation, as part of a reduction and reining in of public services. Nevertheless, social work services have developed as a discretionary response to cutbacks in the provision of universal services. The resolution of this in the 1990s has seen progression towards a more negotiated role for public welfare in general, and an emphasis on effectiveness, responsiveness to user needs and wishes and multi-agency and multiprofessional provision. This places more emphasis on social work as part of wider professional, agency and community networks, and regulation, management and development of it will take place within this context. Thus, a separate local government department for social care dominated by social workers and their professional values is declining in influence, whereas opportunities for influencing other professions and community networks by effective social work in a variety of settings, although not always called social work, are likely to increase.

This discussion suggests the analysis that has informed the arrangement of the rest of this book. I shall argue throughout that the development of social work is affected by the social, cultural and political view of social problems and the potential clientele for its services (Chapter 5), the cultural, political and social ideas that provide the context for its work (Chapter 6), the agency, legal and policy context that forms its role in any society (Chapter 7), the professional and occupational organisation of social workers (Chapter 8) and the knowledge (Chapter 9) and education (Chapter 10) that socialises social workers into their profession.

It is only possible to understand the position of social work both in general and in particular countries and consider its potential and future if we examine the interaction of these factors together. Social workers will have to work in a range of contexts and with many different roles. Understanding those that affect them, where they have come from historically and what the range of possibilities might be, by exploring comparative perspectives in different countries, will help social workers to manage and develop their role in new professional and service contexts.

CHAPTER 5

Perceptions of Social Work's Role

Social work's social roles

As Wilensky and Lebeaux (1965: 14) put it: 'No social problems – no welfare services, no profession of social work.' The way we understand personal problems and social issues affecting societies and individuals creates the form of social work provided. To be seen as justifying social work, social issues must go through a social process (Payne, 1998). First, they are defined symbolically as 'social' in character, then as requiring some political response and finally as requiring a social work response in situations where social work has or can develop a technology that is accepted as an appropriate response. Drug misuse, for example, might be seen as a social evil deriving from alienation, a medical problem arising from personal inadequacies or stresses, or a problem of international crime and global economic policy. In each of these, the contribution of social work, if relevant, would be different.

Two factors affect perceptions of people who become social work clients. One is demographic: people exist whose circumstances seem to require intervention. The second concerns social perception: particular social categories are conceived as relevant to the provision of social work.

Three continuities in social perception have defined the role of social work:

- poverty and the social responses to it
- reliance on families and local communities as the primary response to poverty

- a wish to control social and state responses to those social groups structurally affected by poverty, to reinforce family and community as the main providers.

Social work in the West emerged from a concern for poverty and idleness that raised the risk of social disorder in a rapidly changing society. The starting point of any analysis of social work's development must therefore be reactions to poverty. This chapter looks first at poverty as the basis for the origins of social work, drawing on the account of social work's development in Chapters 2–4, then at issues of family and community as supports in times of poverty. Finally it looks at two groups, elderly and mentally ill people, whose poverty and therefore need for services comes from their inability to work and the lack of family and community support for them.

Poverty, unemployment and care

One characteristic of life throughout much of history is the grinding poverty of much of the population. Concern about paupers from medieval times was about survival and behaviour control in relatively isolated communities. As a social issue, poverty emerged primarily in the late 1800s, at the same time as unemployment, after a period of intensive economic growth. In Britain, for example, the average person was three-and-a-half times better off in 1914 compared with 1830, was living in a successful imperial state with a consumer economy and increasing state social regulation (Floud, 1997). Thus, poverty became a general political issue in the context of a growth in wealth and collective political and scientific power.

Poverty is connected with unemployment because it arises from people not working, creating economic dependence on others, through age, sickness and disability, inadequate means of subsistence or the absence of economically rewarding work. Trattner (1999) proposes that a continuing debate in societies has been about the extent to which it is the duty of the better off to provide help and the right of those in need to receive it. Chapter 2 identified debates about whether people have a duty to give, as opposed to whether the duty is to ensure the effectiveness of charity. This issue also arose around social work's foundation, since it aimed to make philanthropy efficient through the social work method, in the same way that today's 'evidence-based' practice seeks to make social work effective rather than 'just' caring.

Guy (1995) suggests that a characteristic of nineteenth-century developments is a preoccupation with dependency, arising from the assumption that poverty derives from not providing for oneself by not working, an assumption related to liberal philosophies (Chapter 6), which are concerned that incentives to work may fail because of welfare. Chapter 4 showed how this concern arose with the New Right political philosophies of the 1980s, and 90s, and in American welfare reforms of the 1990s, as well as during the period when Victorian liberal philosophies had their strongest impact. Perceptions of work began to change during the late nineteenth century, and in the depression of the 1890s, the idea of involuntary unemployment because of economic changes arose, as opposed to stigmatising views of workless people in the USA (Marshall, 1995) and elsewhere. For unemployment to exist, there have to be people who do not work: the demographic requirement mentioned above. Also, the idea that identifying 'unemployment as a social fact to be studied independently of its individual expressions' (Topalov, 1994: 495) emerged at the end of the nineteenth century in several countries, partly influenced in Britain by riots in 1886 by unemployed people in London. Unemployment as a social work issue, therefore, could not have been relevant before the early twentieth century, since the social category 'unemployment' did not exist. It emerged as a 'social' problem at the same time as social work, in a context in which a range of social concerns were being explored. However, concern about idleness has been a consistent problem throughout medieval times and later.

In Britain activity on unemployment developed between 1900 and 1914 (Brown, 1971), as public awareness grew of the failure of both the Poor Law and private charity to deal with poverty, signalled by social unrest and changing attitudes to the state. Early social science surveys such as the work of Rowntree (1902; Briggs, 1961) and more journalistic activity by Booth and the socialist writer Jack London in the USA (1977) drew attention to serious poverty. The poor health of men volunteering for the forces in the Boer War, the first major war for half a century, led to the same concerns about the 'stock' of the population as the French concerns about the birth rate (see below).

Poverty because of non-employment has always been an underlying social issue in the development of social work and activities like it, but it is not central to what social work does. Social work's role in poverty and unemployment is to provide the care for those who are dependent because they are not or cannot be employed, or to care for those who cannot be dependent on a wage-earner because of unemployment. It is, thus, to mitigate the social problems caused by poverty through unemployment, so that social unrest cannot be justified by failure to care for the dependents of the unemployed. Caring is necessary so that social justice to dependents of unemployed people does not mitigate the disciplinary effect of unemployment on working people. This is why social work's services focus on social justice specifically for dependent people in need of care, rather than more generally on tackling unemployment and poverty directly, which since the late nineteenth century has been the role of more universal social security services. Twentieth-century welfare states sought more universal benefits because of political concern, especially after industrialisation and urbanisation, to reduce unrest and protest from working-class movements. An example of this is the social insurance of the Bismarck period. Universalisation is also a reaction to working-class movements developing self-help and demanding social provision through political means.

Therefore, social work's clientele are not all those in poverty, but particular sub-groups: children and families, elderly people, mentally ill people and people with physical and learning disabilities. In many cultures, gender division means that women perform caring and community roles. Others depend on them for this. Men work for wages or subsistence. However, where there is no economically sustaining work, instead of depending on wages, people depend on family or community networks. Dependence on family and community is often negotiated and arises from past exchanges (Finch and Mason, 1993). Chapters 2–4 showed that much of the political and professional debate at crucial times in social work's development revolved around the responsibility of the state as compared with families and communities, and important movements in different countries, particularly in the East and Catholic countries, focused on retaining family responsibility as the basis for social provision.

Social work focuses on the family and community rather than poverty through unemployment and therefore, even though it emerged from nineteenth-century concerns about poverty, largely works with poor people. There are two main reasons for this. First, we saw in Chapter 2 that social work emerged initially through women's voluntary work in such movements as the American 'women's benevolence movement'. Subsequently, it became professionalised as a way in which women could escape domestic roles into employment. Women transferred their 'caring power', the acceptance of their role as carers that gave them power in social relations, from the domestic sphere to a professional role. They fought for services for women and children, since their caring power gave them understanding and power to achieve some development in this sphere. Where the domestic and personal were important, social work gained influence and importance. The second reason for the family and community focus of social work lies in the importance of social traditions about the organisation of societies. Debate about social problems often turns around the loss of effective families and community traditions and the ways in which they may be reconstituted. Often such debate harks back to rural communities or seeks reconstituted families by adoption and fostering or rehabilitation of delinquent or disturbed children. There are many examples of this in Chapters 2–4. The second part of this chapter examines some of the historical traditions from which the importance of family derives.

Much of this discussion has been about perceptions of poverty in developed countries in the West. Developing countries in Africa have equally been affected by perceptions of their poverty. Structural adjustment programmes have sought to provide general economic answers to widespread poverty: economic development without social help has been the main prescription. However, these have been criticised both because this is likely to lead to disorder and social disruption, but also because it neglects important social elements of economic success. The development of community facilities, such as water sources, and the importance of women as contributors to rural and developing economies has required social interventions before large-scale economic development programmes may be successful. Some late-developing Asian countries, aware of the historical precedents, developed social provision as an aspect of general social development (Chapter 4). Many of the rapidly developing economies of the Asia-Pacific region developed social security and anti-poverty policies during the 1960s and 70s explicitly to avoid social disruption and disorder as a result of extensive structural change and urbanisation: one example was Korea (Ro and Oh, 1988).

On the other hand, in some countries, social security for unemployed people and state subsidy for housing declined in impact during the 1980s. This was a widespread trend, exacerbated in some countries by local factors, such as a right-wing, neoliberal political impetus under Thatcherism and Reaganomics in Britain and the USA and in Germany by the reunification of East and West Germany in the 1990s (Bujard, 1996). As a result, discretionary provision such as social work became more important in dealing with poverty and homelessness. While this emphasises the role of social work as an individualist provision at times of difficulty, it also emphasises its role in maintaining a system where inequality is growing. Bujard (1996) suggests that as universal welfare state provisions decline, three damaging consequences arise:

- State intervention leads to dependency for poor people, as they rely on handouts and individual help rather than universal efforts to improve the economy or social provision.
- State funds are spent on professional help rather than direct assistance to people in need.
- Regulation, planning, control and surveillance of people increases, rather than democratic and participative measures.

If this were true, social work would thrive, but with a greater emphasis on its role in individualistic social control, as the state withdraws from universal social provision. This was true during the period of the British Conservative governments of the 1980s and 90s and, if we see the Poor Law as a forerunner of social work, it was also true of the Poor Law.

In summary, I have suggested that awareness of and state responsibility for poverty and unemployment was a characteristic of increasing wealth in nineteenth-century societies, leading to responses such as universalist social security and mutual aid insurance systems, increasingly incorporated into the state. Social work has had a limited role caring for the needs of people made dependent by poverty and unemployment, and it is this that makes it a non-universal service focused on supporting family and community care and development or organising services that substitute for it.

Family, children and community

Social work's focus on family and community as the caring element in responding to the general issues of poverty and unemployment arises because family and community are important as social structures that mediate the relationships between individuals and society or the state. Davidoff et al. (1999) see this emphasis as a product of the influence of functionalist sociology, and propose that a critical analysis of the history of the family needs to include Marxist and feminist analyses of social factors influencing conceptions of the family. An important aspect of social work as it emerged in the COS focused on maintaining or developing social support for 'family', seeing it in a functionalist way as an important pillar of social order. The diverse patterns of family life throughout history mean that policies and social work in relation to family and community varies, being constructed by the political and social environment in which policy and social work operates.

All historical approaches to studying family (Anderson, 1995) emphasise how economic and social trends interact with beliefs and values and are closely related to gender assumptions. Therefore, how families are organised to participate in economic relationships in different cultures and how this creates gender relationships crucially defines the role of social work in any society. The word 'family' has Latin roots, from *famulus* (servant). In Rome, a family was the household of master, wife, children, servants and slaves. By extension, *familia* came to imply kinship, people descended from a common ancestor, and blood relatives, that is, people descended from a father and mother. Around the world, the word translated into English as 'family' can denote some or all of these meanings (Zonabend, 1996). In traditional Chinese religion, for example, family is the crucial element in worship and organising life. On marriage, a woman became part of the ancestral group of her husband (Thompson, 1989). External and community relationships are less important.

Within the family, social work has had a particular concern for the balance between children's and parental rights (Tunstill, 2000). Children are often subordinate to paternal and family authority as the family pursues its economic, political and social roles in society. Such ideas have long historical roots in the cultures where Western societies originated. The ancient Middle Eastern societies, during the three millennia of the Sumerian and Babylonian periods, moved from great families forming large social groupings as the basis of land-holding towards a more nuclear structure based on paternal authority (Glassner, 1996). Evidence of the ancient Middle Eastern world's infanticide and exposure of children to die may suggest brutal societies in which they have no identity or rights independent of their family or fathers. Others less judgmentally argue that, in the absence of legal mechanisms for adoption, exposure is a mode of making children available for transfer of care, often through wet-nursing, and of parenthood (Cunningham, 1995) – the ultimate 'freeing for adoption', as current British law puts it. The ancient Jewish family model emphasises collective identity through genealogical history in which the family plays a part as a stable social unit for procreation (Alvarez-Pereyre and Heymann, 1996). The Athenian model saw fathers as citizens, whose political rights to freedom were transmitted to sons through legitimate birth within a family to a recognised daughter and mother (Sissa, 1996). The Roman model of citizenship recognised paternal authority *(patria potestas)* as the basis for household and political management and remained influential in European law even after 1800 (Rouselle, 1996; Thomas, 1996).

In many ancient traditions, important aspects of social relations emerge that still have significance for social work today. Among these are the symbolic social importance allocated to the model of family current in a society especially as a contributor to social stability, the importance of the family as a model of and site to pursue political, economic and social power in societies and the importance of religious traditions in the formation of ideals of family organisation and life. More personally, the family is important in social relations as a site for sexual and social control, often by men of women and children. Some societies see families more as separate nuclear entities, while some see them as incorporated in wider kinship or social systems. These are often based on localities, and seen as communities, but may be part of wider economic, political and social connections. Most societies embody elements of both nuclear families and wider kinship connections.

As social work began to emerge in Europe, external social controls (for example religious life, local institutions) on family life declined from the 1700s, accelerating in later centuries. There was a greater appreciation of privacy, a reduction in street life, segregation of sleeping, eating and business rooms, segregation of servants and concern about opportunities for promiscuity. This led to an emphasis by evangelical Christians on moral reform by emphasising family life on the model of St Paul's attitudes of a manly breadwinner and dependent wife. Men's work outside the home and women's work within it were dignified and approved (Hall, 1998: 16–17). It was this model that social work, as it emerged during the nineteenth century, sought to enforce. An opposing concern came from radicalism, based on traditional ideas of freedom to dissent and protest. These concerns were expressed more strongly in trade unionism and in a tradition of writing on people's rights, represented by Thomas Paine's *The Rights of Man* and Mary Wollstonecraft's reply: *Vindication of the Rights of Women.* Utilitarianism, a philosophy emerging during the 1820s, focused on developing social institutions, among them a strong nuclear family, as well as prisons and the Poor Law, as a way of increasing the happiness of the greatest number (Hall, 1998: 18–19). These ideas on families influenced evangelical reformers in the nineteenth century, such as Lord Shaftesbury, who sought legislation to protect women and children from having to work in degrading conditions in factories and mines.

Social work, therefore, developed at a time when enforcing gender divisions in the new employment market was an important social objective. This had consequences for its priorities and activities. Broadly speaking, men were to develop social relations through work, women in domestic life. Social provision tends to follow that division. Men become important clients where unemployment and financial provision need to be dealt with, for example in some Nordic countries where social workers organise the social security system, or in dealing with homeless single men. Women are important clients where domestic roles and caring are important, with families, children, disabled and ill people and elderly parents, for example, and were the main focus of early social work (Chapter 2). Abramovitz (1985), in a study of female paupers before 1000 in the USA, found that women were regulated differently from men. While the essential characteristic of social security provision for men lies in concern to support the work ethic, for women, the concern has often been to support family life by ensuring that women marry and then remain in the home. Where there was, in the early colonies, a surplus of women because of widowhood and other factors, they were often helped in their own homes rather than by requiring them to work, as men had to. However, as industrialisation developed, a class of women emerged who worked in industry or who, under pressures such as the loss of male breadwinners due to the Civil War, often ended up as prostitutes or beggars. These women were separated by their circumstances from an ideal feminine family life and controlled by surveillance in institutions.

Showalter (1987) shows that, as the psychiatric professions developed during the nineteenth and twentieth centuries, cultural views of the 'proper' behaviour of women affected the definitions of women's mental illness. In the Victorian period, treatment of mental disorder in women was concerned with managing mental instability arising from the physical stresses of the menstrual cycle and uncontrolled sexuality. During the reform period of the mid-nineteenth century, 'moral management' was concerned to regulate and domesticate women's lives as a protection against instability. Later, there was a concern to treat the mental 'weakness' of 'neurasthenic' and 'hysterical' women, associated with social Darwinist ideas and the mental hygiene movement. Freudian psychoanalysis focused on neurotic behaviours, mainly associated with women, and developed an influential theory of sexuality that had a huge impact on social work. As a contrast, Showalter (1987: Ch. 7) shows how similar symptoms in men in battle conditions in the First World War were defined as a specific medical condition, 'shell shock'. Women, diagnosed with depression and related mental illnesses more often than men, were often the objects of intrusive and medically controversial treatments such as lobotomy and electroconvulsive therapy, as medicine became more scientific in its practices during the twentieth century. Even the ideas of Laing (1965), the psychiatrist who in the

1960s proposed that the origins of schizophrenia lay in how people had experienced family life, implicitly blamed mothers for their daughters' illness.

Stronger families have been important at different periods as well as, often by implication, the domestic role of women. During the 1800s, there was a growing ideal of 'domestic womanhood', which emphasised living as a family unit. A Canadian study (Iacovetta, 1998: 316) suggests that a century later the period of the Cold War (between Western and Communist regimes) from 1945-65 was one of 'heightened domesticity', when the family was idealised after a period of relative independence for women, and young people's freedoms were repressed. Working-class parenting was disdained and external social controls were considered necessary to discipline children. All these factors emphasised the nuclear family unit.

Culturally and historically, there is variation in the potential for family patterns and relationships within them. Western social work emerged in a society concerned to develop particular models of the family, emphasising the domestic role of women and the employment role of men. Its ideas and values reflect those particular cultural origins, even though in some periods its approach to those problems varied. The social and economic trends of the moment affected how families and women were seen, within a general pattern of gender role division, and the political role of welfare provision for families varied according to social and professional concerns.

Three groups of social work service users

This section examines briefly three groups for whom social work provides services. Social work emerged from concerns about poverty, and its response was focused on action within the family and community. The first example is of the 'problem family movement', which shows how social concerns about families may construct social work activities in a particular way, shifting them in different directions from their intentions. However, some groups in society are affected by the social consequences of poverty because they are outside the labour market. Unless the family and community meet their needs, they may be excluded from social provision. Elders are important because, in many societies, the numbers of elders are growing. They thus present a serious social issue for welfare provision. Mentally ill people are important because they may lose personal independence and legal rights through actual or assumed mental incapacity, and may therefore be particularly subject to surveillance and external social controls. Social work is often involved in that surveillance and control.

'Problem families' in mid-twentieth-century Britain

Concern for families at risk is reflected in British work on 'problem families' from the 1920s to the 60s. The Wood Report (1929) on mental deficiency suggested that mental defectives and their families were concentrated in the bottom tenth of society: a reminder of Booth's research on the 'submerged tenth' in the 1890s. The idea of the problem family emerged in the 1920s, prompted by the Eugenics Society's attempts to identify 'the social problem group' to pursue its sterilisation policies (eugenics was a movement to breed better human beings). There was also interest in social theories and social policy, partly because of anxiety about social disorder as troops came back from the war and the impact of the socialist Russian revolution spread throughout Europe. Also, the Labour Party displacing the Liberal Party and achieving government for the first time in this period raised interest in social issues within politics.

Research on social problem groups in the 1930s did not lead to clear results. However, reports on schoolchildren evacuated from the major cities led to a debate between Conservatives arguing that the residuum was an obstacle to progress and a 'middle-way' group that argued for improved services. Pacifist Service Units were set up during the Second World War to provide for volunteer social work opportunities for conscientious objectors (people who refused to join the military forces because of their pacifist principles). They did intensive work with families with multiple problems. Their work achieved a good deal of publicity and they metamorphosed into a social work agency, Family Service Units (FSU) (Starkey, 2000). Research in Luton during the war produced a report on 'social problem families' who were assailed by multiple difficulties. Although the association of eugenics with Naziism and declining anxiety about the birth rate in the post-war world led to a decline in support for eugenics, the Eugenics Society grasped the idea of problem families. It set up a committee (Blacker, 1952) which raised concerns about parents unable to cope with children because of 'ineducability' and 'weak and vacillating characters' (see Welshman, 1999 for information about this history). This intersected with amendments to the Children Act to permit investigations of allegations of child neglect and abuse.

The commitment of FSU to intensive work with multiproblem families spawned research and publicity (for example Philp and Timms, 1957), which raised the profile of families with multiple problems. The FSU was seen as a new kind of voluntary organisation, an alternative to the growth of more bureaucratic services in local government. Its success was seen as an example of intensive social work and a contributor to the professionalisation of social work. These ideas also contributed to the pressure for a unified family service within local government, which led to the preventive policies of the Children and Young Persons Act 1963 and the Seebohm reorganisation of social services. Macnicol (1999) argues that psychiatric social workers criticised the problem family movement both in order to distance themselves from the 'cheery amateurism' (p. 88) of the FSU, but also from the biological determinism of the eugenicists. Physical poverty had been conquered, so a poverty of lifestyle had to be substituted. However, the tendency of psychiatric social workers to focus on emotional immaturity, rather than poverty, led in part to a critique of social work from the rediscovery of poverty in the 1960s.

Services for elderly people

Johnson (1998) argues that old age has had little interest for historians, and that generally three issues have predominated in historical writing:

- participation in the labour market and family and community relations
- well-being, both economic independence and the need for family and welfare support and social status, that is, how elders as a group were regarded
- and old age constructed by political, legal, medical and cultural rules and customs.

Generations of studies in the twentieth century have been based on the assumption that family ties and help from kin have weakened, but there has been no evidence of this (Thane, 1998). Minois (1989) argues that societies have been based on physical strength and vigour throughout history and that this has consequences for views of old age, particularly where, as in the eighteenth-century Renaissance, a cult of physical beauty devalues old age. He suggests that where societies have been disorganised and anarchic, frail elders have suffered. Civilisations such as ancient Greece and the Middle Ages that rely on oral tradition and custom have been kinder to elders, because they value experience and knowledge. In antiquity, help for elders depended mainly on families and attitudes were ambiguous: while Cicero, one Roman orator, called for respect, another, Seneca, worried about physical and mental decline (Parkin, 1998). In the Middle Ages in Europe, people were accepted as elderly between the ages of 60 and 70, being exempted from military and public service and receiving more lenient treatment as vagabonds (Shaker, 1998). However, people continued as part of ordinary social and economic systems until they reached complete physical or mental incapacity (Johnson, 1998).

Old age was primarily constructed by late nineteenth and twentieth-century welfare and pensions developments, which normalised retirement as a stage of life (Johnson, 1998) and constructed dependency as a structural element of old age (Johnson, 1989). In most countries, including the UK, policy was dominated by pension provision. Views of elderly people during the inter-war years were sometimes disparaging and stereotypical, with an emphasis on seeing elders as a homogeneous population characterised by psychological and physical decay. However, in the USA, a few social workers advocated active practice to enhance the life experience of elders (Reinardy, 1987). In the post-1945 welfare state reforms in many countries, increasing proportions of populations were surviving beyond the age of 60 for the first time (Harper and Thane, 1989). Hugman (1994: 47) suggests that the ageing of the population is a characteristic of postindustrial society, rather than the industrialisation during which social work emerged, when the higher proportion of young people meant that proportions of elders in the population declined in industrialised Europe and the focus was on families with wage-earners. Old age became a *predictable* aspect of the life cycle, to which cultures have not yet become accustomed, making people uncertain how to treat elders in their social circles (Gilleard and Higgs, 2000). Ageing has been seen as a particularly important issue in many countries, such as China (Zhang and Kilpatrick, 1996: 103) and Japan, where a high proportion of the population is ageing.

Social work and the social services have often given a low priority to positive work with elderly people for many of the historical reasons discussed here. The question for current social workers is whether the growing population of elderly people in many countries will lead to a defensive reliance on the continuities in ideology that leads us to say the elderly people are less important, or will press us to change to find a new social work for elders.

Mental illness

Porter (1987) suggests that the Greek epics are evidence of classical views that madness is the effect of the forces of nature and the gods, beyond the control of people. Later Greek and classical medicine sought to subject nature to reason, and rationality was seen as humanity's most noble capacity. Thus, in Porter's view, the Greeks first made irrationality a problem. External conflicts became, through rational reflection, the objects of internal conflicts. They formed two alternative explanations for irrationality: that it was an extreme of experience or the product of a disease, as delirium may come with a fever. These two alternative views of the origins of madness, psychological or physical, are intertwined in debate over the centuries. They became associated with moral responsibility, because of the importance given to rationality. If mental illness results from disease, the failure in being rational is less the responsibility of the mentally ill person.

However, in medieval Christian thinking, unlike the Greek focus on the individual, mental disorder was seen as the product of a battle of the wider forces of good and evil represented by the person's behaviour, and madness might reveal religious experience, genius or badness. No special provision was made for mentally ill people, but in the 1600s the Bethlem Hospital in London began to specialise in caring for mentally ill people. Porter (1987: 13) identifies a long-term shift in policy-making around this time, which led to the rise of exclusion as a way of dealing with people displaying delinquent or dangerous behaviour: this also affected mentally ill people.

As, with the Renaissance, reason became more important, educated people, while benevolent to people with problems, saw the irrational as alien from humanity. Therefore, ideas of religious ecstasy or prophetic powers were increasingly rejected, and mental illness lost what positive connotations remained. Segregation often led to harsh treatment: mentally ill people's irrationality led to them being regarded as little better than animals, needing to be contained and punished for their failings. From the mid-1700s, the trend towards exclusion and segregation was reinforced by growing ideas about therapy among reformers such as Chiurugi (Italy), Pinel (Paris), Reil and other Romantic psychiatrists (Germany) and the Tukes and their ideas of 'moral treatment' at the Retreat, in York, England (Porter, 1987: 16–19). Proper treatment might lead to improvement or restoration to society. These views, drawing on Locke's *Treatise on Human Understanding*, argued that, unlike idiots (people with severe learning disabilities), mentally ill people did not entirely lose their reason and might regain it.

Increasingly, mental illness was seen as susceptible to the same techniques as delinquency: isolation from bad influences, mental discipline and the retraining of thought. To achieve this, asylums, increasing in size, were to provide the appropriate safe environment. One of the achievements of nineteenth-century asylums was to reject the use of physical restraint and focus treatment on 'moral management', the policy of John Conolly, the physician superintendent of Colney Hatch Lunatic Asylum (later Friern Barnett Hospital) near London (Showalter, 1987). Bartlett (1999) argues that the history of asylums for pauper lunatics during the 1800s suggests that the medicalisation and professionalisation of social control, which is the focus of Foucault's work, was peripheral to the problems of Poor Law administration that preoccupied the administrators of the system. Relatively little restraint was required and people were often restored to normal life; the idea of moral management aimed at docile, routinised living. This was a form of treatment, not a wider aim at the governance of social life. Policies such as this promoted benevolent treatment in good surroundings, but asylums became overcrowded, demoralised and repressive institutions. The therapeutic optimism of the mid-Victorian period gave way to pessimism, associated with social Darwinism and a search for the hereditary basis of mental illness. The trend of increasing the size of institutions both made the personalised treatment of the moral managers impossible and also engendered a pessimism that regarded treatment as impossible. In Britain, 100,000 people were incarcerated in asylums by 1900 and half a million in the USA. Alongside this development, occupations providing care became associated with medicine and nursing, and as social work emerged, it also became involved.

Jones (1972, 1993) characterises the development of ideas about mental illness in the UK as a battle between the legal and medical professions, or between legalism and medicalism, for professional control of the area of mental health; Unsworth (1979) and Ramon (1985) incorporate a social view. In this view, the medical model that treatment for an illness was the paramount objective was incorporated into early legislation such as the Lunatics Act 1845, a product of campaigning by Shaftesbury, the philanthropist more renowned for his campaigns on behalf of deprived children. However, scandals led to concerns that patients were incarcerated contrary to their legal rights, and the Lunacy Act 1890 imposed legal controls, making incarceration a condition of treatment. Nye's (1984) study of mental illness and crime in France shows that a medical and biological discourse on deviance shifted into the public realm and, especially in France, but also in Britain and Germany, was associated with concern about national decline and degeneration. This was related to concern about the adverse impact of urbanisation and the 'residuum' in Britain, an important political issue at the turn of the nineteenth century. Butler (1985) argues that moves like these played a role in building acceptance for a role for the state in responding to social and medical problems. The trend to legalism was reversed by the Mental Treatment Act 1930 which made some provision for community treatment and eventually by the Mental Health Act 1959, deriving from the Percy Report (1957), which originated the term 'community care' and strengthened the role of social work. Unsworth (1979), contrary to Jones's account, shows that a range of views were associated with each of the professions involved. He suggests that the views of all professions are towards intervention in ways that reflect their particular approaches. Professions become the instruments of changes in social views about ways of intervening in and regulating working-class or excluded populations.

Thus, in Chapter 3, we saw that doctors were concerned about the loss of mental health experience among social workers as a result of the Seebohm reorganisation, and a change of attitude to a more critical view of compulsory actions. However, Chapter 4 also notes the influence of a civil rights view of mental health compulsory powers, which led to the creation of approved social workers through the Mental Health Act 1983 to regulate these powers more closely. Social concern about whether people with mental illnesses were being adequately treated and cared for, and whether the public was being protected from dangerous behaviour derived from mounting concern about murders by people discharged from mental illness hospitals, fuelled by public inquiries during the 1980s and 90s (Reith, 1998; Chapter 7). In turn this led to proposals, unresolved at the time of writing, to make provision for easier custodial care for mentally ill people who might be dangerous. This is being resisted by professionals; it is also likely to reduce the civil rights role of social workers in this area, and since the approved social worker role is the basis of their involvement in multiprofessional mental health services, is likely to diminish social work involvement and influence in mental health services generally.

In this brief historical account of views of mental illness, we see how treatments or professional interventions responded to social changes and attitudes, shifting to see mentally ill people in different ways. Looking at the future of present-day social work, its role in multiprofessional services is likely to be affected by changes in public and political perception of mental illness. This would operate in the same way that recent public perceptions of mental health have been affected by concerns about whether community care for mentally ill people is adequate, which have arisen because of the impact of particular cases and the inquiries into them.

Conclusion

Social work was in part a response to the poverty arising from unemployment as it was identified as an issue in the late nineteenth century. Its role in many societies therefore became enmeshed in political debates about the economic system and the role of welfare in poverty. Its focus on family and community also derives from political and social debate about responsibility in poverty. Chapters 2–4 showed how social work was and is primarily concerned with poor people. This chapter has pointed to a paradox, in that although social work is mainly concerned with poor people, its role is to focus on family and community rather than poverty.

As societies became more affluent and developed organised responses to poverty, social work symbolised the individualised and personalised elements of those responses, while social security provision embodied the universal response. In some countries, for example Denmark, the two are managed together organisationally. However, in modern welfare regimes, the universal social security provision is always dominant in political debate and in organisational importance. Social work thus is seen to have a role in maintaining family and community as a secondary element to the attack on poverty. In nineteenth-century Britain, the Poor Law was the main provision and social work, as it developed, provided improving moral guidance for the deserving. In twenty-first-century Britain, the focus is on employment as the answer to poverty rather than on welfare. In the USA, we saw in Chapter 4 that welfare responses to poverty are viewed with caution and hostility; enforced employment is the preferred response.

The historical importance of family and child care thus provides an alternative focus for social work, which has come to be dominant. This is partly because of social work's helping techniques, which partly developed from 'rescue' in the nineteenth century and adoption and fostering in the twentieth, and psychological and social responses to delinquency and child behaviour problems. Social work thus became entwined in debates about the role of women in child care, as societies moved away from a traditional acceptance of paternal authority, and the appropriate responses to child behaviour problems and parental inadequacies. Women used social work to escape the wholly domestic role and created a career based on 'caring power', the social acceptance that caring was a primary social role for women. Thus, the importance of family and community as a focus of social work derives from its implementation of gendered social divisions, in which women were primarily seen as carers and concerned with the social, while men were seen as breadwinners and concerned with the economic. Women provide social work, a primarily caring and restitutive response to social problems, while male administrators provide social security and incentives towards employment as a carrot-and-stick response to the social consequences of economic problems.

How social work's clients are seen in the social traditions and political and social debate are crucial to the role of social work; so too is the social interpretation of social work in gender relations as a site of women's caring power. Families are an important site through which social order and social control are exerted through interpersonal relationships, as we saw in the 'problem families' example. In a different way, concern for elderly and mentally ill people also responds to social attitudes and expectations. Social work is both about the caring element of provision for poor people and social categories such as elderly and mentally ill people and the support of social order by facilitating social change in an important site of social control. The politics of poverty and social need is such that social work's focus must therefore be with family, community and identifiable needs of particular social groups rather than social security and employment. This has placed social work in a particular role in maintaining and changing social order, and means that the role of social work responds to social concerns and expectations about the social groups that are considered relevant to social work. At one stage, social work had a civil rights role with mentally ill people; now this is questioned because of the history of services and the rise of social concerns about dangerousness.

These social concerns and expectations are mediated through political debate, so that social work's social role does not only respond to social problems and how a society defines them, but how, in general, it seeks to deal with caring needs. The next chapter, therefore, focuses on philosophical and political debates about the nature of welfare.

CHAPTER 6

Values and Philosophy

The main focus of this chapter is the values embedded in the social care system that form social work. Social work is placed in tension because its history has led it to incorporate values from conflicting political and religious ideas. It does so because it is embedded in the political systems and social thought of the societies in which it exists. We cannot separate it and its values and methods from the whole system of social policy formation and implementation. The social policy of governments, therefore, and to some extent other organisations, and the political and philosophical debates that inform social policy are important in determining the form and nature of social work in any particular society. This is because, as we saw in Chapters 2–4, social work is to some extent a product of the involvement of the state in welfare and because any social development is the product of the ideas, policies and social structures of its time.

While the starting point of this chapter is political value systems, and how social work values connect with them, recent ideas such as communitarianism, participation and empowerment have been important in social work. This chapter also examines localism and centralisation, because social work in the 1800s developed partly around local influences and in many countries is part of a conflict between the central and the local. Finally, because social work has emerged from the secularisation of the welfare roles of organised religion, I examine the relationship between the religious and the secular in social work.

Liberal, socialist and social democratic ideas

The ideological changes that social work has faced during the 1900s can partly be seen in the political philosophies affecting Western states during that time. The following account looks at three main sets of ideas. Liberal and socialist ideas emerged from the social changes in Europe in the 1700s, following the philosophical and scientific revolution after the Enlightenment. Liberal ideas may be traced to the British Enlightenment, where the Scots, particularly the philosophers Locke (1632–1704) and Hume (1711–76) and the economist Adam Smith, were important (Porter, 2000). Socialist ideas were influenced by the French philosopher Rousseau and his book *The Social Contract*, and the German philosophers Hegel and Feuerbach, who in turn influenced Marx and his followers. Towards the end of the 1800s, social democratic ideas emerged, and were particularly important in creating state welfare.

Liberal ideas

Liberalism emerged from the social changes that followed the loss of the power of monarchies, early in Britain, and from secularisation. Traditional sources of power, the monarchy and the church, bound people within a system of thinking in which they were subject to the authority of all-embracing social institutions. They were replaced by the idea that people were individuals who were free to make their own decisions, had rights to protect them from the arbitrary power of the monarchy and the state, and were part of more personal social institutions such as the family and their local community, which protected and nourished them. This individualism has been an element of social work values. The importance of self-determination in ethical codes (McDermott, 1975; Payne, 1989) and individualised or tailored responses in British care management and American managed care to personal needs are examples. In Asian countries such as China, India and Japan, on the other hand, the state remained a distant and arbitrary instrument, and religion and family remained part of a total social system of interdependence. State interventions such as social work have, therefore, not developed so strongly, and as Western models have been applied in limited measure, they have sometimes been seen as inappropriate. In the late 1900s, Western social work has been substantially adapted in these cultures to a model that recognises the religious and social role of interdependent family relationships and the importance of spiritual harmony and social and personal integration.

In the West, the development of science offered the possibility of rational thinking as the basis for deciding on sensible courses of action, rather than following tenets of religion and the authority of social power emanating from the monarch or the church. Industrialisation meant a shift away from interpersonal dependence in small traditional communities. Instead, individual labour for wages was followed by the social disruption of urbanisation. These ideas influenced social work's high valuation of practice based on rational science (Chapter 10).

Liberalism was about people's *liberty* to pursue their own lives and interests supported by individual rights to enjoy their own property, with the state operating by their consent. Personal rights and freedoms, in Locke's view, were 'natural' and came from people's humanity, rather than being granted by the state. Consequently, the liberal view is that the state's role in people's lives should be minimal, allowing people to pursue their own interests as individuals. Adam Smith applied these ideas to economic life. He saw nations growing wealthier by individuals pursuing their own economic interests, competing for goods and services. The economic cycle of growth and recession was a natural part of the world in which human beings pursued their individual interests and state interference would prevent the growth of wealth. Anything more than minimal welfare help to individuals would prevent a nation from becoming more wealthy and would interfere with people's natural human right to pursue their interests.

Thus Jeremy Bentham wrote in 1843 (quoted in Schultz, 1972: 7–8):

> With the view of causing an increase of the means in the mass of national wealth, or with a view to increase of the means either of subsistence or enjoyment ... the general rule is, that nothing ought to be done or attempted by government. The motto, or watchword of government ... ought to be – *Be quiet*. For this quietism there are two main reasons: 1. ... Generally speaking, there is no one who knows what is for your interest so well as yourself – no one who is disposed with so much ardour and constancy to pursue it. 2. ... Each individual ... is likely to take a more effectual course than what, in his instance and on his behalf, would be taken by government. It is, moreover, universally and constantly pernicious in another way, by the restraint or constraint imposed on the free agency of the individual.

These ideas influenced first Britain and then other Western nations as they began to industrialise. The British Civil Wars in the mid-1600s, the War of American Independence and the French Revolution of the 1700s and then later political reform in Britain and elsewhere began to deplete the political power of monarchies and the agriculture-based economic power of the aristocracy. Manufacturers and industrialists gained increasing political influence and their interest in maintaining free markets became a dominant political concern. In Britain, the Whig Party, representing land-owning interests, metamorphosed into the Liberal Party. Its first period of power, in the 1830s, led to stronger political influence for the new industrial cities, the beginning of effective local government. John Stuart Mill (1806–73) underpinned these shifts in power with a political philosophy that argued that democratic structures enabled the governed to hold the governors accountable and created a balance between an individual's needs and the interests of citizens as a whole. Through the new Poor Law, local management of unemployed labour was based on a national policy that emphasised the needs of the free market. We saw in Chapter 2 that in Germany, a new urban middle class of industrialists and their wives gained influence in local government and welfare work.

Political views also distinguished between people who knew how to use their freedom in the economic system to accumulate wealth, and the poor, who had demonstrated that they were unable to use their economic freedom successfully to manage their lives and they had not achieved the capacity to employ labour and contribute to the growth of wealth. The influential self-help movement reflected a concern for enabling poor people to develop educationally and socially, but political power is excluded from any such developments. Samuel Smiles, the guru of self-help, representing commonplace attitudes, wrote in 1882 (quoted in Schultz, 1972: 9–11):

> Even the best institutions can give a man no active help. Perhaps the most they can do is, to leave him free to develop himself and improve his individual condition. But in all times men have been prone to believe that their happiness and well-being were to be secured by means of institutions rather than by their own conduct. Hence the value of legislation as an agent in human advancement has usually been much over-estimated. ... Though only the generals' names may

be remembered in the history of any great campaign, it has been in great measure through the individual valour and heroism of the privates that victories have been won ... Daily experience shows that it is energetic individualism which produces the most powerful effects upon the life and action of others, and readily constitute the best practical education.

Hence, the poor were excluded from political participation. Eventually, these ideas were part of the support for the development of social work's intervention in how poor people managed their household affairs.

The oppressive impact of liberal ideas was limited by the extensive development of charitable work during the 1800s (Chapter 2). In Britain, more than four times as many people received relief from charity as from the Poor Law (O'Brien and Penna, 1998: 25), partly because of the restrictions of the Poor Law. Chapter 2 suggests that the method of social work in Britain developed from alternatives to the Poor Law, while the state organisation of the social services eventually derived from the Poor Law's public employment base. Humanitarian move ments led to the use of legislation against extreme forms of exploitation, and eventually the social hierarchy deriving from the agricultural past began to break down. Industrialists and merchants displaced the aristocracy and collective action by working-class people, such as trade unions and friendly societies, began to protect and defend them against exploitation. It became apparent that people did not start equal, and so their fate could not be left to the market (Carr, 1960).

An important aspect of Enlightenment thinking was the idea that societies were making progress, developing stronger economic and social institutions as they became more wealthy and successful. Henriques (1979) argues that the impulsion to social reform in the 1800s came from both Bentham's philosophy, aiming at planned reform on rational lines, and a humanitarian movement, often impelled by evangelical Christianity and responding to events and proceeding incrementally, building on apparent social needs. Both had their impact on the competing COS and evangelical rescue movements that contributed to the development of social work.

During the 1800s, culminating in Darwin's biological work on the origin of species, evolutionary thinking emphasised how successful societies made economic progress that permitted the development of effective social institutions. Consequently, economic development led to social progress and not the other way round. People who were unable to make economic progress, including the poor and, as many African and Asian countries were colonised, people of other 'races' came to be considered biologically inadequate and therefore not justifying social equality. Political rights were appropriately accorded to people who had achieved economic and social success because they had demonstrated the capacity to provide leadership, and had the economic interest and developed education to achieve social progress for the benefit of all. Although the French philosopher de Tocqueville and the British philosopher John Stuart Mill emphasised the liberal vision of government by representative democracy, in which individual interest was represented by general enfranchisement so that people could vote, political *leadership* would remain with the enlightened classes. Throughout the 1800s, therefore, working-class and colonial agitation and revolution was feared and resisted by liberal political thinking. The same applied in the USA to social equality for non-European 'races'. This is important for the development of social work, because it became one of the ways of enlightening the working classes and, later, developing them and the colonial 'races' to ensure their participation in the state. It is also a strand of the thinking that sees social work as a controlling or disciplinary practice.

Social Darwinist thinking, such as that of Spencer, emerging in the later 1800s, applied evolutionary ideas to the organisation of society. Social institutions were the organs of the state, and contributed like the organs of the body to the development and growth of the individual. Social progress depended on social institutions playing their role effectively. Higher order institutions, such as Parliament, the church, and charitable institutions led by the economically and socially successful, formed the body within which lower order institutions such as families and communities played their part in maintaining interpersonal relationships at a more personal level. These institutions needed to be encouraged, supported and developed. On the international scene, successful economies created development and social progress through free trade and colonial influence.

Experience of local politics in the large industrial cities redirected liberal humanitarianism towards social democratic ideas, through municipal socialism. For example, the great political leader of Birmingham city council Joseph Chamberlain said, in a speech in Hull in 1885:

I believe that the great evil with which we have to deal is the excessive inequality in the distribution of riches. Ignorance, intemperance, immorality, and disease – these things are all interdependent and closely connected; and although they are often the cause of poverty, they are still more frequently the consequence of destitution ... I look for great results from the development of local government amongst us. The experience of the great towns is very encouraging in this respect. By their wise and liberal use of the powers entrusted to them, they have, in the majority of cases, protected the health of the community; they have provided means of recreation and enjoyment and instruction, and to secure for all the members of the community the enjoyments which, without their aid and assistance would have been monopolised by the rich alone.

(Quoted in Schultz, 1972: 57–8)

The idealist philosopher T. H. Green adapted liberal thinking by arguing that, while there should be no political interference in people's economic freedom, it must act to enable 'moral freedom' so that people might overcome social and economic obstacles to self-realisation. We saw in Chapter 2 that these views were important to many early COS workers.

By the early 1900s, the politics of the Liberal Party had incorporated both municipal socialism, humanitarianism and idealism. Lloyd George, the leading Liberal politician, argued in a speech in Swansea in 1908:

Poverty is the result of a man's own misconduct or misfortune. In so far as he brings it on himself, the state cannot accomplish much. It can do something to protect him. In so far as poverty is due to circumstances over which the man has no control, then the State should step in to the very utmost limit of its resources, and save the man from the physical and mental torture involved in extreme penury.

(Quoted in Schultz, 1972: 86)

Socialist ideas

Socialist ideas picked up many of the same issues, but ran counter to liberalism in important respects. Rousseau (1712–78) argued that people as a collective sanctioned governance and laws for the benefit of the 'common good'; through elections they showed what the 'general will' was. People should therefore participate in their own governance, developing a 'social contract' between those in power and those they governed, limiting oppression by the powerful through the influence of law. Hegel (1770–1831) saw history as a process during which people developed full self-consciousness. This process was 'dialectical', involving the use of the mind to develop and understand opposition to and criticism of existing ideas, enabling them to be transformed into new consciousness. People are socialised in families, which in turn are part of civil society in which wider organisations interact. There may be conflict between the interests of the poor and the rich, but this may be mediated by a rational, autonomous 'legal state', which would bring together reason and ethical behaviour in managing social conflicts. All these views contested the liberal assumption that, as part of achieving a successful market economy, elites should govern those unable through their various inadequacies to govern themselves.

Marx (1818–83) built on and criticised Hegel's views to produce a system of socialist thought, opposing liberal thought. It rejects the way liberal ideas value people individualistically seeking their own interests, and focuses on the possibilities for social cooperation. In Marxist views, capitalists who can finance the ways in which goods are produced (the 'means of production') become a separate class of people from workers, who must sell their labour to capitalists. This contrasts with an earlier period when the worker owned their own tools and could often produce goods from home or their own workshop. Workers thus become cut off or 'alienated' from the means of production, and their interests become different from those of capitalists. Because, as we have seen, industrialists and entrepreneurs displaced the aristocracy in political control in industrialising countries such as Britain and Germany, Marxists argued that they began to develop the state to form society for the advantage of capitalists. The state increasingly became a site for struggles between capitalist advantage and workers' attempts to create institutions and services that enabled them to resist control and pursue their own interests. Working-class organisations, such as trade unions, developed during the 1800s and because they were associated with the world of work, seemed to oppose the interests of capitalists. Related organisations such as cooperatives and friendly societies sit uneasily between working-class movements and self-help. Marxism had its origins in European revolutionary movements in the mid-1800s, and its impact on social work initially lies in the corporatism of German social provision (Chapters 2). As the German state formed in the midst of rapid industrialisation, it incorporated social provision in response to the fear of social disorder and resistance. Institutions providing for social security and social care would secure the state by incorporating within it some responses to working-class demands for participation and service provision. Such ideas also contributed to the influence of psychological and COS ideas in social work of the early 1900s because of the anxiety in European countries after the Russian Revolution in 1917 about the possible influence of socialist ideas leading to revolution. Younghusband (1981: 11) proposes that sociology was underdeveloped for the first half of the 1900s and Marxism had little impact on social work at this period.

Marxism is 'materialist' in the same way that liberalism is, since both look for an explanation of human social structures in the external or material world and see economic imperatives as the drivers of social systems. However, later developments have incorporated broader ideas. For example, the Frankfurt School of critical theorists focused on how ideas and cultural values created hegemony for powerful elites in societies, that is, domination through assumptions about how the world is.

Social democracy

Social democratic, democratic socialist and parliamentary socialist ideas emerged at the beginning of the 1900s, as the state became an important site of social and economic management. They promote the possibility of social change for the benefit of working-class people, while suggesting that reform is possible through the democratic processes offered by liberal thinking. Fabian thinking in the late 1800s, for example, argued that if the state could be made more democratic, it could be fashioned as a tool of social reform (Sullivan, 1999). This is different from seeking reform through legislation from a humanitarian point of view: in social democratic ideas, legislation is used to accord socially accepted rights to both provision and participation. Such ideas influenced the thinking of the reforming Liberal Party administration in Britain in the 1906–14 period. However, the quotation from Lloyd George, above, shows how this was still based on humanitarian concern for the poor and insurance principles following German policies, rather than reform to give people social rights. Similar ideas influenced the progressive movement and its politics in the USA during the same period.

The period after the First World War, particularly after the experience of the Depression in the 1930s, led increasingly to a consensus about welfare thinking, centred around democratic socialism. The Conservative politician Macmillan, MP for a working-class town in northern England and later prime minister in the 1950s and 60s, promoted the idea of the 'middle way' between socialism and laissez-faire (Ritschel, 1995). The Labour Party had two periods of minority administration. Most important, the economist Keynes (1883–1946) developed economic ideas that proposed establishing a world economic order, permitting flexibility in how countries responded to economic problems (Williams and Williams, 1995). As a result, trading countries would support each other in managing the international economy, so that they would not experience successive serious depressions and rapid growth. As a negotiator for the British government in the post-war settlements, he used these ideas to achieve considerable influence on the economic system that permitted stable growth during the period after 1945, and the development of welfare states. An important element of the proposed flexibility was using government expenditure to support full employment policies. The academic and administrator Beveridge (1879–1963) also gave priority to dealing with employment, alongside many people following the experience of the 1930s. His report (Chapter 3) on social insurance in 1942 was a substantial influence in establishing the British welfare state.

The separation of social democratic from socialist ideas in British thinking and their impact on the Labour Party as it developed during the 1920s and 30s meant that Marxism was distinguished from social democratic ideas about reform. In the USA, on the other hand, there was a greater association between ideas promoting radical social change and socialism. Thus, in the 1930s the radical rank and file movement of social workers in federal services, concerned particularly with New Deal provision for the poor, associated social work with Communism (Chapter 8). British social workers continued in a relatively liberal mode of thinking, in which social work was concerned with individualised extensions of charity and philanthropy, and those committed to social change became associated with more general social change through legislative and institutional reform. The British separation between social work and 'the dole', the Liberal unemployment insurance scheme that displaced the stigmatised Poor Law for working men in the Depression of the 1930s, meant that social work was not radicalised. However, the brief accounts of the lives of Aves and Younghusband (Chapter 3) show how important figures in developing state provision in the 1950s and 60s started from middle or upper-class origins and were regarded as radical in their association with charitable action among working-class people in the 1930s.

Welfare state ideas

During the welfare state period (Chapter 3), social democratic ideas were in the ascendant and social work was associated with them. The welfare states of the mid-1900s were a product of the impact of social democratic thinking and the economic system created as part of the reconstruction of European states. This accepted, unlike socialist thought, that the economic market as the generator of wealth was the fundamental base of social organisation. The social development of colonies similarly emerged from social democratic thinking applied to the independence movement.

A crucial element of this thinking developed in the 1940s and 50s as ideas about citizenship (Marshall, 1970) applying social democratic thinking to welfare provision, updating Fabian ideas. Citizens were entitled because of their participation in the state, to support and care when in difficulty. The British post-war welfare state assumed that participation was based on male employment, and the state managed the economy to achieve substantially full employment, which then allowed men to maintain other members of the family. Dependence on welfare provision was thus minimised and restricted to easily identifiable groups, who could be accorded help as of right.

These developments incorporate a tension for social work. On one hand, the aim of improving and developing social provision strengthened the role of social work. More state services were provided and welfare was more securely funded by rising budgets. Although most welfare state expenditure was in social security, social protection, health, housing and education, all these services came to incorporate personal social services, and in many countries the range of social work provision was increased. On the other hand, social work remained a largely discretionary provision, a residual or fall-back position where wider welfare state provision was unsuitable, except in some Nordic countries, where an emphasis on providing social support for women's employment made welfare provision more central to universal state provision. Child protection was necessary because public health education of parents was unsatisfactory; child care because family income support and education was inadequate. Old people needed residential care because health care, pensions and family support did not meet all needs. Social development was necessary in developing countries because economic development had not driven up prosperity to the point where Western standards of social organisation were routinely available.

Citizenship and welfare in the 1980s

We saw, in Chapter 3, the importance of welfare states of different kinds in the development of social work, and in Chapter 4, how economic rationalism, based on the neoliberal critique of welfare during the 1980s and 90s led to doubts about the role of the state in welfare, and consequently to a questioning of social work's universalistic role. Neoliberalism applies liberal thinking of the 1800s to the economic and social situation of the 1980s, when the oil price shocks and other economic instability produced doubts about the possibility of sustaining the increasing social expenditure of welfare states. This led in the 1980s to concern about 'squaring the welfare circle' (George and Miller, 1994), that is, paying higher costs of care for ageing populations as medical and staffing costs increased, due to better technology and higher expectations, when political support for increased taxation to meet the costs was in doubt. Bonoli et al. (2000: Ch. 5) summarise the neoliberal argument for cutbacks in state provision of welfare as follows. Social welfare creates benefits for unemployed people to such an extent that it encourages an unwillingness to work and provide for themselves. It therefore adds to the costs of employment, reducing the financial efficiency of industry and commerce and reducing the level of employment. As the state expands, it makes people dependent on it, rather than their own efforts, and so reduces individual freedom, since state control comes to be exerted over more aspects of life.

The British Conservative governments of the 1980s and 90s followed this approach to emphasise individual responsibility for personal welfare and social protection, reducing dependency on state provision, and transferring social costs to the private sector, where they enhance rather than restrict social entrepreneurship. Thus, citizenship conferred rights to participate in and use the market, rather than gain welfare benefits separately from the market. Social work increased at this time, partly because it was less important than health and education, so less of a target, but also because its individualising methods made it a useful residual service, mopping up individual hard cases.

However, Chapter 4 showed how substantial debate about the neoliberal critique and attempts in various countries to respond to it led to a much more mixed pattern of welfare provision in different welfare 'regimes'. Kautto's (2001) study of European welfare states in the late 1990s shows that distinctions between Nordic universal welfare states and less broad provision in other European welfare state regimes continued to exist during and after this period. However, regimes did come closer together, mainly because of retrenchment in the universal welfare states. States also varied more in the priority that they gave to different needs, so there was a good deal of differentiation.

Communitarianism, participation and empowerment

In the 1990s, communitarianism became important as an individualist, liberal view of citizenship. Communitarians propose that rights to welfare are conditional on citizens making a contribution to the community in a social exchange. They gain welfare rights on the basis of past contributions, for example if they are elderly, or by current participation in the market through employment and social responsibility by being good parents and not becoming criminals. These ideas, similar to the social Darwinist ideas of the late 1800s discussed above, place social work in its historic tension between individual help and social justice and reform. It seeks to achieve general social progress by individual improvement, but rejects the punitive market consequences of exclusion if the individual client is unable or unwilling to make a social contribution.

Social work's response in the late 1900s to this tension has been to emphasise client and citizen participation in social provision and the empowerment of clients and social groups from which clients are drawn to achieve such participation. The idea of self-determination was recognised as oversimplified; in the face of professional and state power, clients were often not free to direct their workers' practice (McDermott, 1975). Analysis of the 1950s and 60s saw workers as having professional and legal authority conferred by their training, their agencies' social responsibilities and, in welfare states, legislation (Foren and Bailey, 1968; Yelaja, 1971). This view sought to legitimate workers' interventions. Early codes of ethics, developing in the 1950s and 60s, focused on managing worker–client interactions ethically.

However, an influential Marxist analysis of power in the 1970s, particularly in radical social work (Chapter 10), emphasised that social workers often used state power to oppress disadvantaged people. Writers such as Illich et al. (1977) argued that interventions by professions sometimes worsened social problems, in the same way that some illnesses are caused by medical interventions. Radical social work in the 1970s emphasised the value of enabling people to learn cooperation through activities such as groupwork and community work. Radical views exaggerate the impact of professional influence and the extent of state power, and undervalue the protection offered by the importance of state welfare. However, this analysis had impact on social work professional values. The American code of ethics was rewritten during the 1970s to include a role for advocacy on behalf of clients and the first British code sought to balance the role of social action on behalf of clients with responsibility to agency managements (Payne, 1985).

The radical approach to social work lost influence during the 1980s, with the general political shift towards New Right thinking. However, its perspective was maintained in two streams of work. Consumerism shifted its emphasis during the 1970s from protecting consumers buying retail goods and commercial services towards more comprehensive action including public services. Influential studies of consumer opinion about social services emerged from better funding for research after the British Seebohm reorganisation increased the importance of social services, and the development of social sciences internationally. Allied to this was a movement in Britain for citizens' participation in public decisions, such as planning (Skeffington Report, 1969). Internationally, American movements for equal rights and the 'great society' reforms and Latin American radical movements such as liberation theology and the reconceptualisation movement in Brazilian social work provoked similar radical movements for participation and advocacy. The replacement of self-determination was 'client participation' in decisions affecting them, and access to records about them (BASW, 1980, 1983). Developing from this during the 1980s was a stream of work concerned with emphasising citizen participation for excluded social groups, which was relevant to many of the social groups served by social workers. Disabled people, 'survivors' of mental illness and its treatment and minority ethnic groups among others formed pressure groups and movements to promote equality in social acceptance and services that recognised their needs and wishes.

The second important radical movement of the 1980s and 90s went beyond participation of excluded groups, instead seeking to reduce and ultimately eliminate the impact of what was initially seen as discrimination against them. The analysis developed towards a focus on the oppression of minority groups, particularly minority ethnic groups in Western countries as oppressed by the institutional arrangements in public services and the market. In the anti-oppressive analysis, oppression is seen as the product of market and capitalist systems. Thus, this analysis sees social work as having a duty to correct social injustices. However, other countries have emphasised sensitivity to ethnic and cultural difference, so that professionals can be aware of and respond to particular minority needs, taking a social democratic rather than socialist approach to these issues.

A related approach focuses on empowerment, so that clients may become more aware of oppressions, learning skills and confidence to overcome it. This redirects the radical analysis towards work with individuals, groups and communities, rather than political or social action to combat social injustices and is more social democratic or even liberal.

These debates about approaches to citizenship rights for people receiving welfare services demonstrate the incorporation within social work of the tensions between the different political philosophies that inform it. This is reflected in current codes of ethics. The responsibility within welfare services to discipline clients to conform with participation in market economies by maintaining employment and responding to efforts at social inclusion lead to social work value statements maintaining elements such as confidentiality, which are designed to manage the conflict between helping objectives in a disciplinary service structure. The *International Code of Ethics* (IFSW, 1994), for example, continues to refer to the 'unique value' of every human being and individualistic requirements such as maintaining 'the client's right to a relationship of trust, to privacy and confidentiality, and to responsible use of information'. It also refers to the duty of 'clients to take responsibility, in collaboration with them'. The American code (NASW, 1996) refers to self-determination and informed consent as important principles. However, social work value statements also contain elements of commitment to social justice and anti-discriminatory actions, explicitly, for example, in the IFSW code. The American code also contains references to understanding culture as part of society and knowing about clients' cultures. Thus social work codes of ethics contain, in tension, liberal, social democratic and socialist approaches to these important issues.

Community: localism and centralisation

Chapter 2 identified the importance of central–local relations in the history of social work in many countries. There are many examples.

In the UK, the history of the Poor Laws reflected an uneasy relationship between central and local concerns. The first Poor Laws stressed local responsibility for poor people, at least partly to prevent poor people roaming the countryside. The Poor Law

Amendment Act 1834, which created the new Poor Law, compromised this local responsibility with national inspection and regulation. The 1948 welfare state reforms established social work in local authority welfare and children's departments and probation with local management, each service coordinated by central inspection, advice and support. This was distinguished from a national management of social security and health services, even though the latter had strong elements of local administration. In the last quarter of the 1900s, significant centralisation took place, in pursuit of economic management and policy control by centralised political machines in the Thatcher (1979–91, Conservative) and Blair (1997 to date, Labour) administrations.

In many European countries, unlike the UK, this tendency towards centralisation is absent, since local administrations have independent constitutional rights, greater freedom of independent action and policy-making and more strongly federal legal and administrative structures (Hague et al., 1998: 180). In many cases provision for social care is at the lower levels of administration, often responding to ethnic and community differences in quite complex ways. For example, Belgium, from 1970 a federal state, has three types of government power: the central state, the communities (Dutch-, French- and German-speaking groups) and regions, the Flemish (Dutch) and Walloon (French) areas and the capital. Social services are administered by communities covering the relevant region and part of the bilingual area of the capital (Mostinckx, 1993).

Moreover, in much of Europe, the Catholic principle of subsidiarity, designed to defend the predominance of the Church in interpersonal social matters, was incorporated into German social organisation and EU policy. This principle proposes that social provision should be made informally, if possible, and if not at the lowest level of administration. Thus, what is possible informally or locally and how it relates to a nationwide pattern is a crucial element of understanding welfare systems.

In the USA, in many periods there has been a stress on local state rather than federal responsibility for welfare. For example,in the 1830s and 50s, Dorothea Dix campaigned for federal provision for mentally ill people, having persuaded her local state, New Jersey, to set up a hospital for the insane, then finding that other states could not afford or agree to follow suit. While Congress passed a bill facilitating this, it was vetoed in 1845 by President Franklin Pierce, who said:

> Can it be controverted that the great mass of the business of Government that involved ... the relief of the needy, or otherwise unfortunate members of society, did, in practice, remain with the States; that none of these local concerns are, by the Constitution, expressly or impliedly prohibited to the States, and that none of them are, by any express language of the Constitution, transferred to the United States ... Can it be claimed that any of these functions of local administration and legislation are vested in the Federal Government by any implication?
>
> (Quoted in Pumphrey and Pumphrey, 1961: 133)

At times of social difficulty, such as the New Deal responding to the Depression in the 1930s and the war on poverty of the 1960s, responding to civil rights and anti-war movements, there have been shifts towards more universal federal provision. However, this has often been resisted and reversed in times when less social pressure has been applied to governments, or when political impetus has been towards local autonomy.

The religious and the secular

Chapters 2–4 identified the association of social work with trends towards secularisation and the limitation of the social work role in societies where secularisation had not taken place. These trends raise the historical question whether secularisation is a necessary condition for the development of social work, and whether the religious or spiritual is inconsistent with social work practice. These questions connect with questions of political philosophy since social work is associated with Western secular societies and important societies where religion is a considerable social force are Eastern. However, there are exceptions, among them Western Catholic countries. Ireland is a good example. Here, the Catholic Church opposed the development of state welfare until Catholicism became less important in the state in the late 1900s. Southern European countries with less well-developed welfare states may reflect a similar trend. This confirms the idea that states strongly influenced by religious ideologies resist secularisation; this is associated with less strong development of social work. Even in the Netherlands, Koenis (1999) argues that the dominant Calvinist Church resisted state provision of personal welfare, as opposed to social security prior to the 1950s. Coman (1977) studied the development of Roman Catholic social thought in Britain during the 1900s, built on revived medieval social teaching emphasising the diffusion of ownership and individual responsibility. Until the 1950s, he found that there was a separatist approach, in which the Catholic Church tried to isolate its members from 'damaging influences in the wider society' (Coman, 1977: 109). Separate education through specifically Catholic schools was associated with misgivings about the NHS and national insurance. However, from the 1950s, concerns about maintaining Catholic dogma in other areas, such as birth regulation, gained greater priority. From the 1960s, Marxist thinking in Catholic liberation movements led to a greater concern for third world poverty and social development issues, through organisations such as CAFOD (the Catholic Foundation for Overseas Development). Thus, a long-standing Catholic critique of state intervention and bureaucratisation in Britain lost its impact. Coman (1977: 110) suggests that minority social thinking makes little headway against long-term economic and social trends.

Ray's (1993: Ch. 7) case study of the Islamic revolution in Iran also offers some explanatory information. During the early and mid-1900s, the Pahlavi regime sought to modernise Iran, using authoritarian power supported by a bureaucracy and participation in global economic structures. The international connections of the social work school described by Farman-Farmaien (1992) related to this regime and its bureaucracy, whose approach to modernisation avoided engagement with and recognition of potential democratic opposition. The state and political development thus became isolated from civil society and social aspiration. Consequently, opposition became centred round Islamic beliefs, and the Islamic revolution swept away modernising influences. Thus the Islamic tradition of *zakat*, the duty to give a proportion of wealth as alms, remained separated from secular developments such as social work, which was part of the alienated modernising state. Ray proposes that building bridges between modernisers and important traditional beliefs might have enabled a secular state to relate to traditional social forces. In Farman-Farmaien's account of the work of the social work school, it is shown as inevitably bound up with the authoritarian state, rather than being based in local traditional beliefs and hence did not survive the revolution.

Ray (1993: Ch. 6) connects this with his analysis of the crisis of state socialism in the soviet Communist world during most of the 1900s. Social work based in local and traditional social structures was absent, although informal mutual help was extensive. Authoritarian state organisation provided extensive but largely impersonal welfare services (Table 3.1). When state Communism collapsed under internal and external pressures in the 1980s and 90s, a weak civil society did not provide the impetus for participation in a democratic political system. Equally, it did not provide the basis for well-developed social welfare provision. Thus, social work is only weakly embedded in state and social provision in former Communist countries. In Communist China, on the other hand, while it was underdeveloped in the first half of the 1900s and excluded from provision from the 1940s to the 1990s, attempts to develop it extensively and make it part of local provision and make social work education widely available using indigenous concepts (Chan and Chow, 1992; Tsang and Yan, 2001) may permit a greater embeddedness.

Examining the position in Latin America, the Catholic Church was influential and social work was slow to develop, emerging mainly as a result of post-war American and UN intervention. However, social development approaches were influential. In Africa, on the other hand, while spiritual life was important to many indigenous peoples, the colonial states were relatively secular after the initial influence of Western missionaries. There was a similar experience in the Asian states developing in the second half of the 1900s, such as India, Southeast Asia, Korea and Japan. In all these countries social work provision was small scale, associated with necessary state provision, around the courts and child welfare, and associated with missionary welfare (particularly residential care) and NGO activity. However, social development formed the most important enhancement of social provision.

Moreover, spiritual and religious ideas have had considerable impact on social work. In Western societies many social workers are motivated by religious commitment and Christian and other religious traditions have had influence on social work ideas.

Biestek's ([1957]1961) influential social work text of the late 1950s, explicitly based on Christian ideas, is an example. Some countries, for example Germany, Norway and the USA have religiously based social work schools. Moreover, spiritual and Christian ideas have regained prominence in the later 1990s, alongside a theoretical interest in exploring the potential impact of spiritual beliefs among minority ethnic groups as part of social work practice.

To sum up this discussion, therefore, three points emerge. First, religion and spiritual beliefs and values have at times had an important impact upon social work, and this interrelationship continues, varying in intensity. In largely secular societies, this is a minority interest but occasional developments have their impact. The worldwide influence of family group conferences, emerging from Maori cultural and spiritual ideas is an example. Second, the development of social work as a profession and as part of organised state provision is strongly associated with secularised Western societies, and strong religious influence counterbalancing the state inhibits the development of social work. However, this seems to be mainly because the embeddedness of religious and spiritual beliefs in social relations lessens the impact of organised state services. Where states have failed to engage with important social traditions, cultural and spiritual beliefs remain powerful antagonists to organised social work. Personal social welfare is organised around religion. Where states develop social work separately from social traditions, as in post-Communist Eastern Europe, or pre-revolutionary Iran, it may become bureaucratised and separated from social life. However, where, as in Western societies, it emerges from a strong civil society with roots in social and cultural traditions, it becomes a strong secular profession, able to interact with spiritual beliefs and church organisation of social provision.

This draws attention to the importance for social work's effective development of embedding it in social cultures and beliefs within an effective civil society.

Conclusion

Because social work is closely bound up in the role of the state, examining it requires exploring its political roots, and these rely on important philosophical and ideological debates, outlined in this chapter. Social work, however, often incorporates these different perspectives alongside each other. Consequently, tensions about the values that social work represents often emerge within its practice. Other tensions on localism and centralisation and the relationship between the religious and secular are also present within social work. A historical analysis does not allow us to say that social work has shifted from liberal towards socialist or social democratic values, from centralised to localised services or from the religious to the secular. These issues reappear in social work in different forms at different historical junctures, sometimes mirroring more general social debates.

One of the central tensions for social workers is how these philosophical and value tensions are played out in practice. The representation of tensions in practice is mediated, however, by the legal and organisational contexts within which social work is practised, and the next chapter explores that context further.

CHAPTER 7

Agencies, Law and Social Order

This chapter examines how social work forms social order. It examines the relationship between social work and social order, as practice is mediated through the law and social agencies, and as examples of its role in the social order functions of the state, it looks at the development of state agencies in the UK and how social work is situated within them, the development of institutional and residential care as a site of social work, and at scandals and inquiries in UK social work.

Social work and social order

Social work is a social order. That is, it is a recognisable social practice that has developed in many societies and has become part of official and non-official social structures. It varies within and between these societies and cultures, but in its various identities it is made up of connected ideas and practices, so that all these may be understood as 'social work' (Chapter 9). The social roles discussed in Chapter 5 and the ideas and values discussed in Chapter 6 are mediated through the law and the organisations within which social work is practised. Law and social agencies are social work's context, making it a social order that is part of a wider social order because it is partly constructed by the sources from which it gains its authority to act. Authority in this case implies a mandate, legitimated by some social processes, that gives socially accepted power. That authority is required because social workers are outsiders to the situations in which they act, and their intervention has to be accepted by the people in the situation. However, authority is always contested, and so a social worker's right to intervene might be resisted. For example, Chapter 2 identified a long history of support for self-help, Chapter 3 a debate about whether and how the state should intervene in people's lives, Chapter 5 identified the historic importance of support for family and community as preferred ways of intervening, and Chapter 6 identified a historic political debate about the role of welfare. On the other hand, there are reasons why social work intervention might be accepted. For example, workers might gain authority when they are seen as competent to make an intervention that is seen as beneficial, or from the knowledge that the police or a court will enforce the intervention.

Such sources of authority always connect social workers to a social order: in the first example, an order of knowledge and skill; in the second, an order created by the structures for enforcement of socially approved behaviour. The connection between professional knowledge and skill and social structures raises the possibility that challenges to organisational and political power to intervene may come not only from challenges to social work, but also from challenges to the social orders that social work is a part of, in particular the state. Thus, we saw in Chapter 4 that challenges to social work's expertise and role were raised when there were challenges to the state.

That social work is connected with social order is made clear by the way in which social welfare often developed as a way of combating potential disorder. Previous chapters have shown that modern social work developed partly as a response to the nineteenth-century fear of social disorder from the working class and new urban areas, for example in Britain and Germany. Other examples are Japanese responses to rioting in the early twentieth century, and colonial powers dealing with economic change and urbanisation disrupting the order previously derived from African tribal patterns. The domination of the churches withered as welfare shifted from the church to religiously based organisations, to secular organisations and to the state in many countries, including Britain. The Catholic Church fought against the loss of power over family and marriage in Ireland and mainland Europe and failed. These examples show that social work often replaces powerful social orders, as social institutions change.

Social work does not, however, make social order as an independent entity; it does so as one of several aspects of social order. The form of the agencies that it operates in, whether private, voluntary or state, constructs how it contributes to social order. The legal and social authority for its actions create its particular role in making social order. Social work is a formally educated middle-class workforce, with substantial moral and practical authority. That authority is drawn from organisations with moral authority, especially religion, and financial and practical authority, especially business. However, much of social work's authority has come from social discipline on behalf of the state and representing the interests of groups in society that benefit from social order. Examples include responsibility for child protection, involvement in restraint of people with mental disorders, involvement in criminal justice and in care requiring long-term institutionalisation. All these and other roles place social workers in a position of offering social discipline. However, all attempts at discipline are likely to be resisted, both by the state, which seeks to control the behaviour of its agents, and by the people who are watched and controlled. Thus, the authority of law and organisation and the authority of skill and expertise are always likely to be questioned.

Since, as we have seen in Chapters 2–4, the development of social work derives at least partly from the acceptance of responsibility for welfare by the state, this often gives great importance to the law and political policy-making which sets the parameters of state action. Some countries, for example Finland (Satka, 1995), give great importance to legal authority; others, such as the USA, give greater importance to professional and other forms of mandate.

Legal authority, however, should not obscure other sources of professional and social authority, and other possibilities of resistance. Debate about the sources and role of authority and power has been a continuing theme in social work writing. The psychoanalytically based social work of the first half of the twentieth century (Chapter 9) developed from a medical and psychiatric perspective. Its emphasis on patients' (clients') right to determine their 'treatment' was allied to the concern for professional status. The worker's authority, therefore, derived from expertise, knowledge and professional standing and, according to functional social work, also the role of the agency. Thus, exercising authority was considered to be particularly associated with those agencies that had a legal function, in particular probation and parole workers. The literature of the 1950s and 60s contains much discussion of the problems for the professional view of non-directive social work espoused at a time when social work accepted tasks of legal enforcement. This trend in thinking extends in the USA to a literature (for example Rooney, 1992) that is concerned with the 'involuntary clients' and the special requirements for dealing with them. This is because a significant focus of social work in the USA is in voluntary family agencies, clinical private practice and counselling-related work so that social work ideas drawn from these settings do not offer useful practice guidance in enforcement.

Social work exercises considerable 'caring power' in social relations through its particular role in families and domestic welfare (Chapter 5). Since much of social work is done by women with women in the domestic situation, it may have a significant impact on personal, private and family relations in a way that no other profession achieves. In education, for example, teachers are often said to have little influence on children's total education compared with home life, with its early and continuing role in child care and development. Similarly, criminal justice professions feel themselves powerless in the face of strong family and peer influences towards chaotic or criminal lifestyles. Caring power to some degree counteracts gender discrimination against women which has continued throughout the twentieth century, particularly in employment. This has often excluded women from ownership of property and forced them into low-income employment, subsidiary to a male primary earner. This is emphasised by the state welfare provision developed in many countries during the mid-twentieth century. Social work is the aspect of state welfare that particularly focuses on family and domestic welfare through the use of caring power and its growth in importance occurred during the period when the state was concerned to strengthen the family after the Second World War.

The role of social work in creating social order is ambiguous and controversial. Because it is a replacement that may be more neutral or supportive to oppressed peoples in its action than the application of direct power by religion, the state and the rich, it may have a revolutionary or critical element within its implementation. However, because it is often a subordinate representative of these powers, it may also implement surveillance and oppression over the powerless.

Related to these competing tendencies is the low importance of welfare in most powerful agendas. Rich and powerful organisations or individuals have more important things to do than help others, tending to focus on economic growth and the accumulation of wealth. Therefore, welfare systems, once set up or enacted in law, may persist for many years, changing infrequently, and economic power becomes important in the impact of social services systems. One example of this is the long history and international impact, through the importance of the British Empire, of the British Elizabethan Poor Laws. In another era, social care matters changed little for most of the period of the Conservative Thatcher government in Britain (1979–90), when education and health services were subjected to ceaseless change, impelled by a right-wing ideology that focused on economic growth as the driver for social development. Another example is the long continuation and adaptation of AFDC in the USA.

Because change is slow, evils may persist, an example being the slow reform in Britain of the new Poor Law between 1834 and 1948. Rose (1989) shows how the system of American social security has continued to be affected by lawmakers' concerns at enactment in the 1930s about the 'ideology of the dole', that is, the concern that people who seek relief are undeserving and idle. This is an example of classical liberal ideologies and their continuing impact on daily social care services and attitudes. However, Morton (1988), in a study of homes for 'fallen women' in Cleveland, USA, suggests that, in spite of pressures from policy changes, other professionals and membership of coordinating organisations, these homes continued merely to conform to policy changes on the surface. They maintained their oppressive and stigmatising religious policies from the 1800s well into the 1960s. Professional practices may also, therefore, persist in the face of movements in thinking and attitudes.

Moreover, internationally, Chapters 2–4 have demonstrated continuing debates around using legal measures to constrain expenditure on services and dependency among the undeserving. The Poor Laws are a classic example of the use of the law for constraint and control of the poor. On the other hand, reformers have used the law to promote and develop services and rights to them. The American and British legislation of the 1980s and 90s on disability and advocacy is an example. This example also illustrates the importance of the interaction between law on the one hand and public attitudes and the political process within which policy-making takes place on the other.

Liberal thinking (Chapter 6) gives great importance to the 'rule of law'. This emphasises legal support for personal freedoms, in particular economic freedom. According to this view, law enforcement should be separated from the political process of legislating and the executive which implements government policy, the law should serve general social needs rather than private ends and it should be enforced impartially (Green, 1993). In nineteenth-century Britain, the foundation of the police force (from 1829) and the process of municipalisation of local government displaced the personal responsibility of the local aristocracy for enforcing the law and managing the local social fabric and invested it in more formal and independent organisations. Chapter 2 showed how these provided the context in which formal social work provided an important element of moral and social constraint within services run by 'local bureaucratic elites'.

Local bureaucratic elites in many Western countries were often successful businessmen, with their wives forming a local social elite that took on social work and domestic roles. Such elites are also influential in voluntary and charitable organisations, so that their social and political attitudes and business training in management can have a significant influence on social work. The impact of business and management thinking on international, national and local politics has always been considerable, and continues (Harris, 2002). Chapter 6 drew on evidence in some situations that professionals in welfare systems had imbibed liberal economic thinking and integrated it with decision-making processes. They thus influenced politicians and decision-makers. In Nordic countries, there is evidence that this has led to a separation of decision-makers' values from those of the general public who are more supportive of welfare funding (Blomberg and Kroll, 1999). In addition, we noted in Chapters 4 and 6 that there is a reaction against 'something for nothing' social provision, and a communitarian ideal of people taking responsibility for themselves and others.

In summary, social work relies on many different elements of authority, partly deriving from its middle-class status, including religion, business, women's caring power in domestic and family life and liberal and communitarian ideologies that emphasise social responsibilities. These historical sources of authority are in tension with its emphasis on human rights, equality and anti-oppressive action. These tensions have been played out in the development of social work and continue their impact on daily practice. Moreover, social work's reliance on organisational and legal authority is likely to be resisted and contested, and such contests have also been characteristic of social work's history.

State agencies and social work

Social agencies and social law provide the context within which social work exercises caring power. Some examples of how this works are explored in this chapter. First, the organisation of state agencies in the UK shows how state agencies have developed over time to offer social work services. British social agencies have developed a pattern of using caring power to manage working-class problems. In contrast, Nordic agencies have developed to provide services that ensure that women can work, since this is required to support economies more reliant on female employment than the UK. Thus, as Sipilä et al (1997) argue, the defining characteristic of Nordic welfare is not the welfare of poor people as in the UK, but general provision of care services to support stable employment.

Britain

Chapters 2–4 show that Britain's social services developed from three elements: Poor Law provision, leading to local government services; friendly visiting in the charitable sector, progressing to a range of voluntary sector provision; and private sector provision emerging at the time of the New Right challenge to social care in the 1980s.

Central to these developments is public sector provision, from the Poor Law onwards. Figure 7.1 shows the stages of the break-up of the Poor Law until the creation of social services departments (SSDs), together with prospective moves towards 'joined-up' management.

The first crucial period of changes was the late 1940s, when the Poor Law was broken up. The Poor Law hospitals went to the new NHS, social security went to the pensions administration and the then National Assistance Board. Welfare services continued

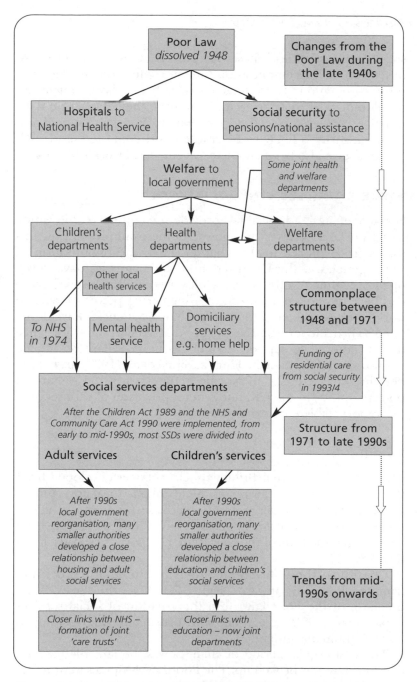

Figure 7.1 Development of English social services structure 1948–2000

in local government administration. A children's department was established in each authority by the Children Act 1948. Usually there was also a welfare department and a health department; sometimes these were combined. The health department usually organised domiciliary services, such as home helps, and eventually, after the Mental Health Act 1959, also became responsible for mental health community services in a mental health department. All these developments encouraged social work. The Children Act 1948 emphasised caring for children in the community by regulating foster care or 'boarding out', welfare departments stimulated the creation of a group of community social workers, and the Mental Health Act 1959 created a role for social workers in community mental health.

The next important stage was the early 1970s when, as a result of the recommendations of the Seebohm Report (1968), local authority SSDs were formed. This was implemented in 1971 in England and Wales, incorporating children's, mental health, welfare and domiciliary services; occasionally education welfare was also included. In Scotland, probation was included in similar social work departments (SWDs), formed in 1970 following the implementation of the Kilbrandon Report (1964). In Northern Ireland, social services formed a division of health and social services boards; probation was separate. After local government reorganisation in 1974, social work in the NHS was transferred to SSDs and most social services authorities became larger. This created an important social position for social workers as professional leaders of a major local government department with substantial expenditure and a high public and political profile. In the 1980s a large private residential care sector mainly for elders but also for other groups needing long-term care grew up, funded by fees paid by the state for care in private care but not in statutory provision. Local authority social work became much more limited as priority was given to statutory activities that regulated behaviour, such as child protection, and to meet high-priority care needs, rather than offering a general social work service.

This structure was maintained, but further changes took place in the 1990s. One reason was that the legislation, the Children Act 1989 and the NHS and Community Care Act 1990, was implemented in such a way that a division into adult and children's services was virtually required. These changes formed a new social work role, care management, in adult services and emphasised social work roles in child protection. Both tasks seemed to deprofessionalise and bureaucratise social work, seeing it as mainly concerned with management or protective procedures. Also, until 1997, the Conservative government implemented a rolling programme of local government reform creating many unitary authorities whose responsibilities included social services. These were too small to have many separate departments, and often merged housing and social services, following a pattern developed by the relatively small urban metropolitan authorities created by the 1974 reorganisation. After 1997, the New Labour administration provided for greater flexibility in local government structure, encouraging new forms of corporate management in search of joined-up government and policy. This sometimes led to adult services being merged with housing, while children's services merged with education. Setting up local trusts for children and mental health services was encouraged by the government as a model for coordinating health and social care services formalised by the Health and Social Care Act 2001. All these changes led to a greater range of organisational forms for British social services.

There are various views of this sequence of events. One is that the creation of state social services took place in two steps. In this view, the 1948 dissolution of the Poor Law was a preliminary stage, completed by the formation of SSDs in the Seebohm reorganisation of 1971. An alternative view is that the sequence represents a cycle in which the problems of a generalist structure are displaced by a specialist structure. In turn, the problems of separate structures become evident, and they are displaced in turn by merger into a renewed generalist structure in 1971. As the expertise problems of this structure became apparent, especially in child care and mental health scandals, proponents of coordination with health and education became more influential and this led to the swing of the 1990s back towards more formal connections with health and education.

Neither view seems quite right to me. The missing element is the development of the social work profession (Chapter 8). Until social work was clearly formed as a separate occupational group in the 1960s, and had begun to unify and professionalise, the creation of an organisation with a social services identity was not possible. Once established, SSDs strengthened the formation of the occupational group. However, by incorporating most social work into local government in one agency, the Seebohm reorganisation created a social work identity that was also a local government identity. In the Poor Law era, social work was clearly in the voluntary sector, even though much the same work was undertaken in the better Poor Law departments. After the Seebohm reorganisation, social work was clearly within the state and stood or fell by its identity with SSDs (and SWDs in Scotland).

British social work around 2000 was formed and changed by political, administrative and managerial changes directed at local government, as British (and much European) social work around 1900 had been formed by municipalisation. The period of Conservative administration in the 1980s increasingly subordinated local government to central government financial and policy control. Although this was not mainly directed at social services, whose organisation was largely unaffected until the mid-1990s, social work was carried into the managerialist, policy-centralising trends. This was reinforced by the growing concern of the New Labour government of the late 1990s about the effectiveness of public services. However, the establishment of the profession had advanced so much that it could not simply be displaced. In the Conservative period to 1997, the reduction in universal social provision required an increase in social work, primarily to provide assessments for access to increasingly selective services. In the Labour period from 1997, the intention to regulate the profession demonstrates that its role was established. However, the creation of specialist multiprofessional services using social work skills, for example the Connexions service for young people in transition from school to work, also demonstrates a valuation of social work skills, even if these are not directly connected to the organised social work profession.

Non-state social work and occupational social work

Settings for social work vary across different countries and it is offered in private organisations in some countries. In the UK, where the state became the major provider of social work in the 1970s, this is defined in relation to public sector provision. Thus, voluntary agencies are seen as pioneers of new service and as filling gaps in public provision, especially where particular groups, such as HIV/AIDS sufferers, may be excluded from political support. Increasingly, voluntary organisations are seen as an alternative structure of provision, which contracts to provide services on behalf of the state. Private provision, that is, for profit, is also organised around the provision of services, mainly using state funding. In the USA, by contrast, elite professional practice lies in important not-for-profit family and community agencies.

However, in some countries, occupational or industrial social work exists, where, as in occupational health, social care is provided at employees' workplaces. Straussner (1989: 3) places the origins of such provision in the 'welfare capitalism' of the late nineteenth century, when employers provided benefits and services 'to socialise, retain and control a raw unskilled and badly needed labor force'. In the USA, it emerged when, after the Civil War (1861–5), more women entered the labour market and needed female 'specialists' to deal with gender-related problems. Mrs Aggie Dunn, probably the first, was hired as 'social secretary' in 1875 by Heinz in Pittsburgh. This practice developed in the early twentieth century and by 1919 a survey of 431 large companies in the USA found that 141 employed a full-time welfare secretary and 154 contracted with outside providers. In 1920, more graduates of the New York School of Social Work were employed in industrial settings than in any other area, although most industrial welfare was not provided by social workers; one, for example, was described as a 'house mother' for female clerks. By 1926, 80 per cent of the 1500 largest companies in the USA had a welfare programme. All these had disappeared by the end of the 1920s, and reappeared again during the Second World War, in the armed forces, government agencies, some trade unions and some private companies. However, current American occupational social work is traced to projects concerned with mental health in the workplace in the 1960s. The movement away from public sector services in the 1970s and increasing private practice led to social workers contracting to provide social work help in the workplace, and growing workplace welfare and equality legislation pushed employers towards providing independent counselling and welfare services to their employees. In all these examples, we can see social work being used to manage workplace disruption.

A similar pattern can be identified in Swedish developments but the philosophical base of Swedish occupational welfare was different. Digby (1989: 13) argues that Swedish social welfare is based on labour market policies to achieve social policies, so programmes of temporary work and extensive training are integrated with unemployment benefits. In the USA, work programmes in the New Deal of the 1930s were seen as undesirable temporary expedients. Thus the Swedish system built up support at work, developing occupational welfare through employers.

Similar provision is also common in China, Japan and African countries, although for different reasons. In China, the Communist system was centred around work communities. In Japan, it is because of the tradition of large employers taking responsibility for their workers' welfare, as family and community support declined with urbanisation and the reduction of self-employment in the nineteenth century. Work took over from the family. In many African countries, large employers take responsibility in order to maintain a healthy and problem-free workforce in the absence of public services.

Residential care

Chapters 2–4 document the importance of shelter and refuge as an aspect of social order throughout history and residential care as an aspect of social care. The basic requirement of shelter led to the provision of places such as almshouses and hospices for travellers and the poor, the old and the sick by charitable activity and the church from antiquity. This was certainly true throughout Europe, but reflected a traditional assumption that they were for deserving people without family support (Woolf, 1986). This could be caring, but it could also be concerned with the control of travellers, vagrants and vagabonds. The Elizabethan Poor Law, from which so many aspects of social work ultimately emerged, provided poorhouses at least partly to deal with the potential crime and disorder arising from economic change and the consequent loss of work and family life. The new Poor Law of the nineteenth century, the direct antecedent of official British social work, was concerned to use residence as a form of social control, both directly, by controlling regimes in prisons and workhouses, and indirectly, by the incarceration of people whose behaviour was out of control, since this allows other institutions to be managed effectively (Parker, 1988).

Residential care, therefore, incorporates both caring and social order aspects of social work, expressing caring within services aimed at social control and control with services intended to be caring. Consequently, residential care has always been stigmatised because of its controlling elements, associated with destitution, madness and criminality (Parker, 1988: 8). Nonetheless, it persists partly because having been established, important institutions, particularly churches and local political elites, have an interest in maintaining its role. Crenson (1998) notes this in relation to the origins of the American child welfare system as Parker (1988) identifies it in British residential care. Professionals also have an interest in its practices, and Crenson (1998) shows how professionals involved in early American children's homes reformed the system to reflect their approaches. Because what goes on in residential institutions is often hidden, professionals may be influential in the ways in which they operate, the ways they maintain their practices unchanged often for long periods of time and in their reform.

Parker (1988: 31–4) notes other factors in changes in the role of residential care:

1. It serves purposes for other systems. Examples include the relationship between asylums, which dealt with uncontrolled behaviour so allowing workhouses to operate as disciplined organisations; the way children's residential care relieves pressure to deal with difficult children in the education system and the way providing 'bed and breakfast' accommodation relieves the pressure to provide public housing for homeless people.
2. Financing always becomes an issue for residential care. Examples include how the cost of maintaining mental hospitals in the 1980s while also trying to develop community care to allow discharge of their patients led to the slow development of community care; how the provision of social security funding for private and voluntary sector residential homes in the 1980s permitted the growth of a private residential care sector; and how the house price inflation in the 1980s permitted capital gains to support the cost of private residential care.
3. Women's employment is always the mainstay of residential care, as of other routine care services. Examples include the availability of unmarried women due to the high male death

rate in the First World War to staff small family group children's homes in the 1950s. Once they retired, the homes became uneconomic and larger specialised homes developed. Another example was the availability of nurses formerly employed in the declining geriatric hospitals to start private residential care homes in the 1980s.

4. The standards in and images of residential care. Examples include the frequent scandals in institutions and, on the other hand, the image of sexual and social freedom in some communes in the 1970s, which encouraged the development of ideas of therapeutic communities in education and social care.

5. Demography is also always a factor in the development or reduction in residential care. Examples include the increase in the population of elders in many Western countries and Japan, encouraging the development of old people's homes.

However, residential care as a form of social work does not solely derive from the nineteenth century history of institutions. Throughout history, building on ideas of shared community in religious institutions such as monasteries and convents (Brandon, 1998), a living community in which responsibility and mutual commitment have been shared has led to the foundation of utopian communities (Moss Kanter, 1972). Many groups migrating to the developing USA in the nineteenth century formed religious and socialist communities (Holloway, 1966). The major wars of the twentieth century were also important, since they led to an increased need for psychiatric treatment of former soldiers who could not easily be stigmatised by their mental illness. A more recent flourish of such interests arose in the twentieth century as communes grew up during the 1960s and 70s, started by people who wanted to live in democratic groups larger than nuclear families (Mills, 1973). The antipsychiatry movement (Laing, 1965), which criticised authoritarian psychiatry, also influenced a trend to a more democratic approach to treatment in residential care. Important aspects and aspirations also came from radical education and its incorporation into therapeutic community ideas. An important early centre run along democratic lines for young people with behavioural difficulties was started towards the end of the First World War by an American, Homer Lane. His 'little commonwealth' attempted both practical help and guidance through domestic and agricultural work, but was closed after a scandal in which he was alleged (although the inquiry was inconclusive) to have sexually abused girls in his care (Wills, 1964).

Finally, ideas about groupwork have been imported into institutional life to include therapeutic objectives as well as custody. Lewin's (1936) field theory of the 1930s, which suggested that groups of people, operating in their life space, developed group forms of behaviour independent of their individual personalities, influenced residential work through groupwork. Therapeutic ideas were also drawn from radical education movements. These included attempts to introduce democratic forms of government, where pupils were allowed to set rules and choose whether or not to attend classes. The UK's most famous democratic school of this kind was Neill's Summerhill. Such ideas influenced boarding schools for delinquent and maladjusted children (now called children with emotional and behavioural difficulties). Work during the Second World War with children disturbed by evacuation from the cities built on this. The charismatic David Wills, in several pre-war and wartime children's homes, especially Q-camps, and other colleagues in education for maladjusted children such as George Lyward (Burn, 1956) had an effect on the more therapeutic approved schools and led to the concept of 'planned environment therapy' (Wills, 1971, 1973).

Also, after the Second World War, treatment for people affected by mental illness arising from their experiences, what would now be called 'post-traumatic stress disorder', were treated by groupwork and eventually in democratically organised hospital wards. Bion's (1961) influential groupwork ideas and the therapeutic communities, devised by Maxwell Jones (1968) and colleagues at the Henderson Hospital, grew out of such work and had a wider influence on mental hospital treatment and, in the 1960s on prisons (Cullen et al., 1997; Kennard, 1998; Harrison, 1999). The main features of therapeutic communities were the use of group meetings of residents and staff to organise the facility and shared authority between staff and residents in an informal atmosphere. Such ideas had international influence, particularly through 'concept' houses such as Syanon and Phoenix House for drug abusers, with a sometimes authoritarian regime, where successful residents often became the staff. Other ideas about group counselling and working with couples had wide influence during the 1960s and

70s. When the Mental Health Act 1959 encouraged the development of community facilities for mentally ill people, these developments extended to community provision. The most extensive development was the international network of residential homes run on therapeutic community lines by the Richmond Fellowship (Jansen, 1980).

Normalisation, an important idea for residential work, emerged from work with mentally handicapped people, now called 'people with learning disabilities'. This first emerged in Denmark as a result of the Mental Retardation Act 1959, which encouraged, as with the British Mental Health Act 1959, provision of services in the community, with normal housing, education, work, and leisure (Emerson, 1992). Responding to the rhythms of normal life and enabling people with learning disabilities to participate in the life events of a normal lifespan, such as work and marriage, were important ideas. During the 1970s, the Nordic ideas were taken up in Canada, adapted by Wolfensberger (1972) and his colleagues to incorporate the idea of giving a high value to normal social roles, and training people with learning disabilities to gain competence in the skills necessary to perform normal social roles. This had a significant impact on the British services for people with learning disabilities and mental illness as large hospitals were closed down in favour of community services during the 1980s (Brown and Smith, 1992). This shows how a professional development often interacts with structured changes deriving from economic and policy changes. One does not cause the other: they interact and influence each other's progress, or lack of it.

Residential care for children developed during the 1950s in family group homes, replacing large institutions. Modern homes for elders were built during the 1960s, and local authority sheltered housing for elders also developed during this period. The Williams Report (1967) examined staffing and training needs and led to efforts to provide basic training and more advanced education in this field during the 1970s.

The movement for deinstitutionalisation in many countries during the 1970s and 80s affected residential care homes both for adults and children and long-stay hospitals. It emerged from a reassessment of institutions during the 1950s. Writers from personal experience such as Vaizey ([1959]1986), the sociologist Goffman ([1961]1968), the medical writer Barton (1976) and the social researcher Townsend (1962) produced literature that drew attention to the poor standards of care in institutions, which maintained the stigma attached to them. A professional ideology of avoiding residential care grew up within UK social work, encouraged by the foster care ideology of the Children Act 1948 and the idea of community care, which emerged from the Mental Health Act 1959. Professional attitudes in child care led to the closure of approved schools after they became local authority community homes with education during the 1970s and in some areas led to substantial reductions of residential care provision (Cliffe, 1991; Berridge and Brodie, 1997). The growing expense of institutions and the cost of upgrading buildings mainly established during the nineteenth century while at the same time trying to develop community facilities increased the financial pressure on local government services during the 1980s. The development mainly for elders of a significant for-profit residential care provision for the first time conflicted with the community ideology and led to a shift in practice towards care management as a social work method to organise packages of community services (Payne, 1995). An associated movement towards 'managed care' offering time-limited and financially restricted care packages also affected the USA. The Wagner Report on residential care (1988) promoted the conception of residential care as part of a continuum of care. Related to this, normalisation contributed a focus on normal housing with care provided separately, rather than residential care where care and shelter are combined.

The movement towards community care is an attempt to provide care without the stigma that it attracts because of its controlling elements. However, the impact of the financial cost of care has led to the use of social work as a way of managing costs which negates the possibility that care management and managed care might be flexible and wholly beneficial. It thus underlines the continuing relationship between shelter, care and control that has always provoked criticism and difficulty for the residential care aspect of social work.

Scandals and inquiries in the UK

That criticism of social work is highlighted in a history of scandals and inquiries about social work practice. The experience of the

Poor Law and of Homer Lane and his 'little commonwealth' in the 1920s was only a forerunner. Scandal leading to inquiry is an important mode of authoritative action, a way in which political and public opinion may have a direct effect on organisation, practice and attitudes in social care. More broadly, however, scandal imposes wider social perceptions about appropriate behaviour and relationships on families and communities, using social work as a way of enforcing these perceptions more consistently.

Chapter 2 noted scandals about care in Poor Law establishments and the impact of child care scandals in assisting trends towards the location of children's departments in local government as a separate welfare, and eventually social work, service. Scandals in the separate, centralised approved school system for young offenders included a post-war murder of a staff member (Home Office, 1947) and rioting at Carlton (Home Office, 1959). A scandal over excessive physical punishment at Court Lees School (Home Office, 1967) raised the profile of this system at a time when the treatment of young offenders was under broader consideration, and the schools were seen to be isolated from the trend towards understanding delinquency as mainly caused by deprivation. They were integrated into the children's residential care system with the 1971 Seebohm reorganisation and largely disappeared over the next decade (Cliffe, 1991).

The reform of the children's home system, the creation of social services departments in 1971, and the development of the idea of the 'battered child' led to more public concern about social work because of a series of scandals in which children died in the care or under the supervision of social workers. One set of these inquiries, beginning with the early inquiry into the death of Maria Colwell (DHSS, 1974) led to a strong focus on child protection, and the development of multiprofessional administrative processes to maintain registers of children at risk and secure their effective supervision. Nevertheless, periodic scandals about poor communication between professionals and ineffective supervision continued. Among important inquiries was the Beckford Report (1985), which led to child protection being given priority in child care work, emphasised the need to develop social work education and led to the first publication of guidelines on multiprofessional working. The Cleveland Report (1988) raised public awareness of child sexual abuse, although a factor in the case was public resistance, which led to greater importance being given to parental rights balancing children's rights in the Children Act 1989. A series of cases in the early 1990s, including Orkney (1992), Nottingham and Rochdale, crystallised concern about ritual abuse, and also about excessive and precipitate action by social workers. In the Orkney case, children were taken away from their parents in 'dawn raids' when there were ill-considered claims of abuse by adults in occult ceremonies. The Pindown Report (Kahan and Levy, 1991) led to a focus on poor standards in children's homes and a follow-up review of public residential care (Utting, 1991). Subsequently, the Warner Report (1992) issued guidance on staffing, particularly the selection of staff, in children's homes, which led to efforts to improve the training of residential care staff and personnel procedures in social care. Inquiries in Northern Ireland (Hughes, 1985) and North Wales (Waterhouse, 2000) focused on concerns that groups of paedophiles were gaining access to residential care homes, partly through influence in public affairs. Although this was largely discounted, they disclosed poor regulation of practice in children's homes. The Climbié Inquiry (Laming, 2003) again drew attention to poor communication, management and practice in child abuse cases.

Scandals and inquiries in long-stay hospitals mainly for people with learning disabilities in the 1970s (Martin, 1984) led to a concern for the quality of care, which particularly engaged the political interest of the Secretary of State, Crossman. In turn, this provided an impetus for further development in community care policies. Reith (1998) argues that, in its turn, this led to concerns about community care provision, examined in a series of reports on community mental health services. The inquiry into the death of Isabel Schwartz, a social worker killed by her client Sharon Campbell (1988), led to a new procedure for multiprofessional cooperation in mental health services, the Care Programme Approach (CPA), and tightened aftercare provision by developing consistent arrangements for case conferences under Section 117, Mental Health Act 1983. Reith (1998) identifies 27 further inquiries during the next decade, arising mainly from an administrative requirement to hold an inquiry after a murder. The inquiry into the death of Christopher Clunis (Ritchie Report, 1994) reported poor communication and cooperation among the professionals involved. The victim's fiancée, a social worker, formed the Zito Trust to lobby for improved community provision and public protection. More comprehensive procedures were issued by the Department of Health (1995a), codifying the CPA and the requirement to hold inquiries after a murder. Reith (1998) identifies a steady development of thinking about approaches to multiprofessional risk assessment and cooperation running through the reports. However, questions were asked about the value of costly inquiries. They helped victims' families to deal with their grief and concerns, but their findings were repetitive. The Labour administration elected in 1997 discontinued the practice.

The number and findings of inquiries led to a public impression that community care for seriously mentally ill people was seriously flawed. This was added to an upsurge of concern about paedophiles, partly arising from scandals in children's residential care but also from a number of notorious criminal cases, and led to legislation to tighten the supervision of seriously mentally ill people in the community and make special provisions for paedophiles leaving prison. A review of the Mental Health Act 1983 also took place, and, consistent with the approach of increasing authoritarian control, recommended reducing the civil liberty role of approved social workers (DH, 2000), although at the time of writing this reform is contested.

The historical lesson from this brief account of many inquiries during the development and recent history of British social work suggests that public services will always from time to time generate concern about particular events. To lay this concern to rest politically, inquiries allow for concerns and issues to be explored in detail, proposals for change to be given impetus and people involved to feel a sense of closure and justice. Such inquiries do not only affect social work and related services. They may lead to developments in services and professional practice and in this way incorporate political, public and general social trends into professional practice. The Children Act 1989 change towards balancing children's and parents' rights is a good example. However, political and official concerns shift, and this means that the failings will rouse different concerns in later periods leading to scandals and inquiries of a different character. Reith's (1998) example of the shift from mental hospital to community care scandals and inquiries between the 1960s and the 1990s reflects a service shift from hospital care to community care, rather than an improvement in practice within hospitals.

The impact of scandals and inquiries does not only affect the UK and may also derive from different forms of authority. For example, in Ireland, the residential care home scandals focus on the role of the Catholic Church, which administered the industrial schools system established under British control during the nineteenth century, but continued through much of the twentieth century (Rafferty and O'Sullivan, 1999). While this relates to concern about sexual abuse by Catholic priests, which has affected many countries, the Irish focus on the Church derives from the minimal role of the state in social care provision until late in the twentieth century. Thus, the concern about the failings of the authorities in Ireland is about the Church rather than the state. However, the state has taken responsibility for resolution, through a far-reaching commission of inquiry (for example Commission to Inquire into Childhood Abuse, 2001), which seeks to help people through counselling and the chance to tell their stories, since the abuse raising concern is largely in the past. A similar approach was taken in the South African Truth and Reconciliation Commission (2002), which tried to respond to the history of apartheid and its social effects. The international movement around children who were forced to migrate from the UK to the empire by child care organisations, and then often subjected to abuse and poor services is another example. Initial publicity through the media led to research and self-help movements that revealed personal stories and enabled estranged people to meet (Bean and Melville, 1989; Humphreys, 1995). This emphasis on enabling victims of abuse to tell their stories and confront offenders offers some degree of social reconciliation where long-standing abuses have had a wide effect on societies, and represents a new way in which states give power to the kind of oppressed and disadvantaged groups that social workers often deal with. The Ireland example suggests that it may be a future way of responding to the needs of victims of service difficulties.

Conclusion

The evidence reviewed in this chapter shows how social work is intimately involved in creating social order, but provides ways in which disorders, disorder and the disordered may be managed separately from universal services and sometimes separately from society in institutions. Social work is itself a social order, constructed through powerful organisations and the law and incorporated into powerful organisations, and contested and resisted because of that. Often these are part of the state, but power and authority may also be gained from incorporation into private sector organisations as well, and this may be resisted for different reasons: that a profit is made from human need. Similarly, voluntary sector social work may be resisted because it is provided as 'charity' rather than as a right and mutual aid may be contested because it does not involve support from resources outside poor and oppressed communities. The point is that all forms of organisation may give certain kinds of authority and power, which is contested in different ways. To understand social work, it is important to understand in what ways particular forms of authority may be contested, resisted or supported and by what interests.

Seeing social work as wholly disciplinary in its social role, however, is not a full analysis, since there are also elements of therapeutic endeavour integral to it, as we saw in residential care and mental health work. However, provider agencies are not the only organisations that form the nature of social work: the next chapters look at social work's own representative organisations and knowledge and educational organisations.

CHAPTER 8

Professional and Trade Union Organisation

The main focus of this chapter is on how social workers organise their profession and work activities and its consequences for the perception of social work as a profession or occupational group. This, in turn, needs to be balanced against the importance of the power of organisations and management as a source of the role of social work, discussed in Chapter 7. Chapter 4 noted, for example, trends towards managerialism between 1980 and 2000 and the development of quasi-markets. This focus on the need for regulation through organisational management and market competition contests the emphasis on the individual worker's discretion supported by professional knowledge and values that is implicit in professional organisation. Social work, to some degree, seeks a new position in this debate: against the excesses of occupational and professional self-interest, against the rigidities of excessive managerial control, and incorporating the direct influence and empowerment of user communities as a counterbalance to professional and organisational power.

Why professionalisation?

During the 1920s in several Western countries, social work became a profession as it became the basis of employment for women. Their employment was in practising the method that had been developed in the COS, rather than in organising philanthropic work or state institutions such as the Poor Law. The organisation of employees was needed when employment developed: for example in the employment agency that was the forerunner of the American professional organisation, and in the professional groups of probation officers and almoners in the UK who helped each other with training and professional development. Before this, and alongside it, the organisation of welfare services was around the interests of the organisations that were developing services.

Professional organisation associates the job with a category of distinctive knowledge and social processes. Trade union organisation associates the job with a category of employing bodies or agencies. The distinction incorporates a class distinction: professions imply middle-class allegiances, developed through university education allied to systems of knowledge and values, while trades imply working-class allegiances, developed through apprenticeship training allied to identified practical skills. This distinction has declined during the twentieth century, as practical skills have been displaced by more complex technology and knowledge-based industries, requiring higher levels of education, have become more important in developed economies. In addition, market controls, management and regulation have become important ways of conditioning the relationship between professionals, the agencies that employ them and the people they serve, making professional work more like non-professional work than previously. In the late twentieth century, the technical form of education has, in the UK and as part of an international trend, been generalised through structured education using functional analysis of work tasks and highly defined competencies. These two separate forms of the organisation of knowledge have thus begun to merge. The emphasis on markets, management and skill-based education has been seen as part of a trend towards deprofessionalisation. This is because it contests the importance of knowledge-based discretion and professional values as the director of decision-making.

Professionalisation is associated with increasing organisation alongside increasing knowledge and power. As knowledge is extended, it becomes subdivided into specialised segments, and these often become associated with increasingly specialised professional groupings. Corfield (1995) shows that as legal, medical and clerical (that is, priestly) professions developed in eighteenth- and nineteenth-century Britain, they permitted social mobility into an increasingly secure middle class for their practitioners: she describes them as 'an insurgent group' (Corfield, 1995: 249); more properly, groups. Their expertise and specialist knowledge gave them power over the users of their services and over social thought and policy, even before the legal and administrative formation of professional organisations in the late nineteenth century, which increased this influence further. However, this power was and is never absolute, since other social relations and sources of knowledge and belief also have influence over individuals and policy. Professionalisation may, therefore, give professionals some power and a belief in the role of their knowledge, while this may be resisted and contradicted by other forms of influence, such as political, organisational and managerial power.

The history of the development of these professions, however, gave social work a model for its own institutional development, as it emerged in the latter part of the period in which these traditional professions achieved recognition. As knowledge continued to extend, become specialised and fragmented, other professions like social work began to emerge, claiming interests and expertise over areas of newly developing understanding. Many of these areas were in newly developing areas of state responsibility, in education, health care (other than medicine) and social care. As a result, these professional groups developed a different form of organisation from medicine and the law, where professionals had individual decision-making responsibility and professional organisations regulated themselves. Social workers and other similar professions made their professional decisions about individuals within an agency and employment context. Therefore, professional organisation interacted with employment-based, and sometimes trade union, organisation.

Professionalisation and unionisation

Professionalisation and unionisation came from two different sources. Professionalisation was the product of middle-class, mainly female activism deriving from the voluntary sector, COS tradition of social work; unionisation was from the more male-influenced, local government traditions of many countries. Three phases may be identified. First, in the late 1800s and early 1900s, professional organisations concerned mainly with education and professional support emerged, and up to 1970 were mainly concerned with establishing social work as a recognised profession. With the welfare state period of 1945–80, the incorporation of social work into state activities strengthened trade unionism in the social services, as white-collar trade unionism emerged in government. Where and when welfare states were dominant, as in some of the Nordic states, trade unionism and professionalisation became associated or aligned. In the third phase of social work development, after the 1970s, conflicts over the nature and role of the welfare state placed both movements on the defensive, trying to maintain the recognition of the profession and its role in welfare provision. Moreover, concern about the dominance of worker and 'producer' interests in services and the growing importance given to consumer views also reduced the impact of worker and professional interests in public services, in favour of user and public interests. In this phase, professional associations and trade unions may be in alliance or in competition, and they become lobbyists and interest groups, rather than groups with professional or organisational negotiating power.

The evidence for both the class and organisational distinctions made here and this general progression may be seen in the variations between countries. Professional organisation is dominant where there is a voluntary sector tradition in a strongly capitalist environment: the classic case is the USA. Trade union or industrial organisation is dominant where there is a largely government social service, for example the UK. Where this is professionalised, trade union and professional interests and organisation are aligned, as in the Nordic countries. Where social provision is weak or under attack, organisation is fragmented or non-existent, as in many resource-poor countries: India is an example. This is also true of many of the countries created from the former Soviet Union.

Social work's professionalisation

The professionalisation of social work in the USA is important because professional education and organisation developed there earlier than in other countries, and its strength made similar achievements an aspiration for other countries, particularly in the movement for generic unity in Britain in the 1950s and 60s. Any account of American professionalisation relies, as the following does, on Leighninger's (1987) extensive archival study and on Reisch and Andrews' (2002) study of radical social work.

Lowe (1987) argues that early American social workers focused on gaining professional standing through the graduate status of their education and the recognition of their skills and techniques by developing the casework method. He suggests that they would have been more successful in establishing the profession if they had focused on gaining an organisational monopoly of an area of work, as British social workers did when they gained control of SSDs in the 1970s. Katz (1996: 172) argues a related point that social work failed to limit entry only to qualified people or established professional standing. He also places the reason for this on the emphasis on casework, which was similar to the clinical work of other professions, rather than on the professional skills of advocacy and social reform. Thus, the American emphasis on method rather than service organisation, partly a result of the lack of development of welfare state services, may have served it badly as a basis for securing a wide role for the profession. Also, the emphasis on therapeutic rather than service-providing practice has led to the critique of Specht and Courtney (1994), discussed in Chapter 4, that American social work has abandoned its faith in social progress.

Early phase professional debate was in national conferences about charity organisation. This shifted around the time of the First World War, which America entered late, in 1917, its ordinary social developments not therefore being so strongly affected as in many European countries. A speech by the educationalist and administrator Abraham Flexner (1915) had a strong impact. Speaking in a context in which social work was becoming a career with growing training provision, he argued that it did not display the six 'key elements' of a profession. This was mainly because he perceived social workers as mediating access to other professions who held the responsibility for action, rather than being directly responsible for action and its outcomes. One important aspect was a single, inclusive, highly organised professional association (Austin, 1983). During the 1920s, an American Association of Social Workers was formed (1921), alongside several specialised organisations, pre-eminently in medical (1918), psychiatric (1926) and school social work. These initially included everyone in relevant posts, but eventually limited membership to people with relevant training. Flexner also emphasised the intellectual base of social work, arguing that it was an activity of intellectual quality (1915: 306), and this led both academic developments and professional movements towards creating an identifiable professional knowledge base (Chapter 10). Early on, the Association began to promote international organisation.

As the professional association emerged, the Milford Conference (AASW, [1929]1974) explored the nature of social work and in particular identified generic features of social work: the activities of workers in different settings were claimed to be branches of one activity. The generic–specific debate continued to be an issue for the next three decades. Medical social workers were initially a prestigious group, but their influence declined particularly in the 1940s and 50s as the growth of counselling led to a stronger focus on psychological and psychiatric knowledge. This strengthened the psychiatric social workers. Another important group was the school social workers. Associations of groupworkers, community organisers and researchers also formed important interests. Groupworkers became aligned with social work, seeing groupwork as a therapeutic technique and shifting from a broader allegiance with youth and community work in the late 1930s (Reid, 1981), influenced particularly by ideas about group dynamics from the work of Kurt Lewin. Andrews (2001) argues that in becoming allied with social casework as a therapy, particularly in 1950s USA, groupwork lost its distinct professional identity within social work.

The important 'rank and file' movement of public sector social workers was formed during the expansion of social work as part of the New Deal. Self-protection was important because of conservative opposition to New Deal policies, which allied the policy and its employees with Communism, at the time a concern of right-wing politics, in view of the success of the Russian Revolution and fears that the Depression might lead to social disorder. New Deal agencies employed a much wider range of people in a wider range of settings than the largely middle-class urban females of the charity organisation and settlement movements. It is an important source of radical ideas, including an alliance with women's and workers' organisations and arguments for social change as a role of social work.

This movement disappeared with economic recovery during the Second World War. However, conflicts between public sector workers through their trade unions and city administrations in the early post-war period were rife, and led to social workers being associated with Communism. Thus, when paranoia about hidden Communist influence developed during the 1950s, symbolised by the Committee on Unamerican Activities in the American Congress, chaired by Senator Joseph McCarthy, social workers were targeted. Well-known left-wing social work educators such as Marion Hathway and Bertha Capen Reynolds were attacked.

The American professional associations merged to form the National Association of Social Workers (NASW), and this led to work to develop a 'working definition of social work practice'. Also in the 1950s, Greenwood (1957), in an influential article, examined the professional standing of American social work, just after the formation of the NASW, comparing it with the common traits of more established professions and, as with Flexner, finding that it was not comparable. Bartlett's (1961, 1970) work was influential. She first analysed the knowledge involved, skills and activity of specialised fields, and then identi-fied a common base of knowledge, skill and values. This achieve-ment was influential in encouraging social workers in other countries also to take a generic view of social work. It particularly influenced social workers in the UK, who in the 1950s were divided again after a wartime attempt at federation. Develop-ment of the main UK professional bodies is summarised in Figure 8.1.

The earliest professional developments came in health-related social work and probation. The Hospital Almoners' Committee with eight members was set up in 1903, followed by a Council in 1907, which subsequently became a professional body, the Institute of Almoners (from 1963, the Institute of Medical Social Workers). Training was organised, building on practice placements and the COS training, and a register of qualified almoners was set up (Malherbe, 1980). Eventually, in 1940, this became a one-year course, based in London; the Insti-tute also approved similar courses in universities. The Institute published a long-standing monthly journal, *The Almoner*, later *Medical Social Work*, which included both news and professional articles, both popular and academic.

Soon after this, with the growth of probation provision after the Probation of Offenders Act 1907, the Home Office estab-lished a register of probation officers and a professional associa-tion was set up in 1912, the National Association of Probation Officers (NAPO) (Bochel, 1976). This continued to develop

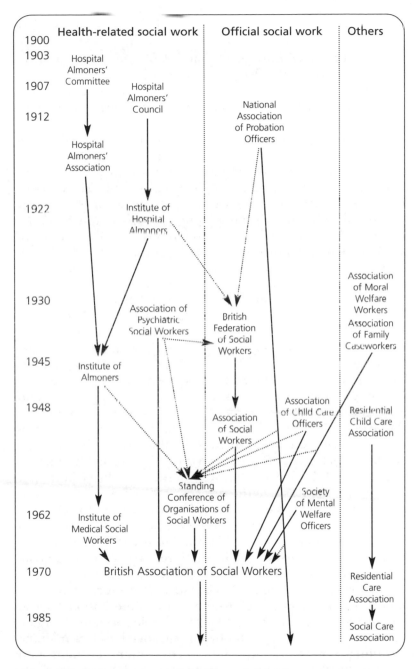

Figure 8.1 Development of British social work professional organisations

Sources: Timms, 1964; Lees, 1971; Bochel, 1976; Hartshorn, 1982; SCA, 2003;

throughout the century as a channel of communication on policy, pushing for the development and professionalisation of the service with the Home Office. It eventually became a trade union in the 1970s. It developed a successful journal, eventually entitled *Probation Journal.*

The next major development was the formation of the Association of Psychiatric Social Workers (APSW) in 1930, with 17 members drawn from the graduates of the first mental health course at the London School of Economics (LSE)(see Chapter 11). Timms (1964) suggests that at its outset it was mainly concerned with mutual support, study groups and maintaining and defining itself as an organisation. It was an active member of the first attempt to unite social work organisations in the British Federation of Social Workers (see below). From this time, until after the end of the Second World War, APSW's main focus was on defining and developing the idea of psychiatric social work. Later, it moved on to considering the role of psychiatric social work in the newly developing welfare state services, which it saw as, to some extent, in opposition to the development of professionalisation in social work (Timms, 1964: 165). Throughout its life, membership was limited to people with university qualifications in psychiatric social work and in the post-war period it and the Institute of Medical Social Workers became the epitome of elite professional organisations. It published a successful biannual professional journal of considerable academic standing, the *British Journal of Psychiatric Social Work.* After the Mental Health Act 1959 led to the development of local authority community mental health services, more psychiatric social workers worked outside clinics and hospitals, and their high status had always led them to consultancy and leadership roles in other areas of social work. APSW established procedures for approving new courses in 1943 and a register for people qualified on approved courses in 1961 (Malherbe, 1980).

The British Federation of Social Workers was formed in 1935, after discussion going back to the second international social work congress in Frankfurt (1932) to enable social work organisations to cooperate in lobbying on social policy matters, including poverty, family allowances, unemployment and housing. In 1950, it proposed a code of ethics for social workers, promoting confidentiality, individualisation, democratic public participation in policy-making and by being volunteers and social workers influencing social policy (Lees, 1971). However, it was wound up in the face of the continuing development of specialisation (Chapter 3).

The Association of Family Caseworkers (for a period known as the Association of General and Family Caseworkers) emerged from the staff of the COS in 1940 as it became the Family Welfare Association, using the COS journal, which became the journal *Social Work* (UK). It involved mainly voluntary sector workers in the major cities, such as the Liverpool Personal Service Society where these existed (Hartshorn, 1982). Other small official and informal organisations also developed: the Moral Welfare Workers, working on adoption mainly in church bodies, and the Mental Welfare Officers, implementing the new Mental Health Act 1959.

After the welfare state reforms of the late 1940s, new forms of social care work emerged and professional groups grew up associated with them. The Association of Child Care Officers (1949–70), formed from the social work staff of the new children's departments of local authorities, was typical of the service-based (that is, open to all employed in the service) professional associations of the 1950s and 60s, although it limited its membership to qualified workers in 1964 (Jacka, 1973). It grew from 35 to 2968 members during its existence, of whom more than a third frequently attended its annual conferences. It published regularly, was actively involved in policy development and in contacts with other professional associations. All this was done mainly through voluntary and part-time work by the members, and a full-time professional general secretary, Keith Bilton, from 1966.

With the increase of local authority specialisms, the time was not right for following the Americans in creating a single social work professional body. After the British Federation dissolved itself in 1951, its successor, the Association of Social Workers, continued to work on uniting and establishing the profession. Younghusband's generic training in the mid-1950s (Chapters 3, 10), involved the cooperation of several of the separate professional organisations.

Even in the separated 1950s, therefore, there were trends towards generic organisation. The Standing Conference of Organisations of Social Workers (SCOSW) was set up in 1962 to develop a unified association based on a minimum qualification standard. Kay McDougall, a psychiatric social worker, editor, publisher and academic, chaired it. Efforts were made to establish registration according to qualification, but the high proportion of unqualified employees meant that this was pointless (Malherbe, 1980). However, SCOSW more broadly responded to trends that stressed the generic character of social work, including the arguments of the Younghusband Reports on training for welfare officers in local government. Other influences were pressure for better coordination among welfare services, particularly in local government, and following the example of the American association. The American theoretical debate on whether social work was a collection of specialised elements or a generic or unified professional discipline was resolved by continuing professional debate (see below). SCOSW continued the trend to professionalisation, eventually establishing the British Association of Social Workers (BASW) in 1970. At this point, NAPO remained separate, an early signal of commitment to criminal justice rather than social work. In the 1990s this led to a separate training for probation officers and, under the New Labour government of the later 1990s, to a national service directed from the Home Office, eventually merged with the prison service.

The British Association of Social Workers was flawed by the unresolved debate about qualification (Payne, 2002), itself a marker of uncertainties about the nature of social work as compared with voluntary community action. After unqualified members of predecessor associations were blanketed in, BASW restricted membership to those with a professional qualification. However, in the radical 1970s, this was seen as a sign of elitism, and members of former ACCO and NAPO (who were entitled to blanketing in, even as NAPO maintained a separate existence) sought 'open' membership for everyone in a social work job. Another group of members sought trade union status, not possible under British law for a company limited by guarantee, the conventional professional association structure. Conflicts about these issues affected BASW for most of its first decade, culminating in a financial crisis in the late 1980s, at a time of high inflation. This gave an impression of instability and poor management, which, allied to the criticism of BASW's role and structure, weakened support for the Association. However, *Social Work Today*, a successful professional journal with good advertising revenues, financed a large secretariat and some useful professional development work, and, during the 1980s, BASW had stable finances and leadership. The financial advantages were lost in the 1990s as commercial competition from the private sector journal *Community Care* drove the journal into loss and finally overcame the publishing operation. *Professional Social Work*, a monthly journal, was published from 1994. The organisation remained weak during the 1990s, in the run-up to the statutory regulation of social care, enacted by the New Labour government in the Care Standards Act 2001. One of BASW's strengths was a project of Kenneth Brill, the first general secretary, to create an academic journal, achieved in 1971 with the publication of the *British Journal of Social Work*, which, by the 1990s, became the leading non-American journal in the world.

During this period of BASW's existence, organisations representing residential care workers were weaker, because the workforce was divided in many different locations, and was generally less well trained. As local government residential care was folded into SSDs with the Seebohm reorganisation in 1971, a variety of specialist groups either disappeared or merged with the Residential Child Care Association to form the Residential Care Association (1972) and the Social Care Association in 1984–5 covering non-fieldwork professionals. It has published various journals, participating in *Social Work Today*, the BASW journal, from 1977 to 1991.

Also with the Seebohm reorganisation, specialist chief officers' associations merged to form the Associations of Directors of Social Services (ADSS) and, in Scotland, of Social Work (ADSW). Because of the chief officers' political strength and seniority, and the weakness of the professional associations and trade unions in speaking on policy issues, this gained greater policy influence than employees' associations. In the much larger organisations post-1971, ADSS and ADSW worked more closely with the powerful local authority associations. ADSS promoted a commercially published magazine, *Insight*, in the mid-1980s, but this did not succeed.

The regulatory approach to social work adopted by the New Labour government from 1997 is ambiguous in its consequences for social work professionalisation. It supports professionalisation in lengthening the minimum length of qualifying training from two to three years, and providing a registration system for social workers. Both these provisions meet EU requirements for the recognition of a profession, and thus strengthen the position of the profession. However, it has done so within the context of systems of regulation for a wider group of 'care workers', from whom social workers are not clearly differentiated. For example, all workers must comply with a 'code of conduct' presented in terms of general accountability, effectiveness and probity, rather than the traditional 'codes of ethics' based on professional values. Allied with registration is a quality assurance mechanism, with inspectorates of care standards in each of the four countries of the UK. This continues and accentuates the centralising trend of the former Conservative administrations in favour of consistency of provision rather than local variation, responding to a national media and political agenda, rather than local responsiveness. On the other hand, the government continues with managed markets, including substantial elements of private and voluntary sector provision of services allied to a strong commitment to consumer choice, even though the delivery of choice is variable. This means that a range of alternative kinds of provision and roles for social work can continue to develop.

Most European countries followed similar patterns of development. During the 1950s, professional organisations of workers employed in the new welfare state services began to develop, as the following examples show. The Danish Association was formed in 1938, soon after a training course emerged (Dansk Socialrådgiverforening, 2003), and developed into a joint professional association and trade union during the 1950s and 60s. The Italian association emerged after the Second World War (AssNAS, 2003). The Norwegian Association of Social Workers was formed in 1960, nine years after the first social work course was established. In 1970, it became a member of the Federation of Trade Unions, giving it a role in the negotiation of salaries and working conditions (Tutvedt, 1995).

Some examples of developments in other countries show a colonialist pattern, following the mother country or American influences. In Australia (Ward, 1962), professional developments began with a social work course in Sydney, provided by the university extramural board of studies (that is, outside the internal degree course structures) and the formation of associations of almoners in Melbourne, Victoria in 1929 and New South Wales in 1932. There was a close tie between the NSW association and the new school of social work with individuals involved in both. By 1948, there were social workers' associations in six states and three institutes of almoners. They went through a merger process during 1946–7, holding the first formal meetings of a national association in 1947.

In Japan, a social work profession on the American model, with a professional association, developed out of changes wrought by the occupation forces, with most employment being in health care and occupational services, an important sector in Japan (Ito, 1995: 266–8). Following the Certified Social Workers and Certified Care Workers Act 1987, a more professionalised local government sector emerged, with a separate professional association.

Unionisation in social work

Unionisation has had an uneasy relationship within social work, partly because trade union membership is associated with the emergence of a working class of non-craft manual workers during the industrialisation of the 1800s, and unionisation of government officials and white-collar workers occurred later, during the bureaucratisation of the state in the 1900s.

Union related activism has been important in social work in two periods: in the USA during the period of radicalisation associated with the Depression and the New Deal during the 1930s, and again as social workers became a more significant group within local government, white-collar trade unionism, as welfare states became significant from the 1970s.

Large-scale social workers' associations with trade union functions developed in Nordic countries during the 1960s, for example, and a period of union activism was characteristic of the 'industrialisation' of social work after the Seebohm reorganisation in Britain during the 1970s. This culminated in a long, bitter, widespread strike in residential social work during the 'winter of discontent' at the end of the period of Labour administration in 1978–9, when many public sector employees also went on strike.

During the 1930s in the USA, the important group among social workers were the 'rank and filers', with their journal *Social Work Today*. However, rather than being trade unionists themselves in social work, they were left-wing activists who saw the value of alliance with the labour movement on behalf of clients (Karger, 1989). These alliances existed around representation on public bodies. They continued in succeeding decades, with NASW, the social worker's professional body, encouraging cooperation with trade unions and for social work managers to support representation of employees. However, American social work has been more characterised by radical socialist activist movements, rather than trade unionism among employees.

In Britain, white-collar unions, including the civil service and local government, were regarded as rather conservative and a different character to the manual working-class union movement. During the period of post-war economic growth and consensus politics of the 1950s and 60s, they became steadily more powerful in government organisations. With the growth in influence of radical and Marxist philosophies in the 1960s and 70s, local government trade unions became more active and critical in their approach. Social workers had often been regarded as a rather separate group within the local government trade union, NALGO, until the Seebohm reorganisation made them a larger, more significant group, bringing them together in one local government department. Moreover, the dominant individualist treatment theories based on psychoanalytic ideas were displaced by a wider range of social theories, including Marxist and socialist ideas in the radical social work movement. Growth in the availability of social work education led such ideas to have a greater impact on younger entrants to social work during the 1970s. These included a view that alliance with working-class movements such as trade unionism should be an aspect of social work as well as a greater personal preparedness to pursue a more conflictual approach to general social issues. Moreover, there was a greater emphasis on the social work role in seeking social change and reform, as well as pursuing individual casework.

The social workers' strikes of 1978–9 were the high point of this activity, covering a wide range of local authorities across the country, and lasted for 42 weeks (Joyce et al., 1988). However, rather than being about clients' concerns, it was an attack on national negotiation systems, seeking locally responsive negotiations on allowances and service conditions. Less obviously, it was concerned with broader concerns about economic policy, since the beginnings of the reductions in social services expenditure, and the control of local government salary policies after the economic crises of the mid-1970s, as the economic and political consensus of the post-war years began to break down.

This experience may have led to a greater acceptance of strikes and other industrial action being used from time to time in social services matters. However, social and legislative changes and government intractability in the face of disputes have led to less active trade unionism during the 1980s and 90s. With the merger of NALGO with other local authority and health service trade unions in 1993 to form Unison, wide-ranging and effective trade union representation has been available. Most social workers have seen this as more important in protecting them against inappropriate action by employers than membership of professional associations during this period. There has, therefore, been an uneasy relationship from time to time with BASW, for example over BASW's ambivalent support for a rival specialised trade union in the early 1970s (Payne, 2002) During the 1990s, there has been conflict over BASW's role in representing social workers in international organisations. Unison claims that its larger membership of social workers justifies a greater role, while BASW argues that its primary professional role is the crucial issue. In Nordic countries, this distinction is not drawn, since social workers' professional organisations are also trade unions and local government trade unionism is organised around professional groups. In some countries, coordinating organisations to represent several social work associations internationally have developed, rather than a united social workers' organisation.

International organisation

International organisation within social work profession emerged during the 1920s. However, we have seen in Chapters 2–4 that social work ideas had a considerable international currency, because of the significance of religious movements across the centuries creating shared philosophies and ideological bases for welfare. International movements arose from the exchange of innovations, particularly between cities as they tried to share the means of dealing with the social change associated with urbanisation.

The first major international development was the social welfare fortnight organised in Paris, inspired by the Belgian Dr René Sand (1877–1953), a doctor and secretary-general of the International Red Cross from 1921 to 1936 (Astbury, 1953), who had been associated with the development of the World Health Organization (Kendall, 1978b). The event included the International Conference on Social Work (8–13 July 1928), which Sand had proposed to the American National Conference on Social Work in 1923. There were 2481 delegates from 42 countries (Lees, 1971). This and other conferences in the period led to the creation of three international organisations:

- the International Council on Social Welfare (ICSW), concerned largely with social policy and social development issues and with a membership of agencies
- the International Federation of Social Workers (IFSW), comprising national professional associations of social workers
- the International Association of Schools of Social Work (IASSW), comprising national and regional organisations of social work education organisations and individual schools.

Two more conferences were organised in Frankfurt (1932) on 'The family and social work' and London (1936) on 'Social work and the community'. At this early stage, the organisations were mainly based on European and American groups and met only for occasional conferences, since intercontinental transport did not permit regular travel across the Atlantic. The Second World War also created a hiatus, but the organisations remained in suspension and were revived during the late 1940s. As air travel became more practicable and economic, and the newly independent countries of Africa and Asia developed social services, membership became truly worldwide, during the 1960s and early 1970s. The organisations now have regular conferences based on continental regions in odd-numbered years and international congresses in even-numbered years, often held in association with each other. An active European region of IFSW and the European Association of Schools of Social Work have provided an important focus for social workers and social work academics since the 1990s, especially in incorporating nascent Eastern European organisations into the international system. IASSW, ICSW and IFSW have a shared journal, *International Social Work*, and regular newsletters and other publications.

Conclusion

Social work professional organisation emerged from the growth of professional courses and state social work during the mid-twentieth century. Early associations focused strongly on defining an identity for social work, and a crucial element of this around the mid-century was establishing a generic rather than a specialist identity. The approach to professionalisation has been to seek mutual support, particularly at a time when social work has been under attack, and to strengthen identity through knowledge and discipline development. Social work has used conferences and journals as crucial elements of professional organisation. However, professional organisations in social work have seen knowledge development as an instrument for development of the profession in political and social influence, rather than being concerned to create more complex and systematic knowledge to benefit service users. Thus, the typical mode of organisation has been to use communication among members as a way of developing shared attitudes and values. In countries where there is a significant group of government employees, however, this is supplemented by trade union activity, which has sometimes gained a priority.

CHAPTER 9

Knowledge and Research

The main focus of this chapter is on the development of social work knowledge, and research as a basis for social work knowledge. The next chapter follows this by considering how social work education disseminates knowledge, research and practice. Control of generating and disseminating knowledge through research and education determines to some degree how a profession becomes established as a social entity and maintains its role. What I describe here and in Chapter 10 as the 'internationalist view' proposes that there is one main stream of knowledge development in social work, which has been disseminated and adopted with variations throughout the world.

A model of social work resolving problems equates to a medical model of curing illnesses. Moreover, a scientific model of knowledge development suggests that social work builds a unified practice on empirical and practice research. I argue that this picture is oversimplified. Although a stream of knowledge development, particularly emanating from the USA, has been influential, there is evidence of alternative perspectives based in other cultures and resistance to American cultural and educational hegemony. Some of these alternative perspectives question the Western, medical model of social work as a problem-solving practice.

Origins of social work knowledge

Soydan (1999: Ch. 2) places the origins of social work knowledge in ideas of sociality and commitment to human progress through a belief in reason. That is, while people may help each other in social relations, it requires the Enlightenment philosophy of making scientific progress through scientific observation and reasoning about the world to create an organised practice that seeks to change social relations. Soydan does not say this, but it would explain why non-Western social work ideas focus on interpersonal social relations, beliefs and values rather than the Western emphasis on applying social science understanding.

To Soydan (1999: Ch. 3), Saint-Simon (1760–1825) is an important source of the basic ideas of social work, influencing the important early sociologists Comte and Durkheim. O'Brien and Penna (1998: 29) show how this thinking connected to the Enlightenment idea of social progress and eventually to Darwinist evolutionary thinking (Chapter 6). Saint Simon's work drew upon Utopian ideas from the 1700s. His social philosophy saw society as sick, and needing change, which could be brought about by using scientific methods, applied by an organised authority, the bearers of knowledge who could plan, organise and lead society. In Soydan's (1999: 43) analysis, the Saint-Simon approach to social work thinking focuses on moving from a philosophical or theoretical position towards practice, and sees social problems as created by society. He sees the charitable tradition of social work knowledge, deriving from the COS, as focusing on moving from practice understanding towards theoretical understanding and explaining social problems as arising from individual behaviour and circumstances.

Scientific charity, philanthropy and the Poor Law

The COS aspect of nineteenth-century social work was crucially concerned with claims about knowledge, particularly in the USA, since it sought to make charity 'scientific'. Other elements in the COS tradition include romantic (Mencher, 1974) and idealist (Vincent, 1992) ideologies emphasising individual development, rather than collective social progress. Personal moral development could only be achieved by personal influence. These views, the religious and cultural partner of the economic individualism of liberalism (Chapter 6), emphasised the spiritual wholeness of individuals, rather than rational and materialistic values. Bowpitt (1998) shows that 'social work', as it entered usage in the 1890s, was particularly associated with this broader conception of philanthropic work, which included social change rather than focusing on individual salvation.

The crucial contribution of this period to the development of social work thinking was the shift from philanthropy to a practice method. The philanthropists had little to use except their Christian commitment, the Protestant work ethic, the belief that it was a duty to work to maintain independence, and the class-based belief that the better off should help the worse off. Younghusband (1981: 11) argues that the success of the COS, settlement and housing welfare workers who developed social work lay in the 'distinctive practice' in which they 'began to keep more or less systematic records, to discuss their experiences and to draw deductions from these'. In the USA, Warner's (1894) book *American Charities*, distinguished philanthropy from practice with people in need and provided an intellectual basis for this emerging practice (Reisch, 1998).

Ultimately, the combination of these trends in thought led to Richmond's (1917) *Social Diagnosis*, which offers extensive detailed checklists of facts to assess. However, Richmond's contribution was to see dealing with individuals as part of a process in which the worker interacted with individuals, family, community and public and charitable services over a period, bringing 'forces' to bear to strengthen the family's own 'forces' (Pumphrey, 1962). Soydan (1999: Ch. 4) characterises this approach as giving primacy to practice as a source of theory, with both interacting with ideals and values. This idea influenced and led to conflicts about the role of practice and theory in early social work education, discussed below. The scientific knowledge used in this period was descriptive (Orcutt, 1990: Ch. 8; Soydan, 1999: Ch. 4), rather than explanatory, with the aim of promoting disciplined thinking rather than the pursuit of formal research, rather in the manner of 'research-minded practice' of the 1990s.

In Europe a different view of scientific development in social work emerged. Hämäläinen and Vornanen (1996: 7) argue that German and Nordic 'social work sciences' produce a theory concerned with the epistemology of social work, that is, how knowledge is acquired and disseminated. This differs from Anglo-American views 'where social work is an institution of professional practice, and a practice, more or less based on scientific discussion, research and theory, developed mostly as a multidisciplinary field based on various particular sciences'. Anglo-American approaches (deriving from Mary Richmond and COS pioneers) produce theories concerned with contributing to the practice of social work. This distinction lies behind the theoretical distinction between social work as an academic discipline and as a practice profession sometimes drawn in Northern Europe.

Ideas on groupwork

Groupwork ideas emerged primarily from the settlement movement and associated informal education, particularly for young people, in organisations such as the Young Men's and Young Women's Christian Associations, and through Jewish charitable organisations, which had and have a strong influence on American practice. In the USA, the educational philosopher Dewey saw schools as a centre of community life, which would develop democracy through voluntary community activity. Dewey, the management and political theorist Mary Parker Follett and the political scientist McIver formed a group, The Inquiry, to pursue ideas about a new democratic state formed from group organisation through neighbourhoods and work organisation (Siporin, 1986). Among members of The Inquiry were the social workers Grace Coyle and Ada Sheffield, who interpreted these ideas as a form of 'discussion method' for enabling individuals to incorporate their interests into group and consequently democratic development. These methodological ideas concentrated on social processes within groups, but were also committed to using groups as a basis for social action (Shapiro, 1991). These ideas came to influence social goals models (Papell and Rothman, 1966: 67–8), which emphasise groupwork as a process of social education, giving experience of democratic life in a personal context which can lead to social change through empowering individuals to act in social settings.

However, there was a debate between protagonists of such views and others seeking a more therapeutic approach to groupwork (Shapiro, 1991). A shift towards seeing groupwork as a therapeutic, enabling approach occurred with the impact of psychoanalysis (also a method with Jewish origins) in American casework during the 1940s and in the UK during the 1950s and 60s (Reisch, 1998). This emphasised the remedial model of groupwork (Papell and Rothman, 1966: 67–8), which used groups as the basis of helping individual personal development. In Britain, groupwork was influenced by the psychodynamic ideas of Bion (Chapter 8), whose theories emphasised that behaviour in groups sought to deal with unconscious psychological needs as well as rational objectives. Subsequently, in the 1970s, groupwork was affected by the group dynamics movement, leading to a model of groupwork, the reciprocal model, which focuses on how people build interpersonal relationships in groups. This developed from Lewin's field theory, humanistic and person-centred encounter groups (Griffiths, 1976). A more pragmatic and activity-based groupwork, where involvement in learning and practical skills development proved an instrument for enabling people's personal and social relationships. This was aided in Britain by legislative and practice developments such as intermediate treatment and community social work (Chapter 4). Radical Freirean educational ideas of the 1970s joined feminist ideas in the 1980s emphasising consciousness-raising and dialogue within equal, democratic relationships. This led to a renewal of the democratic ideal in groupwork, using groups in empowerment (Mullender and Ward, 1991). Many of these ideas also had influence in residential work (Chapter 7).

Social pedagogy

Social pedagogy, like groupwork and community work, emerged from the youth movement, this time in Germany, and from 'reform pedagogy', a movement for social change and development among working-class people (Hämäläinen and Vornanen, 1996). Originally, much of the impetus for this came from the progressive unification of the German state in the mid-1800s, achieved in 1870, since one of the purposes of social development was seen to be integrating all parts of a disparate and rapidly industrialising nation (Lorenz, 1994a: 151). Pedagogy was distinguished from social pedagogy, and according to F. A. W. Diesterweg (1790–1866), the poor could be re-energised if education and personal development could be separated from the church (Lorenz, 1994b: 92–7 from whom this discussion is summarised). Paul Natorp (1854–1924) argued for the direction of people's individual will towards the interests of society as a whole, which should have priority, and social pedagogy should be a means of bringing about better social adjustment between individual development and social needs. Knowledge in this area drew on educational methods and experience, rather than empirical research, using the philosophical and anthropological analysis of organisations and educational and developmental objectives, in the northern European tradition discussed above. Diverse work in residential and daycare settings, mainly with young people, focuses, according to Herman Nohl (1889–1960), on giving people life experiences that promote friendship and solidarity as an instrument of integrative social policy. A substantial programme of social pedagogy failed during the Weimar administration of the 1920s, due to government weakness.

The theoretical source for German social work, on the other hand, was 'social assistance', which developed from the German women's movement, primarily through the work of Alice Salomon (Hämäläinen and Vornanen, 1996). This was more strongly influenced by American psychological work, particularly after the reconstruction efforts after the Second World War. Lorenz (1994b: 96) argues that the American and allied post-war 're-education' of German policy rejected social pedagogy and sought to emphasise social work, particularly casework as more ideologically and politically 'neutral', that is, not associated with social change objectives.

Ideas of social pedagogy have had a substantial influence in several countries as well as Germany, particularly Denmark, France (as *animation*, and in the work of *educateurs*) Norway, the Netherlands and Italy. It relates to the separate tradition in Britain of youth and community work or informal education. Lorenz (1994b) points out that more than half of social workers in France, Germany and Italy are trained under these traditions. These ideas also had an influence on Catholic reformers in Spain, for example the Jesuit Gabriel Palau's *Acción Social Popular*, formed in 1908, which aimed to promote social actions among 'the most needy', Arenal's Organised Social Assistance movement, which encouraged women to participate in responding to social problems, and *Acción Feminina*, formed in 1926, which aimed to work for women's dignity. This led to the creation of the women's school for social assistance in 1932, the first social work school in Spain. However, these developments were interrupted by the disruption of the Spanish Civil War (1936–39) and the subsequent conservative Franco dictatorship (López-Blasco, 1998).

Social pedagogy has also had an impact in Eastern Europe. Helen Radlinska (1879–1954), a leading Polish social worker, also had a view of practice related to social pedagogy and was influential in adult education. She argued for the importance of group and community work to 'uncover, awaken and organize hidden strengths' (Radlinska, 1928, quoted in Brainerd, 2001: 23), particularly in an oppressed population. Janusz Korczak, working in the 1920s and 30s in children's residential care, developed the idea of pedagogy as a style of 'living with people', and such ideas have been influential in Danish social pedagogy and elsewhere when it primarily focuses on residential and daycare work. This interest revived in Eastern Europe during the period of development in the 1990s, partly because of the strength of Eastern European teacher education and educational psychology as an institutional base for the development of social work.

Settlements and social reform

The settlement movement focused more directly than casework and groupwork on work in neighbourhoods, wider communities and broader social change. The strength of the family casework movement meant that these concerns had less prominence in American social work during the 1920s, but they were influential in Britain. The LSE course shifted its focus towards social reform. Clement Attlee, its first social work appointee, (1883–1967) (see Pearce, 1997), had a background in the settlement movement and went on to become the Labour Party prime minister at the time of the introduction of the welfare state reforms. Attlee's book (1920: 220–1) analyses the social worker as a pioneer, 'discovering new social groups and new methods of advance' as a social investigator dealing with the neglect of welfare in rural areas, and as an agitator:

> his particular function being to concentrate attention on particular aspects of the social problem, to spread information or at least the desire for information, and to generate the power necessary to make the slow-moving machinery of society work.
>
> (p. 238)

The same was true of the American tradition emanating from the settlement movement. More strongly based in Chicago than on the east coast, because of the influence of the Abbotts and Jane Addams, American settlement thinking moved away from the evangelical piety of London's Toynbee Hall and emphasised secular, scientific and pragmatic ideas drawing on social science (Farrell, 1967: 52; Davis, 1973). Soydan (1999: Ch. 6) characterises the approach as reflecting a view that knowledge moves from practice towards theory, but focuses on social rather than individual explanations of social problems. Addams (1899: 185) wrote:

> The American settlement, perhaps, has represented not so much a sense of duty of the privileged toward the unprivileged ... as a desire to equalize through social effort those results which superior opportunity may have given the possessor.

Casework ideas 1920–45

From the 1920s onwards, as employment and professional status began to emerge, the focus of knowledge development shifted towards casework. The crucial shift in social work thinking in this period was to become helping and therapeutic, rather than being concerned with social and moral influence. Radical social workers such as Reynolds and more establishment figures such as Lurie (Shriver, 1987) continued to argue for the importance of the social reform role in social work, throughout the first half of the twentieth century.

During the 1920s in the USA, detailed investigation, for example for social histories in psychiatric social work, was an important professional task, often so detailed that psychiatrists refused to read them (Grinker et al., 1961). Associated with this, fact-finding research using case records was important as a basis for knowledge development (Orcutt, 1990: 138) and mirrors the move from cause to function.

Orcutt (1990: 138 ff.) identifies the shift away from responses to poverty and towards family services among elite American agencies as the source of a move towards a greater concern for psychological theories and explanatory hypotheses: the charity organisation became a movement for family agencies. This was also true in Britain where the COS became the Family Welfare Association and the eugenics movement began to promote intervention with problem families (Chapter 5). An increasing influence from psychology emphasised working with the individual in relation to their family rather than working with the family to achieve social, moral and economic security in the COS tradition. Early psychology was Influenced by social Darwinism, the idea that social life led to the development of social structures that proved beneficial. This led to an interest in identifying intelligence and personality traits that benefited societies and excluding characteristics that might be damaging for the survival of humanity. Such ideas were influential in the 'mental hygiene' movement, active especially in the USA until the 1930s. The main American conference on social welfare in 1919 'was a landslide for mental hygiene' (Taft, in Robinson, 1962: 61).

Mental testing consequently became important in psychology during the 1920s. Social work responded to this partly by seeking the inclusion of family and environmental issues in agency decision-making within the functional school of casework (Timms, 1997 – see below). Social workers were interested but doubtful about the focus of psychology and the mental hygiene movement on testing and comparison with population norms, which are the basis of intelligence and personality testing. Hollis (1983), recollecting the period late in life, showed how, through the work of psychoanalysts providing consultation to family agencies, psychoanalytic ideas began to influence American social work. The idea of using relationship therapy as part of a 'process' developed in the 1930s, as part of the influence of the functional school of casework (Grinker et al., 1961).

This influence was later in Britain: the eminent psychologist Dr Cyril Burt told the COS secretary in 1918 that psychology, in its infancy, could not help social workers in a practical way. Many COS workers, with their heavy caseloads, continued into the 1930s to focus on the assessment of needs and problems, making allowance for 'character' and emotional problems (Rooff, 1972).

Practice theories

Psychological and social practice theories

Practice theories emerged from the impact of psychological ideas on the moral and social reform ideology of the COS and settlement movements, initially in the USA. This created a distinctive form of practice, 'casework', based initially on psychoanalytic ideas, which developed until the late twentieth century.

Figure 9.1 shows how these sets of ideas developed and interacted. An upward pointing arrow indicates a theory that criticised and to some degree displaced a previous theoretical position; a downward pointing arrow indicates a development in a theory. More detailed discussion of practice theories may be found in Payne (1997b, 2005).

American casework theory was strongly influenced by psychodynamic theory based on psychoanalytic developments, but was only important in a few elite social work agencies focused on family work. It was displaced by two trends in the 1970s. First, therapies based on psychological behavioural and social learning theories criticised the lack of a scientific evidence base in psychodynamic theory, and a practice that emphasised flexible interpretation of behaviours, and proposed structured alternatives. Social work interpretations of behavioural theories became influential. Later, in the 1990s, cognitive theories were incorporated into behavioural practice. These are the dominant form of theoretically informed individual practice in the early 2000s, although practice in most agencies still maintains a nondirective mode of personal helping, advice giving and support that has its roots in psychodynamic practice.

The second trend to displace psychodynamic theory in the 1970s was socially oriented theories of two kinds. Radical theory was critical of social work's involvement with existing social orders and promoted a equal, dialogical form of practice, to counter the oppressive and controlling approach of psychodynamic practice, which assumed that the role of social work was to help people conform to existing social expectations. Radical social work is the source of the emphasis on community work and advocacy in the 1970s, and laid the foundation for professional support of user movements, anti-discriminatory practice and empowerment theory in the 1980s and 90s. The alternative social approach was systems theory, an ecological interpretation of which has been dominant in the USA from the 1980s onwards, although it has little influence in Europe. Systems theory emphasises a focus on social networks around the individual. Thus, systems practice sees the impact of a whole range of social circumstances on the problems presented to social work agencies, and the possibility of interventions with other agencies and social networks rather than solely with an individual as the main focus of help. This approach incorporates

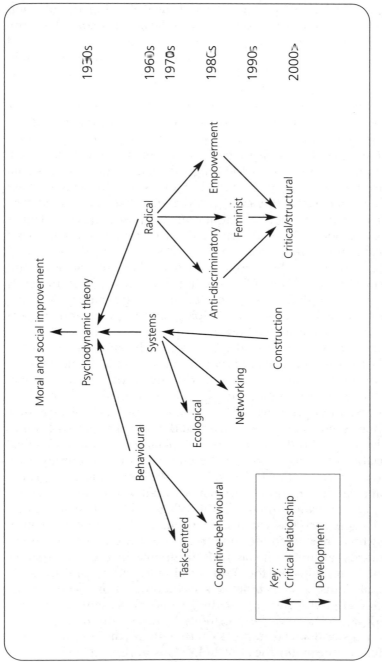

Figure 9.1 Development of social work, psychological and social practice theories

into the individualised practice of psychodynamic social work both help to the local social network and help towards broad social purposes.

Social development emerges

Allied with the Western interest in community work, techniques of social development developed strongly as the newly independent colonies of Africa sought to ally social and economic development through central planning. Concern about how the impact of inappropriate Western, primarily American, knowledge in developing countries was raised in the 1970s, and the concept of indigenisation was first used in the fifth UN international survey of social work: it subsequently developed to reflect a move to adapt Western terminology and ideas to local needs (Walton and El Nasr, 1988). African countries used concepts of social welfare (building up professional helping institutions) and social development (promoting community development and participation in a wide range of social services, including health and education) (Yimam, 1990; 60). After the 1960s, ICSW focused on social development, interpreting it as interventions to seek major institutional and cultural change, focusing on decentralisation and local participation in planning and decision-making in a range of services, not just social work.

Midgley (1997: Ch. 9) distinguishes social development theory from social work and economic development because it seeks social change for the benefit of whole populations rather than particular groups in need, and because its focus is on human well-being, rather than economic development, in order to increase consumption in the economy. It thus imparts a social democratic emphasis into primarily liberal economic development (Chapter 6). Moreover, social development attempts to incorporate poor and deprived people into the development process, in the mode of traditional community work. These techniques were increasingly taken up by developing countries in Africa and Asia, allied to economic development after their independence in the 1960s and 70s. A particular focus in this early period, encouraged by UN funding to IASSW, was on benefits from family planning on health, nutrition and poverty in developing countries (Kay, 1976; Kiu, 1976).

Clinical developments

As the 1970s moved towards the 1980s, developments in practice theory followed a clinical path. Associated with radical theory, some writers focused on the artistic, humanistic and spiritual element of counselling. Rogers' (Rogers, 1951) client- (later called person-) centred counselling was influential, concentrating on non-directive interpersonal work; and writers on social work as art (England, 1986), Zen (Brandon, 1976) and existential ideas (Krill, 1978) and, in groupwork, experiential groupwork (Perls et al., 1973), such as encounter groups, inspired many workers to work therapeutically.

Because of the increasing specialisation in health care during the late twentieth century, several areas of health-related social work also developed specialisation. Signs of this lie in the continuing commitment of workers to specialised groups on forensic and renal social work in the BASW (Payne, 2002) and the increasingly specialised American journals *Health and Social Work* and *Social Work in Health Care*. During the 1990s, this led increasingly to multiprofessional areas of knowledge, with considerable interaction between medical, nursing and social care professionals and journals.

Social science theories towards empowerment and critical practice

Radical social work practice theories lost their general strength in the 1980s, mainly due to the dominance of conservative governments and retrenchment in expenditure during the period (Chapter 4) and increasing evidence of the failure of socialist states in Eastern Europe. Radical concerns in Britain moved towards anti-racist and anti-discrimination practice, focusing on a social justice agenda and seeking structural change benefiting socially excluded groups. Structural social work originated in French-speaking Canada, associated with the work of Moreau (1979, 1990; Carniol, 1992), interpreted in English by Mullaly (2003). Radical social work developed further in Australia, particularly influenced by the work of Fook (2002) and Pease and Fook (1999). Its influence was maintained because Australian social work qualifications and standards were well established as part of public services, and social work was practised in a range of agencies. This gave radical interests a range of issues and settings in which to make an impact. Structural and radical theories developed practices offering a reform agenda and critical analysis of social division and oppression. These came to incorporate a range of critical social science theories, particularly feminist analyses, poststructural and postmodernist theories, which stressed the breakdown of positivist, scientific and generalised analyses of social progress. Instead, they emphasised the social construction analysis in which understanding of social relationships arises from historical, social and cultural contexts. An important influence was the work of Foucault (for example 2002), who provides a critique of the use of power in professions such as medicine and social work to oppress social groups through surveillance and the control of behaviour.

Two streams of practice theory emerged from this work. One incorporated ideas such as solution focused therapy into social work as an explicitly social construction practice theory (Parton and O'Byrne, 2000).

The other stream of development was of ideas about anti-discriminatory practice and ethnic and cultural sensitivity (for example Lee, 2001; Thompson, 2003: Chapter 4). This also became important in international social work, where recognition in social work practices of different cultural expectations of social welfare services in Islamic and Eastern cultures led to a distinctive practice. This was based on fostering interdependence within families and communities, rather than individualistic independence as in Western social work (Kassim Ejaz, 1989; Silavwe, 1995), and promoting personal and interpersonal harmony with spiritual and cultural beliefs rather than confronting difficulties and relationship problems (O'Hagan, 2001). While American social work does not have a strong element of radical or structural social work, the 1990s saw a revival of interest in advocacy and empowerment approaches to practice, concerned with helping minorities and oppressed groups to overcome barriers to personal and social development. This originated with the ground-breaking work of Solomon (1976) and is strongly influenced by practice with oppressed minority ethnic groups (for example Lee, 2001). Advocacy work has been less concerned with individual case advocacy and more with the redevelopment of a macro-social work specialisation of lobbying for social reforms in a practice akin to community work.

The impact of research

As social work came into existence, social science research was characterised by large-scale surveys, such as Rowntree's work on poverty and more journalistic coverage of social ills such as Booth's pen pictures of lower class London life.

The impact of psychological testing in 1920s' USA led social work to develop its own empirical methods. During the 1930s, the classification of casework treatment emerged as an important research aim. The importance given to assessment in diagnostic theory led to the idea of differential diagnosis, where it became important to identify the precise problems the worker was dealing with, so that treatment could be planned accordingly. Following on from this, attempts were made to classify different forms of treatment. Hollis's (1968) extensive classification was tested in empirical studies by Hollis and others.

During the Second World War, a number of studies in sociology and psychology in the USA raised the possibility of empirical research involving a degree of measurement and experiment in social science. From this time onwards, a series of empirical studies became influential in social work. Orcutt (1990: 151–73) has usefully identified the phases of development in these studies and those influential in the USA. Table 9.1 sets out these phases and gives examples of the studies which have had wider impact, and adds studies from the UK. Usually these studies were published in several forms over a period; I have shown the main period of study, ending in the major summary publication.

The first major studies, such as those of Kogan and Hunt (1954) and Giesmar and Ayres (1960) set out to identify ways of measuring change in clients as treatment progressed. These produced scales for use in treatment. Subsequently, studies of the factors which kept clients in contact with social workers were produced. Ripple et al.'s (1964) important study on why clients did not stay in contact with workers (continuance) was undertaken in Chicago; this is important for the subsequent history of empirical research. Hollis's (1968) classification work, building on previous work in the diagnostic casework tradition, was also completed during this period. Building on the Chicago work on continuance, Reid's work with colleagues (Reid and Shyne, 1969; Reid and Epstein, 1972a, b) emerged in the early 1970s,

Table 9.1 Important research projects in social work

Orcutt's (1990) periodisation	Period of publication; country	Findings and importance	Authors
Case study, case record, analysis of change	1948–53, USA	Follow-up study of the results of social casework – measurement of change in clients	Kogan and Hunt (1954)
		Family functioning scale – study of changes in family functioning	Geismar and Ayres (1960)
Prediction of continuance/ discontinuance	1957 64, USA	*Motivation, Capacity and Opportunity* – what factors kept clients in contact	Ripple et al. (1964)
Classification of treatment/ intervention	1956 64, USA	*A Typology of Casework Treatment* – classified range of treatment interventions	Hollis (1968)
Evaluation of outcome/ effectiveness	1965, USA	*Girls of Vocational High* – influential study of social work effectiveness	Meyer et al. (1965)
	1966, UK	*Decision in Child Care* – study of effectiveness of social workers' fostering decisions	Parker (1966)
	1970, UK	*Helping the Aged* study of effectiveness of social work help for elderly people in local authority welfare departments	Goldberg et al. (1970)
Development of practice models	1969–72, USA, international	*Task-centred Practice* – brief casework intervention	Reid and Shyne (1969), Reid and Epstein (1972a,b)
Clinical judgement	1960s, USA	Studies of interpersonal process	Tripodi and Miller (1966)
Interpersonal dynamics/ strategies	1970s–80s, USA	Family therapy studies	Studies cited by Orcutt (1990)
Survey of service/ consumer views	1970, UK	*The Client Speaks* - first major survey of client opinion	Mayer and Timms (1970)
	1973, UK	*Children who Wait* – introduced permanency planning for children	Rowe and Lambert (1973)
	1978, UK	*Social Services Teams: The Practitioner's View* – first broad descriptive study of post-Seebohm SSDs/SWDs	Parsloe and Stevenson (DHSS, 1978)
	1978, USA	*Children in Foster Care* – led to permanency planning for children in care	Fanshel and Shinn (1978)

cont'd

Table 9.1 cont'd

Orcutt's (1990) periodisation	Period of publication; country	Findings and importance	Authors
Service innovations/ outcomes	1984, UK	Community social work	Hadley and McGrath (1984)
	1986, UK	Case (care) management	Davies and Challis (1986)
	1992, UK	Deinstitutionalisation	Knapp et al. (1992)
	1995–8, UK	Child protection	Department of Health programme (Berridge, 1999)
	1996, UK	Community care	Lewis and Glennerster (1996)

first on whether lengthy interventions were more effective than brief contacts and then to develop a model of practice, task-centred casework, using brief interventions based on behavioural techniques. These had considerable impact both in the USA and UK and more widely, because they focused on brief work at a time of costly expansion in social care. They held out the prospect of being able to define aims and objectives in practice and therefore lent themselves to the stronger emphasis on management beginning to affect the social services at that time (Payne, 1997c).

By the 1960s, a number of studies were being published seeking to test whether social work interventions led to improvements in clients' behaviour. Meyer et al.'s (1965) study, *Girls at Vocational High*, was perhaps the best known internationally; Goldberg's (1970) study had considerable influence in the UK. At the same time, consumer studies began; Mayer and Timms (1970) study in the Family Welfare Association, the former London COS, was particularly influential in both the UK and the USA, partly because it connected theoretical criticism of psychodynamic approaches to social work with consumer views. The clients of this primarily psychodynamic agency were bemused by the psychological focus of their social workers.

All these trends came together in a survey by Fischer (1973, 1976) of empirical studies on the effectiveness of social casework in the USA, which demonstrated that there was little evidence of effectiveness. This was confirmed in Britain in Goldberg's

(1970) study of social work with elders, although Davies and Challis (1986) recalculated the results in the 1980s using more sophisticated techniques and propose that this study showed social work to be effective. Consumer surveys also found that social work was often confusing and unfocused to clients, although they often valued it (Glastonbury, 1979). These studies contributed to the growing question marks about conventional social work practice and a greater consciousness of consumer interests (Chapter 4).

Service evaluation

This work in the 1970s represents the end of the line of studies primarily concerned with developing casework as the main mode of practice in social work. Subsequent studies focused on evaluations of services and their organisation, often service innovations, or the experiences of service users. Pawson and Tilley (1997: 2–3) argue that this tradition of evaluation derives from the wish to justify the 'great society' developments in American services during the 1960s, and has been extended by the managerialist approach of New Right thinking in the 1980s, which seeks the pragmatic evaluation of practice, rather than using research to develop theory to inform practice.

Following the Seebohm reorganisation, a new structure for government research funding for the personal social services was introduced in Britain as a result of the recommendations of the Rothschild Report (1971). The commissioning model of research contracting made research liaison groups and chief scientific officers in government departments crucial intermediaries (Stevenson, 1983). This permitted interaction between the social work academic community doing research and civil servants. An important early product was the study of the organisation of and practice within the new SSDs/SWDs (DHSS, 1978). This theme of organisation continued in research funded on community social work (Hadley and McGrath, 1984). Research units were established by the DHSS for continuing social work research at the National Institute for Social Work (now at King's College London) and the Dartington Hall Unit attached to the University of Bristol, but individual projects and academics were also commissioned. Social policy research units were also funded, and the Personal Social Services Research

Unit at the University of Kent at Canterbury produced influential research on adult services and financing policy. Examples in the 1980s are the evaluation research on the care in the community programme concerned with deinstitutionalisation of mental hospitals (Knapp et al., 1992) and work on case (later, care) management (Davies and Challis, 1986). These projects influenced the Wagner Report's (1988) recommendations on residential care and the Griffiths Report (1988) on community care, leading to the introduction of care management, a limited implementation of case management. Work on social networks and innovations such as the All Wales Strategy on mental handicap (now called learning disabilities) (McGrath, 1991) had an impact on service developments. Substantial state funding of research, often through consultancy and evaluation work, on innovations in community care also produced important bodies of knowledge (Robbins, 1993).

This was also true of child welfare research in the UK, an example of how service-based research has developed in the late twentieth century. During the 1970s, important individual studies emerged, often related to specific interests. A substantial body of state-funded research appeared in the early 1980s with nine studies, mainly funded by the then DHSS on social work decision-making, which revealed that children were often admitted to care in crisis and their care careers were marked by poor planning, with frequent changes in placement, no development of links with families and no planning for discharge, This research (DHSS, 1985) was a major factor in the pressure leading to reforms in the Children Act 1989. A coherent programme of research funding continued; Berridge (1999) identifies three areas of work:

- on child protection (DH, 1995b), where narrow child protection investigations were disempowering families and not helping families to improve parenting
- on adolescents (DH, 1996b), where practice lacked strategy and flexibility
- on children in care (DH, 1996a), where many were going missing, wider networks and education were missing for children in care, but factors such as planning and flexibility indicating good residential care were identified.

Despite the difficulties of research influencing practice, there is evidence of research affecting practice in the child care field in the UK, and in the Labour government of 1997 onwards, there were projects to promote practitioners' use of research, including summary and interpretative publications, training and collaboration projects. As part of the development of professional regulation (Chapter 8), the government established the Social Care Institute for Excellence (SCIE, 2004) to promote practice and management based on research outcomes and rigorously reviewed and accepted professional practice. While this organisation mirrored a health service organisation (the National Institute for Clinical Excellence), the less-developed state of social work research promoted smaller scale reviews and practice guidelines. Collaborations between agencies and academic institutions, such as Research in Practice (2004), the Centre for Evidence-based Social Services (CEBSS, 2004) and the higher education learning and teaching network covering social work (SWAP, 2004) also disseminated research findings for practice and practice developments. Social work academics campaigned for social work to be recognised by the Economic and Social Research Council, and this led to a seminar series funded by the Council, which reviewed the state of social work research and led to better training opportunities in academic research (TSWR, 2000).

In most Western countries, and in regional organisations such as the EU, similar information resources were developed, increasingly relying on the internet and electronic information. In Nordic countries, for example, the Nordic Council of Ministers promoted comparative research across the Nordic region while individual countries set up research agencies, such as the Finnish STAKES (2004).

Research movements

During the 1980s and 90s social work research was affected by movements concerned to promote research as an aspect of practice. The Anglo-American tradition of research and knowledge development has been contested throughout by a practice-oriented development of theory, that is, bodies of thought providing 'an organized description and explanation of the purposes and content of social work as both a social phenomenon and as an activity' (Payne, 2000a: 332). Three notable movements focused on research-minded practice, practitioner research and evidence-based practice.

The idea of research-minded practice (Everitt et al., 1992) encouraged social workers to be aware of research that might affect their practice, while recognising that the amount and strength of research available meant that often it would not be directly applicable. Workers might interpret and adapt ideas and think rigorously about their work, rather than be able to apply research knowledge directly.

During the 1980s and 90s, the practitioner research movement (Whitaker and Archer, 1989; Broad and Fletcher, 1993; Fuller and Petch, 1995) encouraged 'research-minded' practice through an increase in opportunities for practitioners to do evaluation research on their own practice, and achieve masters qualifications in social work. This led to a substantial amount of research being published. By doing small-scale research themselves, practitioners would be better able to understand how formal research could be used within their own practice. However, the research outcomes of studies such as these are sometimes criticised because using small samples and less powerful methodologies does not advance causal explanation or produce knowledge that may be widely relevant to workers.

Interpreters of empirical work, critical of the achievements of social work during the 1950s and 60s, took a harder line and created a movement for 'evidence-based practice' (EBP) (Thyer and Kazi, 2004). Writers such as Fischer (1976), and Sheldon (1986, 1987) and his colleagues (Mcdonald and Sheldon, 1992) in the UK began to publish surveys of available research and polemics promoting measured effectiveness as the most appropriate evaluative measure of social work. EBP proposes that social workers should practise using the best available evidence of what actions will be effective to achieve the intended outcomes; they would negotiate with clients. If evidence provides a causal explanation and is generalisable, evidence-based practitioners prefer it. This means that they prefer research designs that suppress subjectivity as far as possible, such as surveys or experiments where statistical and other techniques prevent subjective influence. Random controlled trials of treatment techniques that mimic the tests used to see if medical drugs are effective are ideal. Single-case designs (Kazi,

1998), where workers establish present levels of behaviour and retest after intervention to see what changes have taken place, apply this method to individual cases. Standardised scales are used for assessment.

Using all these techniques together is sometimes referred to as 'empirical practice' or 'empirical clinical practice' in the USA (Witkin, 1991; Faul et al., 2001). Research studies are collected and analysed to accumulate results to increase the generalisability of research to a wider range of circumstances. Single-case evaluations encourage workers to set clear behavioural starting points and test for improvements on the baseline measures (Kazi, 1998). However, this view has been criticised (for example by Gordon, 1954, 1980) as requiring a different kind of social work education, practice and attitude, in which practitioners pursued research studies during their work, creating a cumulative pattern of knowledge drawing on and relating to practice. This contrasted with the existing position, where social work drew on social science knowledge, as a basis for the practical interpretation of events within a policy and administrative framework, but often with little application to practice.

The evidence-based practice movement's focus on effectiveness as defined by 'scientific' measurement was strongly contested from a postmodernist and social construction point of view, and by supporters of a wider range of research methodologies, including interpretive and naturalistic approaches to research (Jokinen et al., 1999; Karvinen et al., 1999; Webb, 2001; Hall et al., 2003). These use less structured interview and other interpersonal methods in often small-scale studies to understand complex social processes and interpretations of behaviour, rather than seeking causal explanations and methods of intervention. The social construction view argues that since social knowledge often depends on the cultural and historical context of social relationships, the evidence-based practice movement's emphasis on causal relationships and practice prescriptions should be displaced by an emphasis on multiple relationships between factors relevant to understanding social situations.

Journals and dissemination of knowledge

An important aspect of the development of knowledge and education and the professionalisation of social work was the publication of specialised books and journals to disseminate knowledge. Important journals include:

- the many journals, papers and books published by the COS to promote its views
- the foundation of academic journals, particularly in the USA from the 1920s
- the development of social science publishing as part of the post-war social reconstruction
- influential journals developed by professional associations from the 1950s and 60s
- a range of social work education and other specialised journals during the 1960s and 70s
- journalistic magazines and a wide range of academic and professional journals in many countries, stimulated in the 1990s by increasingly cheap and flexible computer-based publishing technologies.

Important early journals included the *Social Service Review* published in association with the School of Social Service Administration at the University of Chicago, still the most prestigious English language journal in the world, and *The Family*, founded in 1921 by Family Service Association of America, the main organisation of elite social work agencies emerging from the COS. This journal's history illustrates professional developments: it became *Social Casework* in 1947 and reverted to *Families in Society* in 1987. An important unifying factor for the (American) National Association of Social Workers when it was founded in 1955 was its journal *Social Work*, now the most widely circulated journal in the world.

Social work was a small market until the 1960s, and most books were published by university presses, pre-eminently Chicago, Columbia (New York) and North Carolina in the USA. However, in the UK, Routledge & Kegan Paul published an influential social science series originating in social reconstruction after 1945, which published many texts of social work. The sign of growing educational markets was demonstrated by the first British paperback social work book, Noel Timms *Social Casework*, in 1966, which was followed by two series published in association with the National Institute for Social Work (Training) by Allen & Unwin from 1965, Routledge from 1968 and, in a second wave, by Macmillan (now Palgrave Macmillan) in association with BASW from 1982. American textbook publishers entered the market, particularly as bachelor courses promised a larger sale with substantial general texts. CSWE, the American association of schools of social work, produced a social work education journal in 1964, now the *Journal of Social Work Education*, and two education journals also appeared in Britain in 1979/80, merging in 2000.

British professional journals are considered in relation to professionalisation in Chapter 9. Many large countries or regions produce national or regional journals, for example the *Indian*, *Hong Kong* and *Asia-Pacific Journals of Social Work* and the *Journal of Social Development in Africa*.

Nordic countries are typical of the position in many smaller countries. Each country has its own magazine, associated with the professional association, supported by job advertising, and there is a shared academic journal, *Nordisk Socialt Arbeid*, and some also have academic journals, often with a broader social policy, social welfare or social science remit, such as the Finnish *Janus*. A sign of increasing commercialisation was the foundation in 1990 of the *Scandinavian Journal of Social Welfare*, with an empirical focus and an emphasis on social policy, from a Danish publisher, financially supported by the Swedish Academy of Science. However, in 1998, this became the *International Journal of Social Welfare*, published by a British-based international group and jointly edited from Sweden and the USA, being unable to sustain influential impact from the Nordic base.

Conclusion

Since the outset, social work has sought a knowledge base in support of its professionalisation. It has moved from trying to draw its knowledge from its own internal resources to an increasing incorporation of its knowledge development as part of the wider social sciences, in the impact of social science research on social work, the development of a commercial market in publications and journals and the way in which debates about appropriate forms of social science have been drawn into the social work debate.

The growth of knowledge development and academisation of a specialist area of social science suggests the establishment of a professional group. However, the constant concern to debate theory and practice links suggests an ambiguous relationship between the profession and its knowledge industry. This is perhaps most clearly seen in the distinction between theory about the nature of social work as a focus of German social science and the Anglo-American focus on creating practice prescriptions from research. It may also be seen in debates about the academisation of social work education, discussed in the next chapter.

CHAPTER 10

Education and Training

Education: the internationalist issue

Social work education emerged from the early social work agencies, and has developed as part of the education systems of the countries in which social work operates. Education therefore occurs in different organisations and became established in different ways in different countries.

Thinking about education raises the relationship between theory and practice and academic and practice institutions as stakeholders of the nature of social work as it develops. Academisation may go alongside professionalisation. At different times, academisation has been resisted, for example in the early attempts of COS workers to resist a university base for training courses. Different countries arrive at different emphases in this debate. For example, Finland's reform of social work education in the 1970s, building on a small base of social work education, aimed to professionalise the discipline, which was producing little research. This involved raising the qualification to masters level and providing it within the context of the broader social sciences, particularly social policy education. This emphasised research and social science roles (Satka and Karvinen, 1999), and ignored the earlier discussion of the role of practice-based casework in the 1950s (Chapter 3). Matthies (cited in Satka and Karvinen, 1999: 121) argued that this move had gender implications, a female-dominated view associated with female practitioners being rejected in favour of an assumption that status could only be conferred by a scientific paradigm where male-dominated social science disciplines were more influential. Satka and Karvinen (1999) suggest that as Finland became more involved in globalisation after the dominating presence of the USSR was removed by the collapse of the formerly Communist regime, the role of social work was reviewed in the late 1990s. This created a more separate form of education and professionalisation, with more substantial practice elements.

The historical questions concern what processes lead social work education to emerge and how it becomes established. The evidence reviewed in this chapter suggests that at different historical periods, and in different national and social contexts, social work education developed in different ways. This disputes an internationalist view of social work education, which is propounded by writers such as Salomon (1937) in her early report on world social work education in the 1930s, Younghusband's reports from the mid-century, and Kendall (1978a, 2000), up to 2000, all associated with the International Association of Schools of Social Work. This proposes that there is one basic form of social work education, allied to one diverse social work, and bypasses debate about alternative conceptualisations of social work based in different cultural and political positions, accepting the dominant American influence.

For example, Younghusband (1963) identifies three main phases of development:

- early developments in particular countries in the late 1890s
- the first expansion (1920–39) to about 20 schools mainly in Europe and North America, characterised by the influence of Dr René Sand (see Chapter 9) who supported the supporters of social work organising internationally and the development of schools in Spain and South America
- the second expansion (1945–65) developed by international action through UN agencies, supported by Fulbright fellowships funded from the USA, Canadian technical assistance and in Catholic countries by the Catholic International Union for Social Service.

This view stresses the coherence of many different forms of social responses, including casework, groupwork and community work and ignores the impact of different forms of local organisation, like social pedagogy, and French and Dutch *animation* and cultural social work. It largely emerges from an American tradition, regarding this as central and other traditions as add-ons. Social work education, on the other hand, is seen as extending from early historical examples disseminated across different countries, where it may acquire diversities, but is otherwise a coherent whole.

The evidence in this chapter suggests, contrary to the internationalist view, that we may identify at least five different patterns in histories of social work education:

1. In nineteenth-century industrialising countries, practical training emerged from agencies and was developed in the early 1900s as part of similarly developing education systems.
2. The systems were taken up to some degree in developing or newly industrialising countries particularly in the 1930s–50s. These countries drew on conventional models of Western social work education.
3. Different needs in such countries led to forms of education that were not consistent with the Western form of social work education. These countries accepted some aspects of Western social work, but made substantial adaptations or developed indigenous models of practice and education for it. As the colonial powers relinquished their grasp in the 1950s and 60s, social development became more important in resource-poor countries than individualistic Western social work. By the 1970s, Yelaja (1970) and Nagpaul (1972) were commenting on the need for a greater emphasis on social change and social development. Eventually Midgley's (1981) authoritative assessment of the failure of Western social work to make a valid contribution in many developing countries had a decisive impact and the crucial importance of social development ideas formed a separate social work education.
4. In Western countries, and some others, for example Japan, recognition of professional status as social workers through accreditation systems developed in the 1980s–90s.
5. In the 1990s, countries developing from Communist regimes developed social work education by establishing and adapting conventional Western models of social work education as part of the process of developing their own social work professions. These countries used social work education as part of the attempt to create democratic forms of government. Developing social work agencies and professions as part of a social change process was supported by developing systematic professional education, often before there was a professional practice

for it to feed. Since both education and psychology were strong in Eastern Europe and Russia, and Germany was close and influential, social pedagogy gained a strong influence.

Early developments in the West

In Britain, social work education emerged in several centres, of which London and Liverpool were pre-eminent. Jones (1976) shows that COS objectives in offering education lay in the promotion of its individualistic, welfare-oriented policies in opposition to the more socialist, collectivist developments emerging through the influence of the trade union and Labour Party movements. Until 1895, the COS favoured developing investigatory skills and appropriate moral attitudes among suitable middle-class women through supervision in the field. However, concern about the quality of charity workers and a wish to claim expertise in relief work for the scientific basis of its casework methods and underlying political policies led it to propose education as part of its campaign 'of dealing with Fabianism and strengthening the Society' (Salter, 1901, quoted by Jones, 1976: 15; Chapter 2). The Joint Lectures Committee was set up in 1895, followed by the formal School of Sociology in 1903, providing a two-year course. At much the same time, the Fabians established the School of Economics, offering more formal social science education, which gained support from the settlement movement. Smith (1965: 38) indicates that there was a concern that social work training should be practical and a university base might make it too theoretical. At the same time, there had been an attempt to establish a shared position, through a conference and a 'social education committee' including university interests. The university interests were explicit, however, about academic freedom and this led the COS to continue with its independent efforts. This wider effort led to a withdrawal of the Women's University Settlement, which only had a remit for London, and the women's education movement became separated in Britain from social work education.

The social education committee led to a Liverpool initiative to create a training course in 1904, associated with Liverpool University, into which it merged in 1918. In 1908, the University of Birmingham established the first university-based course (Elliott and Walton, 1995). The Birmingham University Settlement, founded in 1899, provided practical work placements

(Rimmer, 1980). Such developments continued until 1912 when, probably, financial pressure led to a merger of the School of Sociology with the School of Economics to form the London School of Economics and Political Science (the LSE), creating a Department of Social Science and Administration. The new school accepted the requirement for a significant amount of practical training. After this, the COS continued with training plans by setting up a one-year course in 1915, which formed the basis of a cooperative project with Bedford College, a women's college that became part of the University of London.

Similar debates arose in the USA (Austin, 1983: 358–61), where Mary Richmond, prominent in the COS movement, sought separation from university education, so that the emphasis could be on practical training. The New York COS established a summer school for training charity workers in 1898, with Richmond as a contributor, and a one-year training programme at the New York School of Philanthropy started in 1904 (two years from 1912). Formal links with Columbia University (a major university in New York) were resisted. The emphasis was on casework and social assessment, and attempts to develop the social theory curriculum and a social policy orientation were resisted by the social work establishment (Shoemaker, 1998). On the other hand, Edith Abbott, allied with the settlement movement, developed cooperation with the University of Chicago leading to the foundation in 1908 of the Chicago School of Civics and Philanthropy (School of Social Service Administration from 1920; Abbott became dean in 1924) (Austin, 1983: 359). The focus here, with support from economics professors, was on social reform, rather than individual practice. All this training activity led to organised attempts to create a job market for women graduates and, as a consequence, we saw in Chapter 9 that there was a rising concern to see social work as a recognised profession to secure stability and job opportunities.

The first schools of social work emerged in the 1890s in Amsterdam, London and New York. They became established between 1900 and 1920. An important element was the alliance with the movement for education for women, as in Germany, where most early initiatives grew from colleges for women. Education for the working classes or oppressed rural groups was also important, as in Radlinska's work in Poland (Stelmaszuk, 1994; Brainerd, 2001). Sometimes such early initiatives and focuses persisted for many years, as for example in Norway (see below). There is a distinction between groups of countries that regarded social work as part of industrial and technical education, for example in Germany and Denmark, and those where it became primarily university and theoretically based, for example, Sweden, Finland, the USA and countries based on the British system.

National associations of schools of social work were established in Germany (1917), Britain (the Joint University Council for Social Studies, later 'for Social and Public Administration') (1918–19), the USA (1919) and Belgium (1920) (Crichton, 1953; Wieler, 1988). Attempts were made at standardising social work education internationally through the International Association of Schools of Social Work (IASSW), founded in 1928 at the international social welfare fortnight in Paris by a group of pioneers led by Alice Salomon from Germany (Kendall, 1978b: 170–2). Although the IASSW organisation focuses on social work in the internationalist view as inclusive, some forms of social work, such as social pedagogy in some Nordic countries and Germany, were substantially separate until almost the end of the century, with separate educational and professional organisation: an example is Norway, see below. The British tradition of youth and community work, seen as separate from social work and with a commitment to informal social education, is a similar development, often allied in European associations with social pedagogy.

In the 1930s, the first international issue was a conflict between a European model of training in which lecture courses taught social issues academically in universities, followed by an apprenticeship in agencies, and an American model in which universities controlled education, incorporating practice through field teaching in agencies. I noted in Chapter 9 how this distinction arises from different German and American conceptions of theory. However, two competing organisations in American social work education emerged because of the growth of a non-urban government service with the New Deal of the 1930s (Chapter 2). Developments in social and behavioural sciences left the mental hygiene movement behind, so that by the 1940s psychoanalysis was the dominant American source of psychological understanding in the elite social work universities. This was picked up by European and international developments, influenced by post-war reconstruction in the late 1940s and the attempts to secure developing countries against encroaching Communist influence in the 1950s.

Social work was very much a marginal occupation in Britain during the interwar years (1918–39). Much training was by evening classes or short courses, although some social science education was available, often as two-year diplomas in social science, which included some practical element, the early basis of Younghusband's training (Chapter 3). Astbury, the last secretary of the COS, was trained on a two-year, external course at the School of Social Work in Liverpool in the Poor Law in its relation to social work (Rooff, 1972). Some groups, such as the Hospital Almoners' Council, organised practical training for new workers through placements with existing services, with students who often possessed the social studies certificates. An important development began when groups of English social workers went to the USA in 1927–8 with grant aid from the Commonwealth Fund, which was supporting the development of the idea of a child guidance clinic. The newly created Child Guidance Council financed a 'mental health course' at the LSE, led by Sibyl Clement Brown, one of the visitors to the USA, and which marked the foundation of psychiatric social work in Britain (Timms, 1964). It redirected the focus of education towards psychological, mainly psychodynamic, thinking (Jones, 1984: Chs 4–5), but isolated psychiatric social work from the mainstream of the development of public social services. Further psychiatric social work courses were developed in Edinburgh (1944), Manchester (1946), Liverpool (1954) and Leeds. Later generic courses at various universities also included training for psychiatric social workers. Until the Association of Psychiatric Social Workers (Chapter 8) merged with the British Association of Social Workers in 1970, it maintained control of the curriculum and the organisation of courses offering psychiatric social work training.

At much the same time as the first psychiatric social work course, the arrangements for training police court missionaries at the LSE course and by correspondence at Ruskin College, an adult education college in Oxford, were developed in 1930 by a Home Office training scheme for probation officers. It involved practical training, placements and attendance at social science courses at a local university (Bochel, 1976). The Probation

Training Board organised this from 1936. A London Police Court Mission training centre for probation officers was established at Rainer House in London in 1946 and later became a Home Office centre for probation training.

Western social work education

A second expansion of social work education was occasioned by public agencies in welfare state countries, which were difficult to staff, and for which training presented difficulties partly because of the lack of supervision. This was true of many Western countries in the 1950s: Britain (Younghusband, 1963) and Australia (Ward, 1962) were typical. Development of the post-war local government social services went hand in hand with government involvement in training. In the USA, by contrast, the organisation of social work education had been in conflict. Separate associations promoted education for the elite organisations derived from the charity and settlement movements in the major cities and, on the other hand, growing numbers of public sector workers, where courses gave importance to rural issues and were often attached to universities in colleges in less important cities. There was a related conflict over whether education should be at postgraduate (masters) level or undergraduate, which was a central preoccupation of the 1940s (Leighninger, 1987: Ch. 7). This was resolved following the Hollis–Taylor Report on the curriculum (1951; Taylor Davis, 1988), drawing on the concurrent UN statement about social work. The foundation of the Council on Social Work Education (CSWE) in 1952 from its two predecessors was an important factor, since it pressed forward the accreditation of courses, first for masters programmes and from 1974 also including undergraduate programmes (DuBois and Miley, 1999). The succeeding Social Work Curriculum Study, published in 1959 (Dinerman and Geismar, 1984), provided a comprehensive basis for establishing and evaluating curricula.

In Britain, an interim Curtis Report in the mid-1940s, before the main document leading to the establishment of children's departments, recommended provision for training, and this was organised through the Home Office, which was responsible for children's services. The Central Training Council in Child Care was set up in 1947. The Probation Training and Advisory Board of the Home Office was set up in 1949, merging two separate groups, and the Home Office took responsibility for training directly (Hartshorn, 1982). The third Younghusband Report (1959) led to the establishment in autumn 1962 of the Council for Training in Social Work, linked with the Council for Training of Health Visitors by the mandate given by the Health Visiting and Social Work (Training) Act 1962 (*Social Work*, 1963). Another Younghusband enthusiasm led to the creation of a 'staff college' for social work in 1961, the National Institute for Social Work Training (later National Institute for Social Work – NISW), with Robin Huws Jones, Younghusband's vice-chairman on the committee that produced the third report, as director. It had four aims:

- training for social work and for teaching social work
- providing a meeting place for discussion
- promoting inquiries, research and experiments
- publishing teaching materials and providing a library (Huws Jones, 1963).

These activities started in 1963 with a training course, fellowships for teachers, advanced courses and seminars and supervisors groups and these aims were then pursued for all of its life. A research unit developed in the 1970s. NISW hosted the Barclay (1982) and Wagner (1988) Reports of the 1980s on the role of social work. Campaigning for registration of social workers was centred there in the 1990s (Brand, 1999) and it closed in 2001–2, seeing its job as completed, or at least being unable to secure further government funding after government bodies were established to take on some of the responsibilities.

The account has focused on the position in the leading centres. The development of social work education outside these was various, generally later and less vigorous. As an example, in Cardiff, the capital of Wales (Walker and Jones, 1984), early interest in social work, and a Welsh University Society for the furtherance of social work, led to a settlement in 1904 which lasted until 1924. There were further initiatives during the Depression of the 1930s of a homecrafts settlement offering among other things smallholdings for unemployed men. These beginnings were not concerned to develop professional education for social work, but to mobilise students as contributors to welfare. Teaching only developed in 1948 with a diploma in social science in the department of economics. It became more sociological in the late 1950s. An applied social studies diploma developed in 1961, following the generic casework movement building up from Younghusband's LSE experiment. Then a social science degree was developed in 1962, including social administration and professorial posts in sociology (1962) and social administration (1969). After this, sociology became a specialised department and social administration and social work formed a separate school. Here, then, professional education did not develop until the late 1950s and did not become established institutionally within the university until the Seebohm reform led to the institutionalisation of social work into local government services.

After the Seebohm reorganisation, the separate training bodies were merged in 1971 into a Central Council for Education and Training in Social Work (CCETSW) and the training courses were merged into the Certificate of Qualification in Social Work (CQSW). This was developed through a series of consultations in the 1970s (CCETSW, 1977) in which the powerful new social services departments demonstrated a wish for greater control of social work education, at that time dominated by the universities. This led to the creation of the Certificate in Social Service, initially for residential and lower level workers in the social services, and managed by a consortia of local colleges and agencies. This model of management was extended to the new Diploma in Social Work (DIPSW), created by merger of the two previous qualifications in 1991 (CCETSW, 1991), after an attempt to create a three-year qualification, the Qualifying Diploma in Social Work (CCETSW, 1987), failed because of government refusal to underwrite the costs. CCETSW was abolished with the setting up of the General Social Care Council (GSCC) (2004) in 2001 and other similar national bodies under the Care Standards Act 2000, and the creation of a new social work degree beginning in 2003. CCETSW also established a small programme of post-qualifying education, but this had little impact.

A typical example of European developments in smaller countries is the Norwegian College of Local Government Administration and Social Work (NKSH). Pre-war discussions came to nothing, and the College was founded in 1950 to respond to the needs of post-war welfare state developments, and in 1975 incorporated a private college for women, founded in 1920 (Ulsteen, 1995). Eventually, NKSH, after developing a range of courses, a research department, higher degree education and international links in Europe through EU funding and in the former Communist states, including China, became part of the Oslo College in the 1990s and later achieved university status. The administrative focus of education at the outset was partly displaced by the importation of American casework in the 1950s as the basis of teaching and the inclusion of social work methods helped the development of services towards a professional social work model, rather than an administrative service-based model (Tutvedt, 1995). There was a separate college with a church base, and during the 1980s local colleges in different parts of the country developed social work education. These also became part of universities in the early twenty-first century. One university was designated to provide advanced training and research in the area, acting in effect as a staff college like the British National Institute for Social Work.

Norwegian social pedagogues working in welfare work with children and young people in residential care developed community youth work and daycare roles. This development responded to a need for more child care services as a higher proportion of women worked in the post-war period. Later, concern for community education for young people grew, as the phenomenon of the teenager emerged in the 1950s. The College started a one-year course in social pedagogy in 1952 (Bjørnsen, 1995), expanding eventually to three years in 1982 (Grønvold, 1995).

Western social work education 'in question'

Social work or care?

An important development of the 1980s was competence-based education and training, originating in the USA during the 1960s within teacher education (O'Hagan, 1996), but having considerable influence in the UK in the 1990s. It was based on 'behaviourable' models of learning, which sought to define clearly what individuals should be able to do, enhanced by functional analyses of roles and tasks within jobs. Functional analysis emerged in research in the USA on analysing the tasks for social workers (for example Teare and McPheeters, 1970). This was applied in the UK in the professional literature (for example BASW, 1977) as part of a post-Seebohm effort to distinguish between social work tasks and those performed by ancillary or paraprofessional staff (Payne, 1982: 51–3). In the functional analysis of professional tasks, the job is broken down into clearly defined tasks, for which training can develop specific competences, and may be built up into a range of different job roles in which people may demonstrate personal competence.

This approach to vocational training was taken up by government agencies in the UK when the National Council for Vocational Qualifications (NCVQ) was set up in 1986 with the aim of establishing a consistent pattern of training across all sectors of employment. To do so required a system of describing tasks in equivalent ways across different types of work. Following New Right thinking, which was in the ascendant, planning for vocational training was led by employers and was to be based in the workplace, with the aim of promoting entrepreneurialism and business development, even in public sector occupations. At the time, there was considerable development of private sector residential care in the social services, which lent itself to specific practical training.

At the time, social work and its education was being subjected to considerable criticism, and a new way of organising social work education was promoted, involving a consortia of agencies and higher education establishments, so that content and organisation would be influenced by employers and respond to practice needs. In this way, employer commitment to education might be better engaged. Consequently, when the DipSW was established, the curriculum statements were organised into specific competences. This has been criticised as mechanistic, and liable to divide complex and interlocking tasks into oversimplified patterns of competence, with the constant observing and checking of small elements of social work activity interfering with flexible practice (O'Hagan, 1996: 14–18). On the other hand, supporters of the approach have argued that much clearer specifications and more transparent assessment methods have resulted.

Alongside such developments, greater efforts were made during the 1980s and 90s to incorporate the lessons of adult learning within social work education, to respect the mature life experience of many social work students and their consequent need to incorporate life experience within professional learning. An influential experiment on enquiry and action learning, for example, encouraged students to work on professional problems in groups enquiring into alternative ways of dealing with them (Burgess, 1992). Techniques that interpret the educational process as a form of problem-solving akin to practice (Askeland, 1994) are a further example of developing educational practices. Internationally, the widespread location of workers has led to the use of distance and open education techniques in social work education, including full-scale professional education in India, Norway and the UK.

Global developments: a critique?

Many early global developments were based on colonial influences. For example, in India, Clifford Manshardt, an American missionary working in a settlement-style neighbourhood project in Mumbai (Bombay), was instrumental in promoting the American model of social work education in the founding of the Tata Graduate School of social work in 1936 (Mandal, 1995). They were 'not really seeking to meet the felt needs' (Thomas, 1967; 47) but wanted to make available in India opportunities to study and develop a growing body of knowledge. However, the approach placed greater emphasis on social reform than is implied by the later American cultural form of casework (Mandal, 1989). The School then established agencies, such as a child guidance clinic in 1937, to provide placements for its students (Verma, 1991: 70). Subsequent developments in psychiatric social work often arose as students were placed or graduates sought work in other parts of the country, or, as in Madras, where Dr Sarada Menon promoted the employment of social workers because of the skills offered by their training, to support hard-pressed medical and nursing staff in hospitals (Verma, 1991: 69–81).

Another example of colonialist influence is in Latin America (Aguilar, 1995), where the first influential school of social work at Santiago de Chile was founded with European influence in 1925, and subsequently supported developments in other countries, financed and encouraged by the USA from 1940 onwards. A two-year programme in social hygiene in an Argentinian medical school at the University of Buenos Aires started in 1924, applying American models of social work practice (Queiro-Tajalli, 1995). All these initiatives were to some extent the product of colonialist influences, in the empires of the European powers before the Second World War, and afterwards, through the funding and influence of the UN and the USA. The pattern in Central America relied on the example of the South American countries, especially Chile, which was a pioneer. With the exception of a few forerunners in larger and more stable countries, most developments were in the 1950s, often with the support of the UN and funded by the USA as a development activity, and often within ministries of labour or social security. Later, these technical schools were incorporated into university courses (Aguilar, 1995).

Another example is the work of the Iranian school of social work, founded by the American-trained social worker, Sattereh Farman-Farmaian. Her biography (Farman-Farmaian, 1992) describes a school which organised family planning clinics, sought reform of residential care and worked actively with prostitutes, oppressed women and other excluded groups through social welfare centres associated with the school. These developments were lost in 1979, with the Islamic revolution, which deposed the regime of the Shah of Iran. Subsequently, social work has been weak because of the emigration of many leaders in the profession, and the impact of fundamentalist Islamic belief in religious moral prescription rather than liberal, humanist and secular welfare (Midgley and Sanzenbach, 1989; Chapter 6).

Conclusion

Training and education provision during the 1990s in many countries has drawn attention to the distinction between welfare employees and social work. It has become clear that while social work is the leading profession in most social care systems across the world, and usually achieves high-level education, there is a vast army of care workers whose role is more ambiguous. In Britain and New Zealand social services and health and social care 'industry' bodies have become responsible for training for these groups, to a greater or lesser extent excluding social work.

One of the consequences of social change at the start of the new millennium has been a greater complexity of social work, a more complex understanding of knowledge and consequently a more complex form of professionalisation, including a new settlement of the relationships between academic and practice-professionalisation. After the accommodation within social work of the 'new professionalism' of dialogic, equal and involving models of practice respecting clients' independence and citizen status in the 1980s, ideas of empowerment and advocacy had a greater impact and reconstructed the language of social work practice. Within this context, a wholly scientific discourse was impossible, since scientific understanding had to negotiate with and gain acceptance from clients' own perceptions of their position, and a more complex understanding of how knowledge arose came from postmodernism ideas, which argued for a wider range of sources of knowledge interacting with each other. These would include scientific understanding derived from conventional social science research, but not be confined to it.

Managerialist developments in policy thinking often assume that scientific models of understanding and learning such as evidence-based practice and performance indicators can be used to direct and manage practice. Demands for the effective delivery of services and policy created a closer attention to practice allied with managerialism. Thus, the new settlement for social work knowledge, research and education includes a balance between a concern for the effective delivery of policy objectives within a service through effective practice, effective response to citizen and client participation and dialogue and recognition of a more complex relationship between knowledges and different forms of social work.

CHAPTER 11

Social Work's Futures

This chapter brings together the book's analysis by drawing together what present-day social work practice can learn from social work in the past. It argues that continuing discourses about social work and its organisation as a professional practice pose important issues that social workers will always have to grapple with in practice and in the organisation of their working lives and the organisations they work in. Different types of social work influence and learn from each other, are informed by different cultural and theoretical assumptions and traditions and have different objectives. I have argued that we cannot say there is one stream of social work development; rather there are many social works, which influence each other. The main sections of this chapter discuss these two issues in turn.

Continuities in social work

Social order and caring power

Chapters 2–4 of this book contain a summarised chronological account of social work and related social professions. This provides some evidence from a narrative of social work's histories across the world of continuities in its formation. Social care provision is present in all societies, responding to political views, ideological values and social expectations, the nature of all societies and the demands of the moment. Chapters 5–7 show that it is a response to individuals' needs to care and help, a development from political philosophies and values, expressed in a social order that responds to societies' needs to create social order when threatened by problems and disorder. Lubove (1965) argues that one of the factors in the emergence of social work at the end of the nineteenth century was the impact of the concept that benevolence was not an end in itself, but that social objectives should be achieved by charity, although we saw in Chapter 2 that this idea is a continuity – it has appeared repeatedly in discourses about helping others. Consequently, benevolence was converted into a profession committed to efficacy in its interventions. Chapters 8–10 show how the organisation, knowledge development and system of education have created the current mode of implementing social work as part of social welfare in present societies, how that emerged from its forerunners in the nineteenth century and developed throughout the twentieth. Various social professions have emerged responding to the demands and values of particular societies.

An inclusive, internationalist view of social work treats all these social professions as 'social work'. Chapter 10 suggests that this is an ethnocentric view because it categorises all social professions, whatever their cultural and historical origins, as variations on an Anglo-American model of social work. It is more accurate to say that other cultural and historical traditions have interacted with Western social work to create a rich tapestry of social interventions, using a range of interconnected value and knowledge sources. Each welfare regime creates its own pattern of social work agencies to fits its cultural context and political values.

The state's role

In Chapter 6, I identified the impact on the development of social work of liberal and socialist values and the significance in the social democratic tradition of the state's role in social provision. Digby (1989) identifies three different analytical models to explain the development of social care:

1. *Demand-led development*, a 'push' theory, suggests that social welfare responds to variations in need, especially poverty, vagrancy and crime. In this view, social work emerged as a response to urbanisation and industrialisation.
2. *Supply-led development*, a 'pull' theory, proposes that the demand-led view assumes a rational, well-informed assessment of social conditions among individuals, governments and institutions. Instead, changes in motivations and possibilities for action in the supply of welfare may be more impor-

tant. The development of ideas of social welfare, socialism and social responsibility leads to professionalisation, which promotes a 'market' for improved services.

3. *The social change of the state theory,* which proposes that the state emerged as an autonomous actor in the late 1800s leading to its inexorable assumption of responsibilities.

In all ages, there are examples of each of these. Among demand-led explanations are Mitchison's (2000: 5–6) account of how poverty became a particular problem in the sixteenth century because changes in land tenure forced people off the land in many countries, and wars left demobilised and disabled soldiers and sailors without the means of support. The bubonic plague is another example. From its appearance in the East in the 1300s, until it lost its potency in the 1600s, it led to a huge loss of life in the crowded continent of Europe, but while risking the loss of cultural traditions and skills, it also allowed a redistribution of land and property which freed social relations (Herlihy, 1997). The rice riots in early twentieth-century Japan led to developments in social work practice. Fears of social disorder everywhere have led to the development of social care; awareness of this led to developments that were not directly demand-led in late-developing countries in Asia. Shifts in the domestication of women in Western countries in the 1950s led to a more psychological and family-oriented social work, while concern about young people's behaviour and youth culture led to services for offenders and support for community action in deprived areas in the 1960s and 70s. Economic stress led to retrenchment in social services in some Western countries in the 1980s. Similar explanations are often current in everyday debate: the growing proportion of elderly people in the populations of many developed countries is a common concern in the 2000s.

Supply-led views emphasise the importance of economic and political trends in the formation of professions and services, rather than internal development. Examples of supply-led explanations in European history include mendicant preachers in the 1400s–1500s arguing that rich people should reject worldly wealth and the impetus for moral reform from the late 1500s, both encouraging charity (Cavallo, 1995). Increased secularisation after the Enlightenment in the 1600s–1700s led to a decline in charity. Middle-class women's availability for employment and their wish for education in the early twentieth century was an important driver of the development of paid social work, and their focus on family life and child care is an important element in the construction of the preoccupations of social work. Academisation and professional knowledge became available and generated university-level education, demands for the regulation and surveillance of the professional activities that resulted tended to develop. Concern about the ways in which professionalisation may lead services away from the interests of service users and the consequent promotion of advocacy or managerialist performance management in services are also supply-led explanations of developments. Blomberg and Kroll's (1999) study of how professional managers in Finland influenced politicians to accept that anxieties about service costs should lead to managed cutbacks in service contrary to public support of high levels of welfare is another example.

The theory of the state explanations refer to the nation state, rather than official action, since official and quasi-official provision is universal. In early societies where there was little organised state, the actions of a monarch, feudal lord or tribal elders are the equivalent of official action. However, the development of nation states in the nineteenth century was associated with an increasing range of services being undertaken by the state. The economic and social complexity of populous and industrialised states means that collective burdens seem more easily taken up by the state. The emergence of social ideas such as unemployment and a general acceptance of state responsibility for them took place at that time. Universal provision for health, education and social security was taken up as a state responsibility rather later. For social work, the services within which it could make a contribution did not arise until this growth in the state. Moreover, social work did not become a generally available service until countries began to accept wider responsibilities for welfare, in the mid-twentieth century.

However, the role of the state has led to variations of service and I noted in Chapter 6 the importance of a strong civil society and that its role in securing commitment to responding to people's social needs often created a strong social work. The USA and some nation states in the West have varied in their commitment to welfare, and sought to make social work a localised rather than universal responsibility. Others, such as the

Nordic countries, have concentrated on universal services. Some nations with a strong religious culture have not developed social work to any great degree, and Communist states reduced its importance for a period. However, in Chapter 6, I reviewed some of the debate about this, and suggested that no religion was monolithic. All contain a commitment to social change and social care, while all institutionalised religions contain conservative elements that seek to retain family and community issues within the religious sphere. This illustrates that we cannot assume that any organisational or structural arrangement will always promote or hinder social development and social care.

Gender and power

Histories of social work demonstrate that its social order and caring aspects are both gendered. The authority and role of the state to intervene in individual affairs and the value of doing so are balanced with caring and benevolence. Municipalisation and the way new industrialists gained power through the local bureaucratic elite in the nineteenth century shows that male power is not irrelevant to social work. However, women's initiatives have been important throughout the development of the social work method, and the focus on social work as a way of dealing with poverty through concern for families and children was a counterweight to the concern for social control. Caring has been a way to establish female participation and power over social actions.

Social work often throws up this balance between male power in the social order aspects of social work counterbalanced by female power in its caring aspects. For example, Struthers (1987) suggests that in the first half of the twentieth century in Canada, women in social work were more numerous and better trained than men, but were in a minority in leading posts. Exploring the reasons for this, he suggested that they had difficulty in earning the respect of male board members in charities, who were mainly businessmen. Because they were paid low wages, they moved frequently and did not gain seniority. Because they promoted the importance of family and the nurturing role of women in their practice, they became associated with this as employees in their own right. Family responsibilities excluded them from professional acceptability: family came first. It was assumed that because family agencies focused on mothering that women would have the right skills to help, but men had the skills for administration.

Women were assumed to have an orientation to service and caring, which was thought to make them unsuitable for the tough decisions of administration. Pedersen (1994), to take another example, analyses different attitudes of women in Britain and France to family allowances. In France the argument for family allowances derived from a right-wing reaction against liberal individualism, seeking to avoid the 'degeneracy' of birth control and married women working. In Britain, the campaign for family allowances was by socialists and feminists, who supported them to ameliorate family poverty and give unwaged women some financial independence.

Dealing with change in social work

Social workers will always be dealing with change, but the changes they face will always play out these continuities in their practice. The balance at any time and in any situation between social order and caring, between the state and the individual and between male administrative power and female caring power will be played out in their practice. The professional conflict of the 1990s in the USA and Britain between managed care/care management and individualised interpersonal care in services for adults is an example. The post-war conflict between legalistic services and casework in Finland is another (Satka, 1995). The female development of method against the male-dominated management of the Poor Law and charity organisation is a more distant example.

A range of important issues for service users is an important continuity in the development of social work:

- consumers and users and their rights to participate in deciding what happens to them
- the tensions between promoting individual, family and community development
- citizenship, and how it confers rights to service
- inequalities between areas and groups of people and the need for responsiveness to individuals, which also leads to concerns about centralisation or localisation of services.

All discourse is a practice as well as a debate between interests. Therefore, these issues will be played out in practice, in the organisation of social work and its agencies as well as in political and social debate.

Concern about consumerism, choice and rights represents an assertion of the importance of individualised care in the context of a service that has moved through managerialism towards a focus on social order. However, at the same time, by organising clients' interests in organisations to represent consumer power and practices like advocacy to represent individuals and managed care to provide choice, these concerns also represent a formalisation and structuring of responses to them.

Similarly, concern for community may be an attempt to empower individuals in ways that are relevant to their cultural and local preferences and, at the same time, it may be an attempt to use community as a way of enforcing social orders. Community social work in the 1980s was represented as an attempt to engage community interests and initiative, yet it also sought to coopt community concern to a social services agenda.

A policy of universalism may seek fairness and comprehensive provision, or tend to enforce uniformity to particular social orders. The universal British welfare state of the 1940s gave access to social provision by enforcing assumptions about the domestication of women. Individualism may lead to oppressive interventions, or services that are appropriate and delivered through personal relationships.

Chapters 5–10 propose an analysis that may help practitioners sort out these issues in their day-to-day practice. Chapter 5 suggests that a continuity in social work is that it focuses on families and their poverty. Effective practice might consider the balance between the individualisation of needs and social order actions. Chapter 6 examines the way in which social work gains its mandate for intervention from values and traditional sources of authority. Effective practice might consider the balance of value objectives and possible oppression from the sources of authority implicated in the worker's actions. Chapter 7 looks at how organisation within social agencies affects how social work does its work. Effective practice might consider the balance of social order objectives and individual care within the organisation of the agencies in which they participate. Chapter 8 explores professional and trade union organisation and its contribution to the development of social work. Effective practice might question the kinds of priorities and interests that their professional and work structures imply. Chapter 9 examines knowledge development in social work. Effective practice might look at how the knowledge used is created and framed. Chapter 10 examines education for the profession. Effective practice might examine ways in which their education facilitates appropriate balances between individualisation and social order.

Two case examples may put flesh onto these general points. A 15-year-old young person, Julie, 'looked after' by a local authority, that is, in the care of a public agency, was in a residential care home. She wanted to have the chance to return to her mother's care, but a case conference argued that this would not be a safe option and proposed to arrange for her to be fostered. The histories described in Chapter 5 draw attention to how care and control of young people have often been used oppressively to incorporate current political and social concerns about changes in family relationships. A wider range of patterns might be possible; is persuasion without really exploring Julie's wishes an appropriate practice? The issue in this case arose because Julie did not have an advocate and sought one from an independent service. The advocate's intervention used a different form of authority from that which is conventional in social work, and did not conform with assumptions that the public authority should have responsibility for decision making. Having an advocate present to represent Julie's views raised questions of choice and consumer rights. The advocate's practice was criticised by the public agency's workers because the advocate only represented Julie's opinions, rather than joining with other professional workers in arguing for the 'best interests' of the child. The worker pointed to the different values implicit in having advocacy available, and the practice conventions of advocacy, as opposed to those of caring casework and residential care. Moreover, her independent status, as a self-employed contractor for an advocacy agency, led to questions from the public agency workers about her professionalism and financial interests in pursuing the case assertively.

In this case, issues around consumerism, choice and rights were played out within conflicts about appropriate practice, the organisation of practice (the role of the public agency and the position of a self-employed advocate in an 'outside' agency), and the professionalism and knowledge that she used. However, they were played out around the role of families in society, whether the return to birth families is more valued than substitute families. Professional organisation and education also played a part.

In the second case example, a disabled man was cared for through a package of care jointly put together by the local social services and primary care (health service) trust, calling on both health and social care services. His deteriorating condition affected his mental functioning and he behaved inappropriately towards carers, sexually abusing them. The trade union representing some of the workers in the social services demanded that services be withdrawn. A carer's assessment, demanded on behalf of members of the family by a member of the health service advocacy organisation, showed that services were still required, and these were eventually provided by a private agency, which accepted the risks involved. However, a healthcare social worker in the hospital unit where the man had received treatment felt that workers were still very likely to be abused, and the caring service was less well integrated with the other range of services offered. However, hospital or nursing home care was not offered, partly because of the man's choice but also because this was more expensive than a package of care provided at his home. It was also felt that his behaviour would be difficult to manage in a hospital.

In this case, the rights and citizenship of the disabled man and his entitlement to caring services clashed with the citizenship of workers. By privatising the service, in the sense of removing it from public sector provision, the agencies involved privatised the issues, by shifting them from accountable public provision to less accountable contractors. The values represented in services, the individualisation of the disabled man's needs and the role of the trade union as a body representing occupational interests are all issues here. Again, the gendered nature of social care and the way in which social agencies have historically hidden social issues are raised. Historically, hiding social issues by providing inadequate care has often led to excluded communities in residential care, or failure to provide care in the community. At present, some issues of this kind are hidden by the privatisation of care away from public responsibility.

Perspective and context in practice

I do not argue that having some knowledge of social work histories directly provides lessons for social work. Social workers and social care workers might occupy several different roles in these cases, and what they do is affected both by professional knowledge, understanding and competence and the role and policies of the agency in which they work. A social worker trying to act in complex cases cannot apply historical lessons directly. However, I have argued in this book that different cultural and world traditions have produced different social works based on different value positions and organisational structures. Social pedagogy, social development and the different approaches to social work found across the world are not just variations of one international social work, they offer alternative prescriptions for a social profession. Understanding something of the history of social work, and examining some of the detailed histories that I have merely indicated within this book, offers some understanding of the continuity of the issues that social workers face and the range of ways in which over the years social workers have struggled with them. We still struggle with them, we will continue to struggle with them. Social work's futures will involve changes and continuities. Understanding something of the differences around the world within the histories of the social professions give us a perspective to understand that present struggles enact the changing and continuous nature of social work. It is important to continue to struggle, as social workers in the past have done. There is now just as much opportunity to achieve change where it is needed and continuity where it is valued as there was in social work's histories.

Further Reading and Resources

This book provides only a brief overview of general social work histories, and readers will find that the bibliography leads them to a range of sources for further reading. This list offers comments on a few major texts to provide the basis for more extensive further study, citations to classic texts, some journals that contain good coverage of historical research and some useful organisations and websites. Several of these books and much of the detailed American research cited in the text are developed from PhDs, which are clearly an important basis for research into social work history.

Modern texts

Cree, V. E. (1995) *From Public Street to Private Lives: The Changing Task of Social Work* (Aldershot: Avebury).
A well-researched detailed historical account, which provides a good example of historical evidence applied to social conceptualisation.

Davies, B. (1999) *A History of the Youth Service in England,* Volume 1: *1939–1979, From Voluntarism to Welfare State;* Volume 2: *1979–1999, From Thatcherism to New Labour,* (Leicester: Youth Work Press).
An important and comprehensive history of a service related to social pedagogy, which would be regarded as social work in many countries, although it is seen as separate in the UK.

Day, P. J. (2000) *A New History of Social Welfare* (3rd edn) (Boston, MA: Allyn & Bacon).
A comprehensive text showing how American social welfare builds on earlier traditions, although its judgments are affected by hindsight bias and present-day concerns.

Gilchrist, R. and Jeffs, T. (eds) (2001) *Settlements, Social Change and Community Action* (London: Jessica Kingsley).
The welcome publication of this book of useful papers on the origins and current role of settlements offers an up-to-date resource.

Katz, M. B. (1996) *In the Shadow of the Poorhouse: A Social History of Welfare in America* (2nd edn) (New York: Basic Books).
A critical history of American welfare, notable for its doubts about the professionalisation of social work.

Leighninger, L. (1987) *Social Work: Search for Identity* (New York: Greenwood Press).
This authoritative book is a history of the American social work profession, based on the archives of the associations.

Means, R. and Smith, R. (1998) *From Poor Law to Community Care: The Development of Welfare Services for Elderly People 1939–1971* (2nd edn) (Bristol: Policy Press).
A comprehensive and interesting history of the mid-twentieth-century development of services for elders.

Reisch, M. and Andrews, J. (2002) *The Road Not Taken: A History of Radical Social Work in the United States* (New York: Brunner–Routledge).
A well-researched general history of an important aspect of social work's development.

Satka, M. (1995) *Making Social Citizenship. Conceptual Practices from the Finnish Poor Law to Professional Social Work* (Jyväskylä, Finland: SoPhi).
This important book is unusual as being a history of Finnish social work in English. It is an important source, with thoughtful analysis based on research in the archives.

Soydan, H. (1999) *The History of Ideas in Social Work* (Birmingham: Venture).
The English translation of a Swedish text, with an important analysis of theoretical history.

Takahashi, M. (1997) *The Emergence of Welfare Society in Japan* (Aldershot: Avebury).
A useful historical analysis of the development of social welfare and social work in a country representative of the Eastern cultural origins of welfare provision.

Trattner, W. I. (1999) *From Poor Law to Welfare State: A History of Social Welfare in America* (6th edn) (New York: Free Press).
A well-established historical text – following the editions through its 30-year history gives a good picture of the changing views on American welfare.

Yimam, A. (1990) *Social Development in Africa 1950–1985: Methodological Perspectives and Future Prospects* (Aldershot: Avebury).
A useful survey of social welfare and social development in Africa during an important period of development.

Classic works

Ehrenreich, J. (1985) *The Altruistic Imagination: A History of Social Work and Social Policy in the United States* (Ithaca, IL: Cornell University Press).

Gilbert, N. and Sprecht, H. (1976) *The Emergence of Social Welfare and Social Work* (Itasca, IL: Peacock).

Leiby, J. (1978) *A History of Social Welfare and Social Work in the United States* (New York: Columbia University Press).
Three classic and widely used general histories of social work and social welfare services in the USA. Thoughtful forerunners of Day and Trattner's works (above).

Kennedy, R. (ed.) (1982) *Australian Welfare History: Critical Essays* (Melbourne: Macmillan).
Interesting set of papers on Australian welfare.

Lawrence, R. J. (1965) *Professional Social Work in Australia* (Canberra: Australian National University).
A history of Australian social work.

Pumphrey, R. E. and Pumphrey, M. W. (eds) (1961) *The Heritage of American Social Work: Readings in its Philosophical and Institutional Development* (New York: Columbia University Press).
Reprints of important historical documents about the history of social work in the USA.

Timms, N. (1964) *Psychiatric Social Work in Great Britain (1939–1962)*, (London: Routledge & Kegan Paul).
The classic history of British psychiatric social work and its important influence in the professionalisation of social work in the UK.

Woodroofe, K. (1962) *From Charity to Social Work in England and the United States* (London: Routledge & Kegan Paul).
This is the classic history of the main nineteenth-century sources of social work, comparing England and the USA; still relevant and useful.

Young, A. F. and Ashton, E. T. (1956) *British Social Work in the Nineteenth Century* (London: Routledge & Kegan Paul).
This important text still has not been displaced as a summary account of British social work during the period.

Younghusband, E. (1978) *Social Work in Britain: 1950–1975, A Follow-up Study* (Volumes 1 and 2 – bound together in paperback) (London: Allen & Unwin).
'Follow-up' to Younghusband's Carnegie reports of the later 1940s and 1950s, a comprehensive survey of British developments in its period, with specialist chapters by other authors.

Audiovisual

NASW and CSWE (2001) *Legacies of Social Change: 100 Years of Professional Social Work in the United States* (Alexandria, VA: CSWE)
An interesting video covering the main points of American social work history and some important personalities.

Biographies

Biographies, autobiographies and memoirs often provide an interesting picture of what practice was like in a different era or place.

Farman-Farmaian, S. with Munker, D. (1992) *Daughter of Persia: A Woman's Journey from her Father's Harem through the Islamic Revolution* (London: Corgi).
Farman-Farmaian was the creator and director of the first social work school in Iran, and her ghosted autobiography gives a valuable picture of the work and demands of social work in a developing country during the 1950s and 60s. Her own history includes her father's harem and being threatened with execution and exiled during the Islamic revolution in Iran.

Hodge, P. (ed.) (1980) *Community Problems and Social Work in Southeast Asia* (Hong Kong: Hong Kong University Press).
This collection of papers forms a memorial to Jean M. Robertson (1908–74), a leading figure in the development of social work in Britain's Asian colonies during the 1950s and 60s and the first professor of social work at Hong Kong University. In addition to biographical material and historical papers, there are papers by Robertson herself giving a picture of the development of social work in Singapore and Hong Kong.

Jones, K. (1984) *Eileen Younghusband: A Biography* (London: Bedford Square Press).
Dame Eileen Younghusband had a huge impact on the development of social work in the UK and internationally. Although a biography, this book is based on her recorded reminiscences, and is a fascinating picture of social work in the first half of the twentieth century.

Keeling, D. (1961) *The Crowded Stairs: Recollections of Social Work in Liverpool* (London: National Council of Social Service).
Keeling was the first general secretary of an important provincial social work agency, the Liverpool Personal Service Society, where the stairs were crowded with applicants for help during the 1930s. She made an important contribution to the development of citizens advice bureaux nationally and had many contacts among influential professionals and educationalists in Liverpool.

Taylor Davis, A. (1988) *Making of a Teacher: 50 years in Social Work* (Silver Spring, MD: National Association of Social Workers).

Alice Taylor Davis was the Taylor of the Hollis–Taylor Report (1951), an important document in the history of American social work education (Chapters 3 and 10). Her autobiography provides a fascinating picture of American rural social work in the 1930s. She also worked in Canada and at Howard University, the leading black university in the 1950s and 60s.

Wagner, G. (1979) *Barnardo* (London: Weidenfeld & Nicolson.)
Lady Wagner's modern biography of Barnardo and her other historical works are masterpieces of careful research allied with a sympathy and understanding of the complex personalities and demands of charitable administration.

Willmott, P. (1992) *A Singular Woman: The Life of Geraldine Aves 1898–1986* (London: Whiting & Birch).
Dame Geraldine Aves was the chief welfare officer at the UK Ministry of Health as social work was developing during the 1950s and 60s, and her committee on volunteering (Aves Report, 1969) led to significant development in volunteering work. Her early life involved welfare work in London during the 1930s Depression and during the war and the book gives a very good picture of this period.

Journals

British Journal of Social Work
While it only occasionally publishes historical research, *BJSW* is the major source for British research focusing on social work history.

European Journal of Social Work
Again, *EJSW* only occasionally publishes historical research, but its country notes and information section often contains material useful for gaining insight into the development of services and professions in European states.

International Social Work
While this journal covers a broad range, content on particular countries or services often contains brief historical information, which can be useful for gaining global information.

Journal of Progressive Human Service
An American journal whose radical focus includes historical perspectives and has a useful column, From the Archives, which contains interesting historical insights. The journal also connects to the Verne Weed archive at the University of Minnesota Social Welfare Archives, which concentrates on socialist social work.

Journal of Sociology and Social Welfare
This American journal is a useful source on policy and historical work, with a high standard of analysis. It often carries historical research, and has occasional all-history special issues.

Social Service Review
This prestigious American journal, based at the University of Chicago's historic School of Social Service Administration, is the primary source for historical research on social work in the USA.

Historical journals
Historical journals only rarely publish material on social work itself, but many local history journals and specialised journals particularly of social history occasionally publish research relevant to welfare history.

National and regional journals of social work
Most countries and some continental regions have social work journals, which occasionally publish papers on historical research.

Organisations

Social Work History Network (UK) (kandm.bilton@virgin.net)
This is an email network, holding occasional meetings, strongly influenced by supporters of the British Association of Social Workers, but most of the writers of British social work history are members.

Social Welfare History Group (American Historical Association)
www.theaha.org/affiliates/social_welfare_his_group.htm – probably the oldest continuing organisation on social work history.

Social Welfare History Archives – see below for website address
320 Andersen Library, 222 – 21st Ave. South, University of Minnesota, Minneapolis, Minnesota 55455; Tel.: (612) 624-6394, Fax: (612) 625-5525. Archivist: Professor David J. Klaassen, email: d-klaa@tc.umn.edu – main repository of social work archives in the USA; some international organisations are also archived here.

Voluntary Action History Society (UK)
This is a network of people concerned with voluntary sector history in the UK. Voluntary Action History Society, c/o Dr Justin Davis Smith, Institute for Volunteering Research, 8 All Saints Street, London N1 9RL. UK; Tel: +44 (0)20 7520 8900, Fax: +44 (0)20 7520 8910, email: Instvolres@aol.com, www.ivr.org.uk/vahs.htm.

Places to visit

Heatherbank Museum of Social Work – see below for the website address
Glasgow Caledonian University, City Campus, Cowcaddens Road, Glasgow G4 0BA; A.Ramage@gcal.ac.uk, Tel.: 0141-331-8637, Fax: 0141-331-3005. Open weekdays and not on public holidays. Interesting displays and a substantial archive collection.

Jane Addams Hull-House Museum – see below for website address
The University of Illinois at Chicago, 800 S. Halsted, Chicago, IL 60607-7017, Tel.: (312) 413-5353. Historic house that formed the basis of one of the first American settlements.

Jedburgh Castle Gaol
Jedburgh Castle Gaol, Castlegate, Jedburgh. Tel.: 01835 863254. Jedburgh is south of Edinburgh and contains this Howard Reform Gaol of great interest.

Lincoln Castle
Lincoln, Lincolnshire is an impressive castle, which still contains parts of the prison, including a prison chapel with seats in which each prisoner is isolated from each other.

Ripon Museums
Ripon Museum Trust, The House of Correction, St Marygate Ripon, North Yorkshire. HG4 1LX. Tel: 01765 690799, email: ripon. museums@btclick.com. These museums include a workhouse and house of correction in very good condition with many interesting contents (see 'websites' above).

The Workhouse, Southwell
Upton Road, Southwell, NG25 0PT. Tel.: 01636 817250, email: theworkhouse@ntrust.org.uk. Victorian workhouse, again with interesting contents, preserved by the National Trust.

Wellcome Trust History of Medicine Library – see below for website address
Wellcome Building (2nd floor), 183 Euston Road, London NW1 2BE. Tel: +44 (0)20 7611 8582, Fax: +44 (0)20 7611 8369, email: library @wellcome.ac.uk. Library of the history of medicine, which includes some historical materials on social work. The Trust building also contains interesting displays, which vary from time to time. Near Euston Station in London, the terminal for trains from the midlands and north.

Websites

Columbia University School of Social Work
http://www.columbia.edu/cu/ssw/about/index.html# – a historic social work school's website contains a brief illustrated history and a link to a paper on its early period.

Heatherbank Museum of Social Work – see above under 'places to visit'
http://www.lib.gcal.ac.uk/heatherbank/index.html – useful information based on the Museum's archives and displays.

How the Other Half Lives: Jacob A. Riis
http://www.cis.yale.edu/amstud/inforev/riis/title.html – full hypertext edition of a famous American book, published in 1890, describing social conditions in New York tenements of the period; illustrated with drawings from photographs by the author.

Institutions website
http://www.rossbret.org.uk/ – this organisation aims to list all historic institutions in the UK, covering asylums, workhouses, orphanages and reformatories. Extensive information and links.

Jane Addams Hull-House Museum – see above under places to visit'
www.uic.edu/jaddams/hull/hull_house.html – contains biographical and historical information about Jane Addams and Hull House.

National Association of Social Workers Centennial Website
http://www.socialworkers.org/profession/centennial/default.htm – extensive site devised for the centennial of American social work in 1998; biographies of important American social workers and information about historic agencies.

National Association of Social Workers Foundation Pioneers Website
www.naswfoundation.org/pioneers/default.htm – contains brief biographies of well-known American social workers.

New York Department of Juvenile Justice History Website
http://www.nyc.gov/html/djj/html/historymain.html – contains an interesting and illustrated history of juvenile detention (residential care for young offenders) in New York.

Poorhouse Story
http://www.poorhousestory.com – American equivalent of the British workhouse website.

Ripon Museums – see 'places to visit' above
http://www.ripon.co.uk/museums/ – this site provides information about three museums in the old Yorkshire town of Ripon, which include a prison and a workhouse.

Social Welfare History Archives – University of Minnesota – see above for organisation
http://special.lib.umn.edu/swha/ – the website contains useful information on the archives and sometimes excerpts from them.

Social Work History Station
www.idbsu.edu/socwork/dhuff/history/central/core.htm – illustrated information about American social work history, based on a CSWE centennial project. Also contains a gallery of American social photography.

University of Chicago School of Social Service Administration
www.ssa.uchicago.edu/aboutssa/history/tour1c.shtml – this historic university department is one of several on the web that carries a brief history; in this case, it is mainly biographical information about major figures, but further information and documents are promised.

US Social Security Administration – Social Security Online History Page
www.ssa.gov/history/history.html – extensive historical information about social security in the USA, including downloadable copies of many historical documents and books and audio and video clips.

Voluntary Action History Society
www.ivr.org.uk/vahs.htm – small site containing useful historical papers and links.

Volunteers in Service to America (VISTA) Living History Website
www.friendsofvista.org/living/index.html – interesting accounts by volunteers in a wide range of projects in the last part of the twentieth century.

Wellcome Trust History of Medicine Library – see above under 'places to visit'.
http://library.wellcome.ac.uk/ – contains an online catalogue of materials available.

The Workhouse Website
http://www.workhouses.org.uk/ – a website containing fascinating information and pictures about the Poor Laws (including the full text of the laws) and workhouses. Excellent links to other related sites.

Bibliography

AASW (American Association of Social Workers) ([1929]1974) *Social Casework: Generic and Specific: A Report of the Milford Conference* (Washington, DC: National Association of Social Workers).

Abramovitz, M. (1985) 'The family ethic: the female pauper and public aid, pre-1900', *Social Service Review*, **59**(1): 121–35.

Abrams, L. S. (2000) 'Guardians of virtue: the social reformers and the "girl problem," 1890–1920', *Social Service Review*, **74**(3): 436–52.

Ad Hoc Committee on Advocacy (1969) 'The social worker as advocate: champions of social victims', *Social Work*, **14**(2): 16–21.

Adams, R. (2002) *Social Policy for Social Work* (Basingstoke: Palgrave – now Palgrave Macmillan)

Addams, J. (1899) 'A function of the social settlement', in Lasch, C. (ed.) (1997) *The Social Thought of Jane Addams* (2nd edn) (New York: Irvington): 183–99.

Addams, J. (1910) *Twenty Years at Hull-House, with Autobiographical Notes* (reprint edition, with additional papers, ed. Brown, 1999) (Boston: Bedford/St Martin's).

Adepogu, A. (ed.) (1993) *The Impact of Structural Adjustment on the Population of Africa. The Implications for Education, Health and Employment* (Portsmouth NH: Heinemann/UNFPA).

Aguilar, M. A. (1995) 'Mexico and Central America', in Watts, T. D., Elliott, D. and Mayada, N. S. (eds) *International Handbook on Social Work Education* (Westport, CT: Greenwood): 43–64.

Ahmad, B. (1990) *Black Perspectives in Social Work* (Birmingham: Venture).

Aldgate, J., Tunstill, J. and McBeith, G. (1994) *Implementing Section 17 of the Children Act – The First 18 Months* (Leicester: University of Leicester).

Alvarez-Pereyre, F. and Heymann, F. (1996) 'The desire for transcendence: the Hebrew family model and Jewish family practices', in Burgière, A., Klapisch-Zuber, C., Segalen, M. and Zonabend, F. (eds) *A History of the Family:* Volume 1: *Distant Worlds, Ancient Worlds* (English translation of *Histoire de la Famille*, 1986) (Cambridge: Polity): 155–93.

Anderson, M. (1995) *Approaches to the History of the Western Family, 1500–1914* (2nd edn) (Cambridge: Cambridge University Press).

Andrews, J. (1992) 'Helen Hall (1892–1982): a second generation settlement leader', *Journal of Sociology and Social Welfare*, **14**(3): 95–108.

Andrews, J. (2001) 'Group work's place in social work: a historical analysis', *Journal of Sociology and Social Welfare*, **28**(4)· 45 64.

Anstruther, I. (1973) *The Scandal of the Andover Workhouse* (London: Geoffrey Bles).

Askeland, G. A. (1994) *Studium og Klientarbeid: Same Arbeidsprosess?* (Oslo: Det Norske Samlaget).

AssNAS (2003) http://www.assnas.it, 11 October 2003.

Astbury, B. E. (1953) 'The passing of a great leader: Dr René Sand 1877–1953)', *Social Work (UK)*, **10**(4): 843.

Atauz, S. (1999) 'Turkey', *European Journal of Social Work*, **2**(2): 212–14.

Attlee, C. R. (1920) *The Social Worker* (London: Bell).

Audit Commission (1986) *Making a Reality of Community Care* (London: HMSO).

Auslander, G. (2001) 'Social work in health care: what have we achieved?', *Journal of Social Work*, **1**(2): 201–22.

Austin, D. M. (1983) 'The Flexner myth and the history of social work', *Social Service Review*, **57**(3): 357–77.

Aves Report (1969) *The Voluntary Worker in the Social Services* (London: Allen & Unwin).

Bagdonas, A. (2001) 'Practical and academic aspect of social work development in Lithuania', in Helppikangas, P. (ed.) *Social Work and Civil Society from an International Perspective* (Rovaniemi, Finland: Lapin Yliopisto): 37–83.

Bailey, R. and Brake, M. (eds) (1975) *Radical Social Work* (London: Edward Arnold).

Barclay Report (1982) *Social Workers: Their Role and Tasks* (London: Bedford Square Press).

Barnes, M. (1997) *Care, Communities and Citizens* (Harlow: Addison Wesley Longman).

Barretta-Herman, A. (1994) 'Revisioning the community as provider', *International Social Work*, **37**(1): 7–21.

Bartlett, H. (1961) *Analyzing Social Work Practice by Fields* (New York: National Association of Social Workers).

Bartlett, H. (1970) *The Common Base of Social Work Practice* (New York: National Association of Social Workers).

Bartlett, P. (1999) *The Poor Law of Lunacy: The Administration of Pauper Lunatics in Mid-Nineteenth-Century England* (Leicester: Leicester University Press).

Barton, R. (1976) *Institutional Neurosis* (Bristol: Wright).

Bastos, M. D. F., Gomers, M. F. C. M, and Fernandes, L. L. (1996) 'Social work in Brazil – conservative and radical perspectives in poor communities', IASSW, IFSW and HKSWA (eds) *Participating in Change – Social Work Profession in Social Development Proceedings of the Joint World Congress of the International Federation of Social Workers and the International Association of Schools of Social Work* (Hong Kong: HKSWA): 70–2.

BASW (1980) *Clients are Fellow Citizens* (Birmingham: BASW Publications).

BASW (1983) *Effective and Ethical Recording* (Birmingham: BASW Publications).

Batten, T. R. (1967) *The Non-directive Approach in Group and Community Work* (Oxford: Oxford University Press).

Bayley, M. J., Parker, P., Seyd, R. and Tennant, A. (1987) *Practising Community Care: Developing Locally-Based Services* (Sheffield: Social Services Monographs: Research in Practice).

Bayliss, E. (1987) *Housing: The Foundation of Community Care* (London: National Federation of Housing Associations).

Bean, P. and Melville, J. (1989) *Lost Children of the Empire: The Untold Story of Britain's Child Migrants* (London: Unwin Hyman).

Becker, D. G. (1961) 'The visitor to the New York City poor, 1843–1920' *Social Service Review*, 35(4): 382–96.

Beckford Report (1985) *A Child in Trust: The Report of the Panel of Inquiry into the Circumstances Surrounding the Death of Jasmine Beckford* (Wembley: London Borough of Brent).

Bell, F. M. (1962) *Josephine Butler: Flame of Fire* (London: Constable).

Bennett, J. (Canon) (1949) *Father Nugent of Liverpool* (Liverpool: Catholic Social Services – Archdiocese of Liverpool).

Beresford, P. and Croft, S. (1993) *Citizen Involvement: A Practical Guide for Change* (Basingstoke: Macmillan – now Palgrave Macmillan).

Berridge, D. (1999) 'Child welfare in England: problems, promises and prospects', *International Journal of Social Welfare*, 8(4): 288–96.

Berridge, D. and Brodie, I. (1997) *Children's Homes Revisited* (London: Jessica Kingsley).

Beveridge Report (1942) *Social Insurance and Allied Services* (Cmd 6404) (London: HMSO).

Biestek, F. P. ([1957]1961) *The Casework Relationship* (London: Allen & Unwin).

Bion, W. R. (1961) *Experiences in Groups* (London: Tavistock).

Birkenhead County Borough (1974) *Birkenhead 1877–1974* (Birkenhead: County Borough).

Bjørnsen, A. (1995) 'The historical development of child welfare work in Norway', in Tutvedt, Ø. and Young, L. (eds) *Social Work and the Norwegian Welfare State* (Oslo: NotaBene): 145–64.

Blacker, C. P. (ed.) (1952) *Problem Families: Five Inquiries* (London: Eugenics Society).

Bland, L. (1995) *Banishing the Beast: English Feminism and Sexual Morality, 1885–1914* (Harmondsworth: Penguin).

Blomberg, H. and Kroll, C. (1999) 'Who wants to preserve the Scandinavian welfare state? Attitudes to welfare services among citizens and local government elites in Finland, 1992–6' in Blomberg-Kroll, H. *Kosta Vad det Kosta Vill? Attitydmönster och attitydförändringar hos befolkning och eliter beträffande välfäldsservicen i nedskäningarnas tid*, Vasa, Finland: Åbo Akademi Institutionem för socialpolitik, 52–86.

Bloor M. (1988) *One Foot in Eden: A Sociological Study of the Range of Therapeutic Community Practice* (London: Routledge).

Blyth, E. and Cooper, H. (2002) 'School social work in the United Kingdom: a key role in social inclusion', in Huxtable, M. and Blyth, F. (eds) *School Social Work Worldwide* (Washington DC: NASW): 15–32.

Bochel, D. (1976) *Probation and After-Care: Its Development in England and Wales* (Edinburgh: Scottish Academic Press).

Bonoli, G., George, V. and Taylor-Gooby, P. (2000) *European Welfare Futures: Towards a Theory of Retrenchment* (Cambridge: Polity).

Borenzweig, H. (1971) 'Social work and psychoanalytic theory', *Social Work*, 16(1): 7–16.

Bowpitt, G. (1998) 'Evangelical Christianity, secular humanism and the genesis of British social work' *British Journal of Social Work*, 28(5): 675–93.

Boyd, N. (1982) *Josephine Butler, Octavia Hill, Florence Nightingale: Three Victorian Women who Changed their World* (Basingstoke: Macmillan – now Palgrave Macmillan).

Brainerd, M. D. (2001) 'Helen Radlinska: expanding conceptualisations of social work practice from Poland's past', *International Social Work*, 44(1): 19–30.

Brand, D. (1999) *Accountable Care: Developing the General Social Care Council* (York: Joseph Rowntree Foundation).

Brandon, D. (1976) *Zen in the Art of Helping* (London: Routledge & Kegan Paul).

Brandon, D. (1998) 'The monastic tradition and community care', in Jack, R. (ed.) *Residential Versus Community Care: The Role of Institutions in Welfare Provision* (Basingstoke: Macmillan – now Palgrave Macmillan): 112–23.

Brandon, D., Brandon, A. and Brandon, T. (1995) *Advocacy: Power to People with Disabilities* (Birmingham: Venture).

Braverman, H. (1974) *Labor and Monopoly Capital: The Degradation of Work in the Twentieth Century* (New York: Monthly Review Press).

Brewer, C. and Lait, J. (1980) *Can Social Work Survive?* (London: Temple Smith).

Bridgen, P. and Lowe, R. (1998) *Welfare Policy Under the Conservatives 1951–1964: A Guide to Documents in the Public Record Office* (London: Public Record Office).

Briggs, A. (1961) *Social Thought and Social Action: A Study of the Work of Seebohm Rowntree 1871–1954* (London: Longmans).

Briggs, A. and MacCartney, A. (1986) *Toynbee Hall: The First Hundred Years* (London: Routledge & Kegan Paul).

Brinton, C. (1949) *English Political Thought in the Nineteenth Century* (2nd edn) (London: Benn).

Broad, B. and Fletcher, C. (eds) (1993) *Practitioner Social Work Research in Action* (London: Whiting & Birch).

Brooks, D. and Webster, D. (1999) 'Child welfare in the United States: policy, practice and service delivery', *International Journal of Social Welfare,* 8(4): 297–307.

Brown, H. and Smith, H. (eds) (1992) *Normalisation: A Reader for the Nineties* (London: Routledge).

Brown, K. D. (1971) *Labour and Unemployment 1900–1914* (Newton Abbott: David and Charles).

Brown, P. (1985) *The Transfer of Care: Psychiatric Deinstitutionalisation and its Aftermath* (London: Routledge & Kegan Paul).

Brown, V. B. (ed.) (1999) *Twenty Years at Hull-House, with Autobiographical Notes by Jane Addams* (with an introduction and additional related documents by Brown, V. B.) (Boston: Bedford/St Martin's).

Buckle, J. (1981) *Intake Teams* (London: Tavistock).

Bujard, O. (1996) 'Social work at the epochal "end of history"', in IASSW, IFSW and HKSWA (eds) *Participating in Change – Social Work Profession in Social Development Proceedings of the Joint World Congress of the International Federation of Social Workers and the International Association of Schools of Social Work;* Volume 3 (Hong Kong: HKSWA): 34–6.

Burgess, H. (1992) *Problem-led Learning for Social Work: The Enquiry and Action Approach* (London: Whiting & Birch).

Burn, M. (1956) *Mr Lyward's Answer: A Successful Experiment in Education* (London: Hamish Hamilton).

Burnett, J. (1994) *Idle hands: the Experience of Unemployment, 1790–1990* (London: Routledge).

Butler, T. (1985) *Mental Health, Social Policy and the Law* (Basingstoke: Macmillan – now Palgrave Macmillan).

Campbell Inquiry (1988) *Report of the Inquiry into the Care and After-care of Miss Sharon Campbell* (Chair: John Spokes QC) (Cm 440) (London: HMSO).

Cannan, C., Berry, L. and Lyons, K. (1992) *Social Work and Europe* (Basingstoke: Macmillan – now Palgrave Macmillan).

Carlton-LaNey, I. B (ed.) (1994) The legacy of African-American leadership in social welfare, *Journal of Sociology and Social Welfare,* special edition, 21(1): 5–152.

Carlton-LaNey, I. B. (ed.) (2001) *African-American Leadership: An Empowerment Tradition in Social Welfare History* (Washington DC: NASW Press).

Carniol, B. (1992) 'Structural social work: Maurice Moreau's challenge to social work practice', *Journal of Progressive Human Services* 3(1):1–20.

Carr, E. H. (1960) *The New Society* (London: Macmillan – now Palgrave Macmillan).

Carson, M. (2001) 'American settlement houses: the first half century' in Gilchrist, R. and Jeffs, T. (eds) *Settlements, Social Change and Community Action* (London: Jessica Kingsley): 34–53.

Cavallo, S. (1995) *Charity and Power in Early Modern Italy* (Cambridge: Cambridge University Press).

CCETSW (1977) *Patterns of Education and Training for Social Work leading to the Certificate of Qualification in Social Work: Policy Issues arising from Consultation Documents 1 & 2* (London: CCETSW).

CCETSW (1987) *Care for Tomorrow: The Case for Reform of Education and Training for Social Workers and Other Care Staff* (London: CCETSW).

CCETSW (1991) *Rules and Requirements for the Diploma in Social Work: DipSW* (Paper 30) (London: CCETSW).

CEBSS (2004) http://www.ex.ac.uk/cebss/ (accessed 29 July 2004).

Chambers, C. A. (1963) 'Social service and social reform: a historical essay', *Social Service Review*, 37(1): 76–90.

Chambers, C. A. (1986) 'Women in the creation of the profession of social work', *Social Service Review*, 60(1): 1–33.

Chan, C. L. W. (1993) *The Myth of Neighbourhood Mutual Help: The Contemporary Chinese Community Based Welfare System in Guangzhou* (Hong Kong: Hong Kong University Press).

Chan, C. L.W. and Chow, N. W. S. (1992) *More Welfare After Economic Reform? Welfare Development in the People's Republic of China* (Hong Kong: Department of Social Work and Social Administration, University of Hong Kong).

Chandler, S. K. (1995) '"That biting, stinging thing which ever shadows us": African-American social workers in France during world war I', *Social Service Review*, 69(3): 498–514.

Chatterjee, P. (1996) *Approaches to the Welfare State* (Washington DC: NASW Press).

China Civil Affairs (1995) *China Civil Affairs: Civil Administration in China* (Beijing: Ministry of Civil Affairs).

Chow, N. (1986) 'The past and future development of social welfare in Hong Kong' in Cheng, J. Y. S. (ed.) *Hong Kong in Transition* (Hong Kong: Oxford University Press): 403–19.

Chow, N. W. S. (1982) 'Development and functions of social services in Hong Kong', in Cheng, J. Y. S. (ed.) *Hong Kong in the 1980s* (Hong Kong: Summerson Eastern): 140–51.

Clarke, J. and Newman, J. (1997) *The Managerial State: Power, Politics and Ideology in the Making of Social Welfare* (London: Sage).

Clarke, J., Hughes, G., Lewis, G. and Moomey, G. (1998) 'The meaning of the welfare state', in Hughes, G. (ed.) *Imagining Welfare Future* (London: Routledge): 1–12.

Cleveland Report (1988) *Report of the Inquiry into Child Abuse in Cleveland 1987* (Cm 412) (London: HMSO).

Cliffe, W. with Berridge, D. (1991) *Closing Children's Homes: An End to Residential Child Care?* (London: National Children's Bureau).

Cole, J. (ed.) (1984) *Down Poorhouse Lane: The Diary of a Rochdale Workhouse* (Littleborough: George Kelsall).

Coman, P. (1977) *Catholics and the Welfare State* (London: Longmans).

Commission to Inquire into Childhood Abuse (2001) *Second Interim Report 2001* (Dublin: CICA); http://www.childabusecommission.ie. (accessed 4 August 2004).

Connolly, M. (1994) 'An act of empowerment: the Children, Young Persons and Families Act (1989)', *British Journal of Social Work*, 24(1): 87–100.

Cooper, J. (1983) *The Creation of the British Personal Social Services 1962–74* (London: Heinemann).

Corby, B., Doig, A. and Roberts, V. (2001) *Public Inquiries into Abuse of Children in Residential Care* (London: Jessica Kingsley).

Corfield, P. J. (1995) *Power and the Professions in Britain 1700–1850* (London: Routledge).

Corrigan, P. and Leonard, P. (1978) *Social Work Practice under Capitalism* (Basingstoke: Macmillan – now Palgrave Macmillan).

Court, J. (1969) 'The battered child', *Medical Social Work* (22): 11–20.

Coyle, G. L. (1961) 'The great tradition and the new challenge', *Social Service Review*, 35(1): 6–14.

Crenson, M. A. (1998) *Building the Invisible Orphanage: A Prehistory of the American Welfare System* (Cambridge, MA: Harvard University Press).

Crichton, A. (1953) 'The place of social work in a social science diploma course', *Social Work (UK)*, 10(4). 841–8.

Cullen, E., Jones, L. and Woodward, R. (eds) (1997) *Therapeutic Communities for Offenders* (Chichester: Wiley).

Cunningham, H. (1995) *Children and Childhood in Western Society since 1500* (London: Longman).

Curtis Report (1946) *Report of the Care of Children Committee* (Cmd 6922) (London: HMSO).

Cushlow, F. (1997) 'Guilded help?' in Laybourn, K. (ed.) *Social Conditions, Status and Community 1860-c. 1920* (Stroud: Sutton): 29–44.

Dalrymple, J. and Hough, J. (eds) (1995) *Having a Voice: An Exploration of Children's Rights and Advocacy* (Birmingham: Venture).

Dansk Socialrådgiverforening (2003) http://www.socialrdg.dk/index.dsp 11 October 2003.

Davidoff, L., Doolittle, M., Fink, J. and Holden, K. (1999) *The Family Story: Blood, Contract and Intimacy, 1830–1960* (London: Longman). p. 125.

Davies, B. P. and Challis, D. J. (1986) *Matching Resources to Needs in Community Care* (Aldershot: Gower).

Davis, A. F. (1973) *American Heroine: The Life and Legend of Jane Addams* (New York: Oxford University Press).

Day, P. J. (2000) *A New History of Social Welfare* (3rd edn) (Boston, MA: Allyn & Bacon).

Deacon, B., Heikkilä, M., Kraan, R., Stubbs, P. and Taipale, V. (1996) *Action for Social Change: A New Facet of Preventive Peace-Keeping – The Case of UNPREDEP*, Helsinki: STAKES: National Research and Development Centre for Welfare and Health).

DH (1989) *Caring for People: Community Care in the Next Decade and Beyond* (Cm 849) (London: HMSO).

DH (1995a) *Building Bridges – A Guide to Arrangements for Inter-Agency Working for the Care and Protection of Severely Mentally Ill People* (London. Department of Health).

DH (1995b) *Child Protection: Messages from Research* (London: Department of Health).

DH (1996a) *Caring for Children Away from Home: Messages from Research* (London: Department of Health).

DH (1996b) *Focus on Teenagers: Research into Practice* (London: Department of Health).

DH (1998a) *Modernising Mental Health Services: Safe, Sound and Supportive* (London: HMSO).

DH (1998b) *Modernising Social Services: Promoting Independence, Improving Protection, Raising Standards* (Cm 42169) (London: HMSO).

DH (2000) *Reforming the Mental Health Act: Part I: The New Legal Framework* (London: TSO).

Dhooper, S. S. (1997) *Social Work in Health Care in the 21st Century* (Thousand Oaks, CA: Sage).

DHSS (1971) *Better Service for the Mentally Handicapped* (Cmnd 4683) (London: HMSO).

DHSS (1974) *Report of the Committee of Inquiry into the Care and Supervision Provided in Relation to Maria Colwell* (London: HMSO).

DHSS (1976) *Priorities for Health and Personal Social Services in England* (London: HMSO).

DHSS (1977) *Priorities for Health and Social Services: The Way Ahead* (London: HMSO).

DHSS (1978) *Social Services Teams: The Practitioner's View* (London: HMSO).

DHSS (1985) *Social Work Decisions in Child Care: Recent Research Findings and their Implications* (London: DHSS).

Dickey, B. (1986) *Ration, Residence, Resources: A History of Social Welfare in South Australia Since 1836* (Netley, SA: Wakefield).

Digby, A. (1989) *British Welfare Policy: Workhouse to Workfare* (London: Faber and Faber).

Dinerman, M. and Geismar, L. L. (eds) (1984) *A Quarter-Century of Social Work Education* (Washington DC: NASW/ABC-Clio/CSWE).

Dominelli, L. (1996) 'Deprofessionalizing social work: anti-oppressive practice, competencies and postmodernism', *British Journal of Social Work*, **26**(2): 153–75.

Dominelli, L. ([1988]1997) *Anti-Racist Social Work* (2nd edn) (Basingstoke: Macmillan – now Palgrave Macmillan).

Dominelli, L. (2002) *Feminist Social Work Theory and Practice* (Basingstoke: Palgrave – now Palgrave Macmillan).

Donajgrodski, A. P. (1977) ' "Social police" and the bureaucratic elite', in Donajgrodski, A. P. (ed.) *Social Control in Nineteenth Century Britain* (London: Croom Helm): 51–76.

Donnison, D. (1975) *Social Administration Revisited* (2nd edn) (London: Allen & Unwin).

DuBois, B. and Miley, K. K. (1999) *Social Work: An Empowering Profession* (3rd edn) (Boston: Allyn & Bacon).

Elliott, D. and Walton, R. G. (1995) 'United Kingdom', in Watts, T. D., Elliott, D. and Mayada, N. S. (eds) *International Handbook on Social Work Education* (Westport, CT: Greenwood): 123–43.

Emerson, E. (1992) 'What is normalisation?' in Brown, H. and Smith, H. (eds) (1992) *Normalisation: A Reader for the Nineties* (London: Routledge): 1–18.

England, H. (1986) *Social Work as Art* (London: Allen & Unwin).

Esping-Andersen, G. (1990) *The Three Worlds of Welfare Capitalism* (Cambridge: Polity).

Everitt, A., Hardiker, P., Littlewood, J. and Mullender, A. (1992) *Applied Research for Better Practice* (Basingstoke: Macmillan – now Palgrave Macmillan).

Fairchilds, C. C. (1976) *Poverty and Charity in Aix-en-Provence 1640–1789* (Baltimore, MD: Johns Hopkins University Press).

Fanshel, D. and Shinn, E. B. (1978) *Children in Foster Care: A Longitudinal Investigation* (New York: Columbia University Press).

Farman-Farmaian, S. with Munker, D. (1992) *Daughter of Persia: A Woman's Journey from her Father's Harem through the Islamic Revolution* (London: Corgi).

Farrell, J. C. (1967) *Beloved Lady: A History of Jane Addams' Ideas on Reform and Peace* (Baltimore, MD: Johns Hopkins University Press).

Faul, A., McMurtry, S. L. and Hudson, W. W. (2001) 'Can empirical clinical practice techniques improve social work outcomes?', *Research on Social Work Practice*, 11(3): 277–99.

Ferguson, H. and Powell, F. (2002) 'Social work in late-modern Ireland', in Payne, M. and Shardlow, S. (eds) *Social Work in the British Isles* (London: Jessica Kingsley): 76–104.

Fido, J. (1977) 'The Charity Organisation Society and social casework in London 1869–1900', in Donajgrodski, A. P. (ed.) *Social Control in Nineteenth Century Britain* (London: Croom Helm): 207–30.

Finch, J. and Groves, D. (eds) (1983) *A Labour of Love: Women, Work and Caring* (London: Routledge & Kegan Paul).

Finch, J. and Mason, J. (1993) *Negotiating Family Responsibilities* (London: Routledge).

Firth Report (1987) *Public Support for Residential Care* (Report of a Joint Central and Local Government Working Party) (London: DHSS).

Fischer, J. (1973) 'Is casework effective? A review', *Social Work*, 18(1): 5–20.

Fischer, J. (1976) *The Effectiveness of Social Casework* (Springfield, IL: Charles C. Thomas).

Flexner, A. (1915) 'Is social work a profession?', in Pumphrey, R. E. and Pumphrey, M. W. (eds) (1961) *The Heritage of American Social Work: Readings in its Philosophical and Institutional Development* (New York: Columbia University Press): 301–7.

Floud, R. (1997) *The People and the British Economy, 1830–1914* (Oxford: Oxford University Press).

Flynn, M. (1989) *Sacred Charity: Confraternities and Social Welfare in Spain, 1400–1700* (Ithaca, NY: Cornell University Press).

Fook, J. (2002) *Social Work. Critical Theory and Practice* (London: Sage).

Foren, R. and Bailey, R. (1968) *Authority in Social Casework* (Oxford: Pergamon).

Forsythe, B. (1995) 'Discrimination in social work – an historical note', *British Journal of Social Work*, $25(1)$: 1–16.

Foucault, M. ([1970]2002) *The Order of Things: An Archaeology of the Human Sciences* (London: Routledge).

Fraser, D. (2003) *The Evolution of the British Welfare State: A History of Social Policy since the Industrial Revolution* (3rd edn) (Basingstoke: Palgrave Macmillan).

French, L. M. (1940) *Psychiatric Social Work* (New York: Commonwealth Fund).

French, P. (1994) *Younghusband: The Last Great Imperial Adventurer* (London: HarperCollins).

Fuller, R. and Petch, A. (1995) *Practitioner Research: The Reflexive Social Worker* (Buckingham: Open University Press).

Gardner, J. F. (1986) *Women in Roman Law and Society* (Bloomington, IL: Indiana University Press).

Gargett, E. (1977) *The Administration of Transition: African Urban Settlement in Rhodesia* (Gwelo: Mambo Press).

Garrett, P. M. (1999) 'Mapping child-care social work in the final years of the twentieth century: a critical response to the "looking after children" system', *British Journal of Social Work*, $29(1)$: 27–47.

Geismar, L. L. and Ayres, B. (1960) *Measuring Family Functioning* (St Paul: Minnesota Family-centered Project).

George, V. and Miller, S. (1994) 'Squaring the welfare circle', in George, V. and Miller, S. (eds) *Social Policy Towards 2000: Squaring the Welfare Circle* (London: Routledge): 6–21.

Germain, C. (1970) 'Casework and science: a historical encounter', in Roberts, R. W. and Nee, R. H. (eds) *Theories of Social Casework* (Chicago: University of Chicago Press): 3–32.

Gilbert, B. B. (1970) *British Social Policy 1914–1939* (London: Batsford).

Gilleard, C. and Higgs, P. (2000) *Cultures of Ageing: Self, Citizen and Body* (Harlow: Prentice-Hall).

Glassner, J-J. (1996) 'From Sumer to Babylon: families and landowners and families as rulers' in Burgière, A., Klapisch-Zuber, C., Segalen, M. and Zonabend, F. (eds) *A History of the Family:* Volume 1: *Distant Worlds, Ancient Worlds* (English translation of *Histoire de la Famille*, 1986) (Cambridge: Polity): 92–127.

Glastonbury, B. (1979) *Paying the Piper and Calling the Tune: Being a Study of Public Attitudes Towards Social Work* (Birmingham: British Association of Social Workers).

Goffman, E. ([1961]1968) *Asylums: Essays on the Social Situation of Mental Patients and Other Inmates* (Harmondsworth: Penguin).

Goldberg, E. M., Gibbons, J. and Sinclair, I. (1985) *Problems, Tasks and Outcomes* (London: Allen & Unwin).

Goldberg, E. M., with Mortimer, A. and Williams, B. T. (1970) *Helping the Aged* (London: Allen & Unwin).

Goldstein, H. (1973) *Social Work Practice: A Unitary Approach* (Columbia, SC: University of South Carolina Press).

Goodman, R. (1998) 'The Japanese-style welfare state and the delivery of personal social services', in Goodman, R., White, G. and Kwon, H.-J. (eds) *The East Asian Welfare Model: Welfare Orientalism and the State* (London: Routledge): 139–58.

Göppner, H.-J. (1998) 'Social work in the German health care system: organization of the health care system and roles and functions of social work' in Ylinen, S. (ed.) *Social Work in Public Health Symposium* (Kuopio, Finland: Kuopion Yliopistollinen Opetusssosiaalikeskus): 105–25.

Gordon, W. E. (1954) 'Scientific training in the social work doctorate', in Council on Social Work Education, *Social Work Education in the Post-Master's Program: Approaches to Curriculum Content* (New York: Council on Social Work Education), Monograph No. 2: 7–21.

Gordon, W. E. (1980) 'Does social work research have a future? A book review', *Social Work Research and Abstracts*, 16: 3–4.

Gorman, H. and Postle, K. (2003) *Transforming Community Care: A Distorted Vision?* (Birmingham: Venture).

Gosden, P. H. (1961) *The Friendly Societies in England 1815–1975* (Manchester: Manchester University Press).

Graham, J. R. (1996) 'An analysis of Canadian social welfare historical writing', *Social Service Review*, 70(1): 140–58.

Green, D. G. (1993) *Reinventing Civil Society: The Rediscovery of Welfare without Politics* (London: IEA Health and Welfare Unit).

Green, E. C. (1999) 'Introduction', in Green, E. C. (ed.) *Before the New Deal: Social Welfare in the South 1830–1930* (Athens, GA: University of Georgia Press): vii–xxii.

Greenwood, E. (1957) 'Attributes of a profession', *Social Work* 2(3): 45–55.

Griffiths, K. A. (1976) 'Social work practice in groups', in Boas, P. J. and Crawley, J. (eds) *Social Work in Australia: Responses to a Changing Context'* (Melbourne: Australia National Press and Publications/ Australian Association of Social Workers): 214–26.

Griffiths Report (1988) *Community Care: Agenda for Action* (London: HMSO).

Grinker, R. R., MacGregor, H., Selan, K., Klein, A. and Kohrman, J. (1961) 'The early years of psychiatric social work', *Social Service Review*, 35(2):111–26.

Grønvold, E. (1995) 'Forty years of child care', in Tutvedt, Ø. (ed.) *40 År for Velfoerdsstaten: Norges kommunal-og sosialhøgskoles Historie 1950–1990* (Oslo: NKSH), 193–4.

GSCC (2004) http://www.gscc.org.uk/ (accessed 29 July 2004).

Guest, G. (1989) 'The boarding of the dependent poor in colonial America', *Social Service Review*, **63**(1): 92–112.

Guillén, A. M. and Álvarez, S. (2001) 'Globalization and the southern welfare states', in Sykes, R., Palier, B. and Prior, P. M. (eds) *Globalization and European Welfare States: Challenges and Change* (Basingstoke: Palgrave): 103–26.

Guy, R. (1995) 'US welfare policy in historical perspective: a bifurcated system', *International Social Work*, **38**(3): 299–309.

Hacsi, T. (1996) 'From indenture to family foster care: a brief history of child placing' in Smith, E. P. and Merkel-Holguin, L. A. (eds) *A History of Child Welfare* (New Brunswick, NJ: Transaction): 155–73.

Hadley, R. and McGrath, M. (eds) (1980) *Going Local: Neighbourhood Social Services* (London: Bedford Square Press).

Hadley, R. and McGrath, M. (1984) *When Social Service are Local: The Normanton Experience* (London: Allen & Unwin).

Hague, R., Harrop, M. and Breslin, S. (1998) *Comparative Government and Politics: An Introduction* (Basingstoke: Macmillan – now Palgrave Macmillan).

Hall, A. (1975) 'Policy-making: more judgement than luck', *Community Care*, 6 August: 16–18.

Hall, C. (1998) 'A family for nation and empire' in Lewis, G. (ed.) *Forming Nation, Framing Welfare* (London: Routledge & Kegan Paul): 9–47.

Hall, C., Juhila, K., Parton, N. and Pösö, T. (2003) *Constructing Clienthood in Social Work and Human Services: Interaction, Identities and Practices* (London; Jessica Kingsley).

Hall, N. (1995) 'Social work education and social development: the challenge ahead', in IASSW, IFSW and HKSWA (eds) *Participating in Change – Social Work Profession in Social Development Proceedings of the Joint World Congress of the International Federation of Social Workers and the International Association of Schools of Social Work* (Hong Kong: HKSWA): 94–9.

Hall, P. (1976) *Reforming the Welfare: The Politics of Change in the Personal Social Services* (London: Heinemann).

Hämäläinen, J. and Vornanen, R. (1996) 'Social work and social security – theoretical and practical challenges in a changing society', in Hämäläinen, J., Vornanen, R. and Larvinkari, J. (eds) *Social Work and Social Security in a Changing Society: Festschrift for Prof. Pauli Niemela* (Augsberg: MaroVerlag): 7–32.

Hands, A. R. (1968) *Charities and Social Aid in Greece and Rome* (London: Thames and Hudson).

Harper, S. and Thane, P. (1989) 'The consolidation of "old age" as a phase of life, 1945–1965', in Jeffreys, M. (ed.) *Growing Old in the Twentieth Century* (London: Routledge): 43–61.

Harrington, M. (1962) *The Other America: Poverty in the United States* (New York: Penguin).

Harris, J. (1997) 'Past patterns, present prospects: social work in the Czech Republic', *International Social Work*, **40**(4): 425–32.

Harris, J. (1998) 'Scientific management, bureau-professionalism, new managerialism: the labour process of state social work', *British Journal of Social Work*, **28**(6): 839–62.

Harris, J. (1999) 'State social work and social citizenship in Britain: from clientelism to consumerism', *British Journal of Social Work*, **29**(6): 915–37.

Harris, J. (2002) *The Social Work Business* (London: Routledge).

Harrison, T. (1999) 'A momentous experiment: strange meetings at Northfield', in Campling, P. and Haigh, R. (eds) *Therapeutic Communities: Past, Present and Future* (London: Jessica Kingsley): 19–31.

Hartshorn, A. E. (1982) *Milestone in Education for Social Work: The Carnegie Experiment 1954–1958* (Dunfermline, Fife: Carnegie United Kingdom Trust).

Harwin, J. (1996) *Children of the Russian State: 1917–95* (Aldershot: Avebury).

Hatcher, J. (1977) *Plague, Population and the English Economy 1348–1530* (Basingstoke: Macmillan – now Palgrave Macmillan).

Hearn, B. and Sinclair, R. (1998) *Children's Services Plans: Analysing Need; Reallocating Resources. A Report to the Department of Health* (London: National Children's Bureau).

Heasman, K. (1965) *Christians and Social Work* (London: SPCK).

Heinenon, T., and Spearman, L. (2001) *Social Work Practice: Problem-solving and Beyond* (Toronto/Vancouver: Irwin).

Henderson, P. (ed.) (1995) *Children and Communities* (London: Pluto).

Hennock, E.P (1987) *British Social Reform and German Precedents: The Case of Social Insurance 1880–1914* (Oxford: Clarendon Press).

Henriques, U. R. Q. (1979) *Before the Welfare State: Social Administration in Early Industrial Britain* (London: Longman).

Herlihy, D. (1997) *The Black Death and the Transformation of the West* (Cambridge, MA: Harvard University Press).

Hietala, M. (1987) *Services and Urbanization at the Turn of the Century: The Diffusion of Innovations* (Helsinki: Societas Historica Finlandiae).

Higgins, J. (1978) *The Poverty Business: Britain and America* (Oxford: Blackwell/London: Robertson).

Hildeng, B. (1995) 'The Norwegian welfare state: its aims and organization', in Tutvedt, Ø. and Young, L. (eds) *Social Work and the Norwegian Welfare State* (Oslo: NotaBene, Ø.K.S. –rapport nr. 95:2): 165–98.

Hofmeyer, E., Kimberley, M. D. and Hawkins, F. R. (1995) 'Canada', in Watts, T. D., Elliott, D. and Mayadas, N. S. (eds) *International Handbook on Social Work Education* (Westport CT: Greenwood Press): 23–42.

Hollis, E. V. and Taylor, A. L. (1951) *Social Work Education in the United States: The Report of a Study made for the National Council on Social Work Education* (New York: Columbia University Press).

Hollis, F. (1968) *A Typology of Casework Treatment* (New York: FSAA).

Hollis, F. (1983) 'How it really was', *Smith College Journal*, 10(2): 3–9.

Holloway, M. (1966) *Heavens on Earth: Utopian Communities in America 1670–1880* (2nd edn) (New York: Dover).

Holman, R. (1976) *Inequality in Child Care* (London: Child Poverty Action Group).

Holman, R. (1981) *Kids at the Door* (Oxford: Blackwell).

Holman, R. (2000) *Kids at the Door Revisited* (Lyme Regis: Russell House).

Home Office (1947) *Report of the Committee of Inquiry into the Conduct of Standon Farm Approved School and the Circumstances Connected with the Murder of a Master at the School on February 15th, 1947* (Cmd 7150) (London: HMSO).

Home Office (1959) *Report of an Inquiry relating to Carlton Approved School* (Cmnd 937) (London: HMSO).

Home Office (1965a) *The Adult Offender* (Cmnd 2952) (London: HMSO).

Home Office (1965b) *The Child, The Family and the Young Offender* (Cmnd 2742) (London: HMSO).

Home Office (1967) *Administration of Punishment at Court Lees Approved School* (Cmnd 3367) (London: HMSO).

Hort, S. E. O. and McMurphy, S. C. (1997) 'Sweden', in Mayadas, N. S., Watts, T. D. and Elliott, D. (eds) *International Handbook on Social Work Theory and Practice* (Westport, CT: Greenwood): 144–60.

Houghton Report (1972) *Report of the Departmental Committee on the Adoption of Children* (Cmnd 5107) (London: HMSO).

House of Commons Select Committee on the Social Services (1985) *Community Care: With Special Reference to Adult Mentally Ill and Mentally Handicapped People* (HC13-1) (London: HMSO).

Hughes Inquiry (1985) *Report of the Committee of Inquiry into Children's Homes and Hostels* (Belfast: HMSO).

Hughes, G., Clarke, J., Lewis, G. and Mooney, G. (1998) 'Reinventing "the public"?' in Hughes, G. (ed.) *Imagining Welfare Futures* (London: Routledge): 152–65.

Hugman, R. (1994) *Ageing and the Care of Older People in Europe* (Basingstoke: Macmillan – now Palgrave Macmillan).

Hui, Y. F. (1989) 'Ideal models for social policies during the transitional period', *International Social Work*, 32(4): 251–9.

Humphreys, M. (1995) *Empty Cradles* (London: Doubleday/Corgi).

Huws Jones, R. (1963) 'The National Institute for Social Work Training', *Social Work (UK)*, 20(3): 12–15.

Iacovetta, F. (1998) 'Parents, daughters and family-court intrusions into working-class life', in Iacovetta, F. and Mitchinson, W. (eds) *On the Case: Explorations in Social History* (Toronto: University of Toronto Press): 312–37.

IFSW (1994) *The Ethics of Social Work: Principles and Standards*, http://www.ifsw.org/Publications/4.4.pub.html (accessed 11 October 2003).

Ikeda, Y. and Takashima, S. (1997) 'Specific features of development of social welfare in Japan in comparison with that of Western European countries', *Japanese Journal of Social Services*, 1: 1–9.

Illich, I., Zola, I. K., McKnight, J., Caplan, J. and Shaiken, H. (1977) *Disabling Professions* (London: Marian Boyars).

Ingleby Report (1960) *Report of the Committee on Children and Young Persons* (Cmnd 1191) (London: HMSO).

Inkeles, A. and Bauer, R. A. (1959) *The Soviet Citizen: Daily Life in a Totalitarian Society* (Cambridge, MA: Harvard University Press).

Ito, Y. (1995) 'Social work development in Japan', *Social Policy and Administration*, 29(3): 258–68.

Jacka, A. A. (1973) *The ACCO Story* (Birmingham: The Society for the Promotion of Education and Research in Social Work).

James, E. (1980) 'From Paris to ASCAP – a short history of the European Anti-Poverty Programme', *International Social Work*, 23(4): 2–9.

Jamur, M. (1996) 'Changement ou permanence: les projets professionals des assiatants sociaux au 1936–93', in IASSW, IFSW and HKSWA (eds) *Participating in Change – Social Work Profession in Social Development Proceedings of the Joint World Congress of the International Federation of Social Workers and the International Association of Schools of Social Work:* Volume 3 (Hong Kong: HKSWA): 40–2.

Jansen, E. (1980) *The Therapeutic Community Outside the Hospital* (London: Croom Helm).

Jay Report (1979) *Report of the Committee of Enquiry into Mental Handicap Nursing and Care* (Cmnd 7468) (London: HMSO).

Johnson, P. (1989) 'The structural dependency of the elderly: a critical note', in Jeffreys, M. (ed.) *Growing Old in the Twentieth Century* (London: Routledge): 62–72.

Johnson, P. (1998) 'Historical readings of old age and ageing' in Johnson, P. and Thane, P. (eds) *Old Age from Antiquity to Post-Modernity* (London: Routledge): 1–18.

Jokinen, A., Juhila, K. and Pösö, T. (1999) *Constructing Social Work Practices* (Aldershot: Ashgate).

Jones, C. (1976) *The Foundations of Social Work Education* (Durham: University of Durham, Department of Sociology and Social Administration, Working Papers in Sociology 11).

Jones, C. (1979) 'Social work education, 1900–1977', in Parry, N., Rustin, M. and Stayamurti, C. (eds) *Social Work, Welfare and the State* (London: Arnold): 72–88.

Jones, C. (1982) *Charity and Bienfaisance: The Treatment of the Poor in the Montpellier Region 1740–1815* (Cambridge: Cambridge University Press).

Jones, K. (1972) *A History of the Mental Health Services* (London: Routledge & Kegan Paul).

Jones, K. (1984) *Eileen Younghusband: A Biography* (London: Bedford Square Press).

Jones, K. (1993) *Asylums and After: A Revised History of the Mental Health Services: From the early 18th century to the 1990s* (London: Athlone Press).

Jones, K. (2000) *The Making if Social Policy in Britain 1830 1990* (2nd edn) (London: Athlone).

Jones, M. (1968) *Social Psychiatry in Practice* (Harmondsworth: Penguin).

Jordan, J. (2001) *Josephine Butler* (London: Murray).

Jordan, W. K. (1960) *The Charities of London 1480–1660* (London: Allen & Unwin).

Joyce, P., Corrigan, P. and Hayes, M. (1988) *Striking Out: Trade Unionism in Social Work* (Basingstoke: Macmillan – now Palgrave Macmillan).

Kahan, B. and Levy, A. (1991) *The Pindown Experience and the Protection of Children: Report of the Staffordshire Child Care Inquiry* (Stafford: Staffordshire County Council).

Karger, H. J. (1987) 'Minneapolis settlement houses in the "not so roaring 20s": Americanization, morality, and the revolt against popular culture', *Journal of Sociology and Social Welfare*, 14(2): 89–110.

Karger, H. J. (1989) 'The common and conflicting goals of labor and social work', *Administration in Social Work*, 13(1): 1–17.

Karvinen, S., Pösö, T. and Satka, M. (1999) *Reconstructing Social Work Research* (Jyväskylä: SoPhi).

Kassim Ejaz, F. (1989) 'The nature of casework practice in India: a study of social workers' perceptions in Bombay', *International Social Work*, 32(1): 25–38.

Katz, M. B. (1996) *In the Shadow of the Poorhouse: A Social History of Welfare in America* (2nd edn) (New York: Basic Books).

Kautto, M. (2001) *Diversity among Welfare States: Comparative Studies in Welfare State Adjustment in Nordic Countries* (Research Report 118) (Helsinki: STAKES, National Research and Development Centre for Welfare and Health).

Kay, B. H. (1976) 'The interdependence of professions and social science disciplines: allies in problem-solving', in IASSW *Asian Social Problems: New Strategies for Social Work Education* (New York: IASSW): 9–32.

Kazi, M. A. F. (1998) *Single Case Evaluation by Social Workers* (Aldershot: Ashgate).

Kendall, K. A. (1978a) *Reflections on Social Work Education 1950–1978* (New York: International Association of Schools of Social Work).

Kendall, K. A. (1978b) 'The IASSW 1928–1978: a journey of remembrance', in Kendall, K. A. *Reflections on Social Work Education 1950–1978* (New York: International Association of Schools of Social Work), 170–91.

Kendall, K. A. (2000) *Social Work Education: Its Origins in Europe* (Alexandria, VA: CSWE).

Kennard, D. (1998) *An Introduction to Therapeutic Communities* (2nd edn) (London: Jessica Kingsley).

Kidd, A. (1999) *State, Society and the Poor in Nineteenth-century England* (Basingstoke: Macmillan – now Palgrave Macmillan).

Kilbrandon Report (1964) *Children and Young Persons in Scotland* (Cmnd 2306) (Edinburgh: HMSO).

Kiu, D. K. (1976) 'Problems of health, nutrition, and family planning in Asia: an allied professions approach', in IASSW *Asian Social Problems: new strategies for Social Work Education* (New York: IASSW): 33–47.

Knapp, J. M. (ed.) ([1895]1985) *The Universities and the Social Problem: An Account of the University Settlements in East London* (London: Rivington Percival; new edn, New York: Garland).

Knapp, M., Cambridge, P., Thomason, C., Beecham, J., Allen, C. and Darton, R. (1992) *Care in the Community: Challenge and Demonstration* (Aldershot. Avebury).

Koenis, S. (1999) 'The uses of social science in the history of Dutch social work, 1900–1980', *European Journal of Social Work*, 2(1): 41–53.

Kogan, L. S. and Hunt, J. M. (1954) 'Two year study of casework uses', *Social Casework*, 35(2): 252–7.

Kosonen, P. (2001) 'Globalization and the Nordic welfare states', in Sykes, R., Palier, B. and Prior, P. M. (eds) *Globalization and European Welfare States. Challenges and Change* (Basingstoke: Palgrave – now Palgrave Macmillan): 153–72.

Kramer, R. and Specht, H. (1969) 'Introduction', in Kramer, R. and Specht, H. (eds) *Readings in Community Organization Practice* (Englewood Cliffs, NJ: Prentice Hall): 1–21.

Krill, D. (1978) *Existential Social Work* (New York: Free Press).

Kumar, H. (1994) *Social Work: An Experience and Experiment in India* (New Delhi: Gitanjali).

Kwan, A. Y. H. (1989) 'Social welfare and services in Hong Kong', in Kwan, A. Y. H. (ed.) *Hong Kong Society* (Hong Kong: Writers' and Publishers' Cooperative): 131–83.

Kwon, H. J. (1999) *The Welfare State in Korea: The Politics of Legitimation* (Basingstoke: Macmillan – now Palgrave Macmillan).

Laing, R. D. (1965) *The Divided Self: An Existential Study in Sanity and Madness* (Harmondsworth: Penguin).

Laming, H. (2003) *The Victoria Climbié Inquiry Report of an Inquiry by Lord Laming* (London: TSO); http://www.victoria-climbie-inquiry.org.uk/finreport/finreport.htm.

Lasch, C. (1997) 'Introduction', in Lasch, C. (ed.) *The Social Thought of Jane Addams* (2nd edn) (New York: Irvington): 1–6.

Laybourn, K. (1995) *The Evolution of British Social Policy and the Welfare State c. 1800–1993* (Keele: Ryburn Publishing/Keele University Press).

Laybourn, K. (1997) 'The guild of help and the community response to poverty 1904-c.1914', in Laybourn, K. (ed.) *Social Conditions, Status and Community 1860-c. 1920* (Stroud: Sutton): 9–28.

Lee, J. A. B. (2001) *The Empowerment Approach to Social Work Practice* (2nd edn) (New York: Columbia University Press).

Lees, R. (1971) 'Social work, 1925–50: The case for a reappraisal', *British Journal of Social Work,* 1(4): 371–9.

Leibfried, S. (2000) 'Towards a European welfare state?' in Pierson, C. and Castles, F. G. (eds) *The Welfare State Reader* (Cambridge: Polity): 190–206.

Leighninger, L. (1987) *Social Work: Search for Identity* (New York: Greenwood).

Lenoir, R. ([1974]1989) *Les Exclus: Un Français sur dix* (Paris: Éditions du Seuil).

Leung, C. B. (1982) 'Community participation: from Kai Fong Association, Mutual Aid Committee to District Board', in Cheng, J. Y. S. (ed.) *Hong Kong in the 1980s* (Hong Kong: Summerson Eastern): 152–70.

Leung, J. B. (1996) 'Community development: past, present and future', in Chi, I. and Cheung, S.-K. (eds) *Social Work in Hong Kong* (Hong Kong: Hong Kong Social Workers Association): 129–37.

Lewin, K. (1936) *Principles of Topological Psychology* (New York: McGraw-Hill).

Lewis, J. (1995) ' "Not alms but a friend": social work, poverty and relief in the late nineteenth and twentieth centuries' in Schwieso, J. and Pettit, P. (eds) *Aspects of the History of British Social Work* (New Bulmershe papers) (Reading: Faculty of Education and Community Studies, University of Reading): 124–47.

Lewis, J. and Glennerster, H. (1996) *Implementing the New Community Care* (Buckingham: Open University Press).

Lin, W-I. (1991) 'The structural determinants of welfare effort in post-war Taiwan' *International Social Work,* 34(2): 171–90.

Loch, C. S. (1883) *How to Help in Cases of Distress: A Handy Reference Book for Almoners, Almsgivers, and Others* (London: Longmans Green) (Reprint 1977, Plymouth: Continua).

Loewenberg, F. W. (1992) 'Federal relief programs in the 19th century: a reassessment', *Journal of Sociology and Social Welfare,* 19(3): 121–36.

Loney, M. (1983) *Community Against Government* (London: Heinemann).

Longford Report (1964) *Crime – A Challenge to us All* (London: Labour Party).

López-Blasco, A. (1998) 'The development of social pedagogy in Spain: the tension between social needs, political response and academic interests', *European Journal of Social Work,* 1(1): 41–53.

Lorenz, W. (1994a) 'Personal social services', in Clasen, J. and Freeman, R. (eds) *Social Policy in Germany* (Hemel Hempstead: Harvester Wheatsheaf): 148–69.

Lorenz, W. (1994b) *Social Work in a Changing Europe* (London: Routledge).

Lowe, G. (1987) 'Social work's professional mistake: confusing status for control and losing both', *Journal of Sociology and Social Policy,* 14(2): 187–206.

Lubove, R. (1965) *The Professional Altruist: The Emergence of Social Work as a Career 1880–1930* (Cambridge, MA: Harvard University Press).

Lundström, T. (1989) 'On Swedish social policy', *International Social Work*, **32**(4): 261–71.

Lurie, H. L. (1959) 'Private philanthropy and federated fundraising', *Social Service Review*, **29**(1): 64–74.

Lymbery, M. (2001) 'Social work at the crossroads', *British Journal of Social Work*, **31**(3): 369–84.

Macey, M. and Moxon, M. (1996) 'An examination of anti-racist and anti-oppressive theory and practice in social work education', *British Journal of Social Work*, **26**(3): 297–314.

Machtinger, B. (1999) 'The U. S. Children's Bureau and Mothers' Pension administration, 1912–1930', *Social Service Review*, **73**(1): 105–18.

Mackintosh Report (1951) *Report of the Committee on Social Workers in the Mental Health Services* (Cmnd 8260) (London: HMSO).

Macnicol, J. (1999) 'From "problem family" to "underclass", 1945–95', in Fawcett, H and Lowe, R. (eds) *Welfare Policy in Britain: The Road from 1945* (Basingstoke: Macmillan – now Palgrave Macmillan): 69–93.

Malherbe, M. (1980) *Accreditation in Social Work: Principles and Issues in Context: A Contribution to the Debate* (CCETSW Study 4) (London: CCETSW).

Maluccio, A. N., Fein, E. and Olmstead, K A. (1986) *Permanency Planning for Children: Concepts and Methods* (New York: Routledge/Chapman & Hall).

Mandal, K. S. (1989) 'American influence on social work education in India and its impact', *International Social Work*, **32**(4): 303–9.

Mandal, K. S. (1995) 'India', in Watts, T. D., Elliott, D. and Mayada, N. S. (eds) *International Handbook on Social Work Education* (Westport, CT: Greenwood): 355–65.

Marsh, P. and Crow, G. (1997) *Family Group Conferences in Child Welfare* (Oxford: Blackwell).

Marshall, J. (1995) 'National depression, the poor, and poor relief: Lafayette, Indiana, 1896–1897, a case study', *Social Service Review*, **69**(2): 285–308.

Marshall, T. H. (1950) *Citizenship and Social Class* (Cambridge: Cambridge University Press).

Marshall, T. H. (1970) *Social Policy* (3rd edn) (London: Hutchinson).

Martin, J. P. (1984) *Hospitals in Trouble* (Oxford: Blackwell).

Matthews, J. and Kemmis, J. (2001) 'Development of the English settlement movement', in Gilchrist, R. and Jeffs, T. (eds) *Settlements, Social Change and Community Action* (London: Jessica Kingsley): 54–68.

Mayer, J. E. and Timms, N. (1970) *The Client Speaks* (London: Routledge & Kegan Paul).

McDermott. F. E. (ed.) (1975) '*Self-Determination in Social Work* (London: Routledge & Kegan Paul).

McDonald, D. J. (1996) 'A social experiment: the impact of recent social inventions on the social work enterprise in New Zealand', in IASSW, IFSW and HKSWA (eds) *Participating in Change – Social Work Profession in Social Development Proceedings of the Joint World Congress of the International Federation of Social Workers and the International Association of Schools of Social Work* (Hong Kong: HKSWA): 160–2.

Mcdonald, G. and Sheldon, B. with Gillespie, J. (1992) 'Contemporary studies of the effectiveness of social work', *British Journal of Social Work* 22(6): 615–43.

McGrath, M. (1991) *Multi-Disciplinary Teamwork: Community Mental Handicap Teams* (Aldershot: Avebury).

McHugh, P. (1980) *Prostitution and Victorian Social Reform* (London: Croom Helm).

Meacham, S. (1987) *Toynbee Hall and Social Reform 1880–1914: The Search for Community* (New Haven, CT: Yale University Press).

Means, R. and Smith, R. (1998) *From Poor Law to Community Care: The Development of Welfare Services for Elderly People 1939–1971* (2nd edn) (Bristol: Policy Press).

Melder, K. (1967) 'Ladies bountiful: organized women's benevolence in early nineteenth century America', *Social Service Review*, 65(3): 231–54.

Mencher, S. (1974) 'The influence of romanticism in nineteenth-century British social work' *Social Service Review*, 38(2): 174–90.

Meyer, H. J., Borgatta, E. F. and Jones, W. C. (1965) *Girls of Vocational High: An Experiment in Social Work Intervention* (New York: Russell Sage Foundation).

Michielse, H. C. M. (trans. Van Krieken, R.) (1990) 'Policing the poor: J. L. Vives and the sixteenth century origins of modern social administration', *Social Service Review*, 64(1): 1–21.

Midgley, J. (1981) *Professional Imperialism: Social Work in the Third World* (London: Heinemann).

Midgley, J. (1997) *Social Welfare in Global Context* (Thousand Oaks, CA: Sage).

Midgley, J. and Sanzenbach, P. (1989) 'Social work, religion and the global challenge of fundamentalism', *International Social Work*, 32(4): 273–87.

Miller, A. (1988) *Poverty Deserved? Relieving the Poor in Victorian Liverpool* (Liverpool: Liver Press).

Mills, R. (1973) *Young Outsiders: A Study of Alternative Communities* (London: Routledge & Kegan Paul).

Ministerial Advisory Committee on a Maori Perspective for the Department of Social Welfare (1986) *Puao-te-Ata-tu (Daybreak)* (Wellington: Department of Social Welfare).

Minois, G. (1989) *History of Old Age: From Antiquity to the Renaissance* (Cambridge: Polity).

Mitchell, B. (1934) Patten, Simon Nelson' in Malone, D. (ed.) *Dictionary of American Biography* (London: Humphrey Milford: Oxford University Press): 14: 298–301.

Mitchison, R. (2000) *The Old Poor Law in Scotland: The Experience of Poverty, 1574–1845* (Edinburgh: Edinburgh University Press).

Monckton Report (1946) *On the Circumstances which led to the Boarding out of Dennis and Terence O'Neill at Bank Farm, Minsterley, and the Steps taken to Supervise their Welfare* (Cmd 6636) (London: HMSO).

Moreau, M. J. (1979) 'A structural approach to social work practice', *Canadian Journal of Social Work Education,* 5(1): 78–94.

Moreau, M. J. (1990) 'Empowerment through advocacy and consciousness-raising: implications of a structural approach to social work', *Journal of Sociology and Social Welfare,* 17(2): 53–68.

Morison Report (1962) *Report of the Departmental Committee on the Probation Service* (Cmnd 1650) (London: HMSO).

Morris, C. (1984) *The Permanency Principle in Child Care Social Work* (Norwich: Social Work Monographs).

Morris, J. (1993) *Independent Lives? Disabled People and Community Care* (Basingstoke, Macmillan – now Palgrave Macmillan).

Morton, M. J. (1988) 'Fallen women, federated charities and maternity homes, 1913–1973', *Social Service Review,* 62(1): 61–82.

Moss Kanter, R. (1972) *Commitment and Community: Communes and Utopius in Sociological Perspective* (Cambridge, MA: Harvard University Press).

Mostinckx, J. (1993) 'The Flemish community' in Munday, B. (ed.) *European Social Services* (Canterbury: European Institute of Social Services, University of Kent at Canterbury): 19–60.

Mullaly, R. P. (2003) *Structural Social Work: Ideology, Theory and Practice* (2nd edn) (Ontario: Oxford University Press).

Mullender, A. and Ward, D. (1991) *Self-Directed Groupwork: Users Take Action for Empowerment* (London: Whiting & Birch).

Munday, B. (1997) 'Social exclusion: its implications for European social services', in Kautto, M. (ed.) *European Social Services – Policies and Priorities to the Year 2000: A Report from a European Expert Meeting on Social Care Services* (Helsinki: STAKES): 59–69.

Nagpaul, H. (1972) 'The diffusion of American social work education in India: problems and issues', *International Social Work,* 15(1): 3–17.

NASW (1996) *Code of Ethics of the National Association of Social Workers,* http://www.socialworkers.org/pubs/code/code.asp.

Nellis, M. (1989) 'Social work', in Brown, P. and Sparks, K. (eds) *Beyond Thatcherism: Social Policy, Politics and Society* (Milton Keynes: Open University Press): 104–20.

Ngai, N.-P. (1996) 'Revival of social work education in China', *International Social Work,* 39(3): 289–300.

Nye, R. A. (1984) *Crime, Madness and Politics in Modern France: The Medical Concept of National Decline* (Princeton, NJ: Princeton University Press).

Nygren, L., with Andersson, M., Eydal, G., Hammarqvist, S.-E., Rauhala, P.-L. and Warming Nielsen, H. (1997) 'New policies, new words – the service concept in Scandinavian social policy' in Sipilä, J. (ed.) *Social Care Services: The Key to the Scandinavian Welfare Model* (Aldershot: Ashgate): 9–26.

O'Brien, M. and Penna, S. (1998) *Theorising Welfare: Enlightenment and Modern Society* (London: Sage).

O'Hagan, K. (1996) 'Social work competence: an historical perspective', in O'Hagan, K. (ed.) *Competence in Social Work Practice: A Practical Guide for Professionals* (London: Jessica Kingsley): 1–24.

O'Hagan, K. (2001) *Cultural Competence in the Caring Professions* (London: Jessica Kingsley).

Oliver, M. (1996) *Understanding Disability: From Theory to Practice* (Basingstoke: Macmillan – now Palgrave Macmillan).

Oliver, M. and Barnes, C. (1998) *Disabled People and Social Policy: From Exclusion to Inclusion* (London: Longman).

Orcutt, B. A. (1990) *Science and Inquiry in Social Work Practice* (New York: Columbia University Press).

Orkney Inquiry (1992) *The Report of the Inquiry into the Removal of Children from Orkney in February 1991* (Edinburgh: HMSO).

Otte, C. (1997) 'Germany', in Mayadas, N. S., Watts, T. D. and Elliott, D. (eds) *International Handbook of Social Work Theory and Practice* (Westport, CT: Greenwood): 122–43.

Otten Report (1974) *Social Work Support for the Health Service: Report of a Working Party* (London: HMSO).

Ow, R. (1996) 'Social services and social work education in Singapore', in IASSW, IFSW and HKSWA (eds) *Participating in Change – Social Work Profession in Social Development Proceedings of the Joint World Congress of the International Federation of Social Workers and the International Association of Schools of Social Work;* Volume 3 (Hong Kong: HKSWA): 239–42.

Panayi, P. (1994) *Immigration, Ethnicity and Racism in Britain: 1815–1945* (Manchester: Manchester University Press).

Papell, C. P. and Rothman, B. (1966) 'Social group work models: possession and heritage', *Journal of Education for Social Work,* **2**(2): 66–77.

Park, J.-S. (1996) 'An evaluation of exploratory study on developing church social work course in Korea', in IASSW, IFSW and HKSWA (eds) *Participating in Change – Social Work Profession in Social Development Proceedings of the Joint World Congress of the International Federation of Social Workers and the International Association of Schools of Social Work* (Hong Kong: HKSWA): 111–6.

Parker, J. K. (1994) 'Women at the helm: succession politics at the Children's Bureau, 1912–1968', *Social Work,* **39**(5): 551–9.

Parker, R. A. (1966) *Decision in Child Care* (London: Allen & Unwin).

Parker, R. A. (1988) 'An historical background' in Sinclair, I. (ed.) *Residential Care: The Research Reviewed* (London: HMSO).

Parkin, T. G. (1998) 'Ageing in antiquity: status and participation', in Johnson, P. and Thane, P. (eds) (1998) *Old Age from Antiquity to Post-Modernity* (London: Routledge): 19–42.

Parry, N. and Parry, J. (1979) 'Social work, professionalism and the state', in Parry, N., Rustin, M. and Stayamurti, C. (eds) *Social Work, Welfare and the State* (London: Edward Arnold): 21–47.

Parton, N. (1985) *The Politics of Child Abuse* (Basingstoke: Macmillan – now Palgrave Macmillan).

Parton, N. and O'Byrne, P. (2000) *Constructive Social Work: Towards a New Practice* (Basingstoke: Macmillan – now Palgrave Macmillan).

Pawson, R. and Tilley, N. (1997) *Realistic Evaluation* (London: Sage).

Payne, M. (1982) *Working in Teams* (Basingstoke: Macmillan – now Palgrave Macmillan).

Payne, M. (1985) 'The code of ethics, the social work manager and the organisation', in Watson, D. (ed.) *A Code of Ethics for Social Work: The Second Step* (London: Routledge & Kegan Paul).

Payne, M. (1986) 'Unemployed at work', *Community Care*, 20 February: 17–18.

Payne, M. (1989) 'Open records and shared decisions with clients', in Shardlow, S. (ed.) *The Values of Change in Social Work* (London: Tavistock/Routledge): 114–34.

Payne, M. (1995) *Social Work and Community Care* (Basingstoke: Macmillan – now Palgrave Macmillan).

Payne, M. (1997a) 'Government guidance in the construction of the social work profession', in Adams, R. (ed.) *Crisis in the Human Services: National and International Issues* (Hull: University of Lincoln and Humberside): 381–90.

Payne, M. (1997b) *Modern Social Work Theory* (2nd edn) (Basingstoke: Macmillan – now Palgrave Macmillan).

Payne, M. (1997c) 'Task-centred practice within the politics of social work theory', *Issues in Social Work Education*, 17(2): 48–65.

Payne, M. (1998) 'Why social work? Comparative perspectives on social issue and response formation', *International Social Work*, 41(4): 443–53.

Payne, M. (2000a) 'Social work theory' in Davies, M. (ed.) *The Blackwell Encyclopaedia of Social Work* (Oxford: Blackwell): 332–4.

Payne, M. (2000b) 'The politics of case management in social work', *International Journal of Social Welfare*, 9(2): 82–91.

Payne, M. (2002) 'The role and achievements of a professional association in the late twentieth century: The British Association of Social Workers 1970–2000', *British Journal of Social Work*, 32(8): 969–95.

Payne, M. (2005) *Modern Social Work Theory* (3rd edn) (Basingstoke: Palgrave Macmillan).

Pearce, R. (1997) *Attlee* (London: Longman).

Pease, B. and Fook, J. (1999) *Transforming Social Work Practice: Postmodern Critical Perspectives* (London: Routledge).

Pedersen, S. (1994) *Family, Dependence and the Origins of the Welfare State: Britain and France, 1914–1945* (Cambridge: Cambridge University Press).

Peebles-Wilkins, W. (1996) 'Janie Porter Barrett and the Virginia Industrial School for Colored Girls: community response to the needs of African American children', in Smith, E. P. and Merkel-Holguin, L. A. (eds) *A History of Child Welfare* (New Brunswick, NJ: Transaction): 135–54.

Peiris, P. (1996) 'The social work profession and changes in ethnic and gender relations', IASSW, IFSW and HKSWA (eds) *Participating in Change – Social Work Profession in Social Development Proceedings of the Joint World Congress of the International Federation of Social Workers and the International Association of Schools of Social Work;* Volume 3 (Hong Kong: HKSWA), 1–3.

Penketh, L. (2000) *Tackling Institutional Racism: Anti-Racist Policies and Social Work Education and Training* (Bristol: Policy Press).

Percy Report (1957) *Royal Commission on the Law relating to Mental Illness and Mental Deficiency 1954–1957* (Cmnd 169) (London: HMSO).

Perls, F., Hefferline, R. F. and Goodman, P. (1973) *Gestalt Therapy: Excitement and Growth in the Human Personality* (Harmondsworth: Penguin).

Peterson, J. F. (1965) 'From social settlement to social agency: settlement work in Columbus, Ohio, 1898–1958), *Social Service Review*, **39**(2): 171–208.

Petrie, G. (1971) *A Singular Iniquity: The Campaigns of Josephine Butler* (London: Macmillan – now Palgrave Macmillan).

Philp, A. F. and Timms, N. (1957) *The Problem of 'The Problem Family': A Critical Review of the Literature Concerning the 'Problem Family' and its Treatment* (London: Family Service Unit).

Pincus, A. and Minahan, A. (1973) *Social Work Practice: Model and Method* (Itasca, IL: Peacock).

Pinker, R. (1982) 'An alternative view', in Barclay Report, *Social Workers: Their Role and Tasks* (London: Bedford Square Press): 236–62.

Pinker, R. (1990) *Social Work in an Enterprise Society* (London: Routledge).

Pinker, R. (1993) 'A lethal kind of looniness', *Times Higher Education Supplement*, 10 September.

Pollis, A. (1981) 'Human rights, third world socialism and Cuba', *World Development*, **9**(9/10): 1005–17.

Pollitt, C. (1993) *Managerialism and the Public Services: Cuts or Cultural Change in the 1990s?* (Oxford: Blackwell).

Poole, H. R. (1970) *The March of the Reinforcements: Experiences of the Liverpool Council of Social Service* (Liverpool: LCVS).

Porter, R. (1987) *A Social History of Madness: Stories of the Insane* (London: Phoenix/Weidenfeld & Nicolson).

Porter, R. (2000) *Enlightenment: Britain and the Creation of the Modern World* (London: Allen Lane).

Powell, M. and Hewitt, M. (2002) *Welfare State and Welfare Change* (Buckingham: Open University Press).

Pugh, G. (1993) 'Thirty years of change for children 1963-1993: an overview', in Pugh, G. (ed.) *30 years of Change for Children* (London: National Children's Bureau): 1–24.

Pumphrey, M. W. (1962) 'Mary Richmond's process of conceptualization' in Kasius, C. (ed.) *Social Casework in the Fifties: Selected Articles, 1951–1960* (New York: FSAA): 3–16.

Pumphrey, R. E. and Pumphrey, M. W. (eds) (1961) *The Heritage of American Social Work: Readings in its Philosophical and Institutional Development* (New York: Columbia University Press).

Queiro-Tajalli, I. (1995) 'Argentina', in Watts, T. D., Elliott, D. and Mayada, N. S. (eds) *International Handbook on Social Work Education* (Westport, CT: Greenwood): 87–102.

Qureshi, H. and Walker, A. (1988) *The Caring Relationship* (London: Routledge & Kegan Paul).

Rafferty, M. and O'Sullivan, E. (1999) *Suffer the Little Children: The Inside Story of Ireland's Industrial Schools* (Dublin: New Island).

Ralphs Report (1975) *Report of the Working Party on the Role and Training of Education Welfare Officers* (London: Local Government Training Board).

Ramon, S. (1985) *Psychiatry in Britain: Meaning and Policy* (London: Croom Helm).

Ramon, S. (1995) 'Slovenian social work: a case study of unexpected developments in the post-1990 period', *British Journal of Social Work*, 25(4): 513–28.

Ramon, S. (1996) *Mental Health in Europe: Ends, Beginnings and Rediscoveries* (Basingstoke: Macmillan – now Palgrave Macmillan).

Rankin, P. (1996) 'Developmental social welfare: a South African perspective', in IASSW, IFSW and HKSWA (eds) *Participating in Change – Social Work Profession in Social Development Proceedings of the Joint World Congress of the International Federation of Social Workers and the International Association of Schools of Social Work;* Volume 3 (Hong Kong: HKSWA): 57–9.

Ray, L. J. (1993) *Rethinking Critical Theory: Emancipation in the Age of Global Social Movements* (London: Sage).

Reid, K. E. (1981) *From Character-Building to Social Treatment: The History of the Use of Groups in Social Work* (Westport, CT: Greenwood).

Reid, W. J. (1994) 'The empirical practice movement', *Social Service Review*, 68(2): 165–84.

Reid, W. J. and Epstein, L. (1972a) *Task-Centered Casework* (New York: Columbia University Press).

Reid, W. J. and Epstein, L. (eds) (1972b) *Task-Centered Practise* (New York: Columbia University Press).

Reid, W. J. and Shyne, A. W. (1969) *Brief and Extended Casework* (New York: Columbia University Press).

Reinardy, J. R. (1987) 'Social casework with the elderly between World Wars I and II', *Social Service Review*, **61**(3): 498–513.

Reisch, M. (1998) 'The sociopolitical context and social work method, 1890–1950', *Social Service Review*, **72**(2): 161–81.

Reisch, M. and Andrews, J. (2002) *The Road Not Taken: A History of Radical Social Work in the United States* (New York: Brunner-Routledge).

Reith, M. (1988) *Community Care Tragedies: A Practice Guide to Mental Health Inquiries* (Birmingham: Venture).

Research in Practice (2004) http://www.rip.org.uk (accessed 29 July 2004).

Richmond, M. E. ([1917]1965) *Social Diagnosis* (New York: Free Press).

Rimmer, J. (1980) *Troubles Shared: The Story of a Settlement 1899–1979* (Birmingham: Birmingham University Settlement).

Ripple, L., Alexander, E. and Polemis, B. W. (1964) *Motivation, Capacity and Opportunity: Studies in Casework Theory and Practice* (Chicago: University of Chicago Press).

Ritchie Report (1994) *Report of the Inquiry into the Care and Treatment of Christopher Clunis* (London: HMSO).

Ritschel, D. (1995) 'Macmillan', in George, V. and Page, R. (eds) *Modern Thinkers on Welfare* (London: Prentice Hall): 51–8.

Ro, K-k. and Oh, S-b. (1988) 'Anti-poverty programmes for the urban poor in Korea', *International Social Work*, **31**(2): 95–113.

Robbins, D. (ed.) (1993) *Community Care: Findings from Department of Health Funded Research 1988–1992* (London: HMSO).

Robinson, V. (1962) *Jessie Taft: Therapist and Social Work Educator* (Philadelphia: University of Pennsylvania Press).

Rodrigues, F. and Monteiro, A. (1998) 'Social work in Portugal', in Shardlow, S. and Payne, M. (eds) *Contemporary Issues in Social Work: Western Europe* (Aldershot: Arena): 93–115.

Rogers, A., Pilgrim, D. and Lacey, R. (1992) *Experiencing Psychiatry: Users' Views of Services* (Basingstoke: Macmillan – now Palgrave Macmillan).

Rogers, C. (1951) *Client-centered Therapy : Its Current Practice, Implications and Theory* (London: Constable).

Rooff, M. (1972) *A Hundred Years of Family Welfare: A Study of the Family Welfare Association (Formerly Charity Organisation Society) 1869–1969* (London: Michael Joseph).

Rooney, R. E. (1992) *Strategies for Work with Involuntary Clients* (New York: Columbia University Press).

Rose, J. (1980) *Elizabeth Fry: A Biography* (London: Macmillan – now Palgrave Macmillan).

Rose, N. E. (1989) 'Work relief in the 1930s and the origins of the Social Security Act', *Social Service Review*, **63**(1): 63–91.

Rosenhaft, E. (1994) 'The historical development of German social policy', in Clasen, J. and Freeman, R. (eds) *Social Policy in Germany* (Hemel Hempstead: Harvester Wheatsheaf): 21–41.

Rosenthal, M. G. (1986) 'The Children's Bureau and the juvenile court: delinquency policy, 1912–1940', *Social Service Review*, 60(2): 301–18.

Rossell, T. and Fernández, J. (1998) 'Social work in Spain', in Shardlow, S. and Payne, M. (eds) *Contemporary Issues in Social Work: Western Europe* (Aldershot: Arena): 117–31.

Rothschild Report (1971) *Organisation and Management of Government Research* (Cmnd 4814) (London: HMSO).

Rouselle, A. (1996) 'The family under the Roman Empire: signs and gestures', in Burgière, A., Klapisch-Zuber, C., Segalen, M. and Zonabend, F. (eds) *A History of the Family:* Volume 1: *Distant Worlds, Ancient Worlds* (English translation of *Histoire de la Famille*, 1986) (Cambridge: Polity): 270–310.

Rowe, J. and Lambert, L. (1973) *Children Who Wait* (London: Association of British Adoption and Fostering Agencies).

Rowntree, B. S. (1902) *Poverty: A Study of Town Life* (2nd edn) (Basingstoke: Macmillan – now Palgrave Macmillan).

Salomon, A. (1937) *Education for Social Work* (Zurich: International Committee of Schools of Social Work).

Satka, M. (1995) *Making Social Citizenship: Conceptual Practices from the Finnish Poor Law to Professional Social Work* (Jyväskylä, Finland: SoPhi).

Satka, M. and Karvinen, S. (1999) 'The contemporary reconstruction of Finnish social work expertise' *European Journal of Social Work*, 2(2): 119–29.

SCA (2003) *Social Care Association 1949–1999,* http://socialcaring.co.uk/full_history.asp.

Schultz, H. J. (ed.) (1972) *English Liberalism and the State: Individualism or Collectivism* (Lexington, MA: Heath).

SCIE (2004) http://www.scie.org.uk/ (accessed 29 July 2004).

Seebohm Report (1968) *Report of the Committee on Local Authority and Allied Personal Social Services* (Cmnd 3703) (London: HMSO).

Seed, P. (1973) *The Expansion of Social Work in Britain* (London: Routledge & Kegan Paul).

Shaker, S. (1998) 'Old age in the high and late middle ages: image, expectation and status', in Johnson, P. and Thane, P. (eds) *Old Age from Antiquity to Post-Modernity* (London: Routledge): 43–63.

Shapiro, B. Z. (1991) 'Social action, the group and society', *Social Work with Groups*, 14(3/4): 7–21.

Sheldon, B. (1986) 'Social work effectiveness experiments: review and implications', *British Journal of Social Work*, 16(2): 223–42.

Sheldon, B. (1987) 'Implementing findings from social work effectiveness research', *British Journal of Social Work*, 17(6): 573–86.

Sheppard, M. (1995) *Care Management and the New Social Work: A Critical Analysis* (London: Whiting & Birch).

Shoemaker, L. M. (1998) 'Early conflicts in social work education', *Social Service Review*, 72(2): 182–91.

Showalter, E. (1987) *The Female Malady: Women, Madness and English Culture, 1830–1980* (London: Virago).

Shriver, J. M. (1987) 'Harry Lurie's assessment and prescription: an early view if social workers' roles and responsibilities regarding political action', *Journalof Sociology and Social Welfare*, 14(2): 111–27.

Sibeon, R. (1990) 'Comments on the structure and forms of social work knowledge', *Social Work and Social Sciences Review*, 1(1): 29–44.

Silavwe, G. W. (1995) 'The need for a new social work perspective in an African setting: the case of social casework in Zambia', *British Journal of Social Work*, 25(1): 71–84.

Simey, M. (1992) *Charity Rediscovered: A Study of Philanthropic Effort in Nineteenth-century Liverpoool* (Liverpool: Liverpool University Press).

Simpura, J. (1995) 'Social policy in transition societies: the case of the Baltic societies', in Simpura, J. (ed.) *Social Policy in Transition Societies: Experience from the Baltic Countries and Russia* (Helsinki: STAKES): 5–22.

Sipilä, J. with Andersson, M., Hammarqvist, S.-E., Nordlander, L., Rauhala, P.-L., Thomsen, K, and Warming Nielsen, H. (1997) 'A multitude of universal, public services – how and why did four Scandinavian countries get their social care model?' in Sipilä, J. (ed.) *Social Care Services: The Key to the Scandinavian Welfare Model* (Aldershot: Ashgate): 27–50.

Siporin, M. (1986) 'Group work method and the Inquiry', in Glasser, P. H. and Mayadas, N. S. (eds) *Group Workers at Work: Theory and Practice of the 80s* (Totowa, NJ: Rowman & Littlefield): 34–49.

Sissa, G. (1996) 'The family in ancient Athens (fifth-fourth century BC),' in Burgière, A., Klapisch-Zuber, C., Segalen, M. and Zonabend, F. (eds) *A History of the Family:* Volume 1: *Distant Worlds, Ancient Worlds* (English translation of *Histoire de la Famille*, 1986) (Cambridge: Polity): 194–227.

Skeffington Report (1969) *People and Planning: Report of the Committee on Public Participation in Planning* (London: HMSO).

Slack, P. (1985) *The Impact of Plague in Tudor and Stuart England* (Oxford: Clarendon).

Smith, E. P. (1995) 'Willingness and resistance to change: the case of the Race Discrimination Amendment of 1942', *Social Service Review*, 69(1): 31–56.

Smith, M. J. ([1953]1965) *Professional Education for Social Work in Britain: An Historical Account* (London: Allen & Unwin).

Social Development Section of the Economic Commission for Africa (1964) *Directory of Regional Social Welfare Activities* (New York: UN).

Social Welfare Department (1965) *Aims and Policy for Social Welfare in Hong Kong* (Hong Kong: Government Printer).

Social Welfare Department (1972) *Social Welfare in Hong Kong: the Way Ahead* (Hong Kong: Government Printer).

Social Work (1963) 'The Council for Training in Social Work' *Social Work (UK)*, 20(3): 3.

Solomon, B. B. (1976) *Black Empowerment: Social Work in Oppressed Communities* (New York: Columbia University Press).

Solomos, J. (2003) *Race and Racism in Britain* (Basingstoke: Palgrave Macmillan).

Soydan, H. (1999) *The History of Ideas in Social Work* (Birmingham: Venture/Social Work Research Association).

Specht, H. and Courtney, M. (1994) *Unfaithful Angels: How Social Work Abandoned its Mission* (New York: Free Press).

Specht, H. and Vickery, A. (eds) (1977) *Integrating Social Work Methods* (London: Allen & Unwin).

STAKES (2004) http://www.stakes.fi/english/index.html (accessed 29 July 2004).

Starkey, P. (2000) *Families and Social Workers: The Work of Family Service Units 1940–1985* (Liverpool: Liverpool University Press).

Stelmaszuk, Z. W. (1994) 'Helena Radlinska and the School of Adult Education and Social Work at the Free University of Poland', in Marriott, S. and Hake, B. J. (eds) *Cultural and Intercultural Experiences in European Adult Education* (Leeds: Leeds Studies in Continuing Education): 224–46.

Stevenson, O. (1983) 'Research and policy in the personal social services', in Gandy, J., Robertson, A. and Sinclair, S (eds) *Improving Social Intervention: Changing Social Policy and Social Work Practice through Research* (London: Croom Helm): 22–50.

Stones, C. (1994) *Focus on Families: Family Centre in Action* (Basingstoke: Macmillan – now Palgrave Macmillan).

Straussner, S. L. A. (1989) 'Occupational social work today: an overview' in Straussner, S. L. A. (ed.) *Occupational Social Work Today* (New York: Haworth): 1–17.

Streatfeild Report (1961) *Report of the Inter-departmental Committee on the Business of the Criminal Courts* (Cmnd 1289) (London: HMSO).

Stroud, J. (1970) 'Forgotten social workers – John Clay', *British Hospital Journal and Social Service Review,* 12 December.

Stroud, J. (1971) *13 Penny Stamps* (London: Hodder & Stoughton).

Struthers, J. (1987) 'A profession in crisis: Charlotte Whitton and Canadian social work in the 1930s', in Moscovitch, A. and Albert, J. (eds) *The 'Benevolent State': The Growth of Welfare in Canada* (Toronto: Garamond): 111–25.

Sullivan, M. (1999) 'Democratic socialism and social policy', in Page, R. M. and Silburn, R. (eds) *British Social Welfare in the Twentieth Century* (Basingstoke: Macmillan – now Palgrave Macmillan): 105–30.

SWAP (Social Work and Policy) (2004) http://www.swap.ac.uk/ (accessed 29 July 2004).

Taithe, B. (1997) 'Working men, old Chartists and the Contagious Diseases Acts' in Laybourn, K. (ed.) *Social Conditions, Status and Community 1860-c. 1920* (Stroud: Sutton): 184–203.

Takahashi, M. (1997) *The Emergence of Welfare Society in Japan* (Aldershot: Avebury).

Tamai, K. (2000) 'Images of the poor in an official survey of Osaka, 1923–1926', *Continuity and Change*, **15**(1): 99–116.

Tayler, W. E. (1860) *The Bristol Orphan Houses, Ashley Down: The History of the New Orphan Houses on Ashley Down, Bristol, under the direction of Mr George Müller* (London: Morgan & Scott).

Taylor Davis, A. (1988) *Making of a Teacher: 50 years in Social Work* (Silver Spring, MD: National Association of Social Workers).

Teare, R. J. and McPheeters, H. L. (1970) *Manpower Utilization in Social Welfare: A Report based on a Symposium on Manpower Utilization in Social Welfare Services* (Atlanta, GA: Social Welfare Manpower Project, Southern Regional Education Board).

Thane, P. (1982) *The Foundations of the Welfare State* (London: Longmans).

Thane, P. (1998) 'The family lives of old people' in Johnson, P. and Thane, P. (eds) *Old Age from Antiquity to Post-Modernity* (London: Routledge): 180–210.

Thomas, P. T. (1967) 'Problems of social work education', *Indian Journal of Social Work*, **28**(1): 41–53.

Thomas, Y. (1996) 'Fathers as citizens of Rome, Rome as a city of fathers (second century BC – second century AD)', in Burgière, A., Klapisch-Zuber, C., Segalen, M. and Zonabend, F. (eds) *A History of the Family:* Volume 1: *Distant Worlds, Ancient Worlds* (English translation of *Histoire de la Famille*, 1986) (Cambridge: Polity): 228–69.

Thompson, L. G. (1989) *Chinese Religion: An Introduction* (4th edn) (Belmont, CA: Wadsworth).

Thompson, N. (2003) *Anti-discriminatory Practice* (3rd edn) (Basingstoke: Palgrave – now Palgrave Macmillan).

Thyer, B. A. and Kazi, M. A. F. (eds) (2004) *International Perspectives on Evidence-Based Practice in Social Work* (Birmingham: Venture).

Timmins, N. (1996) *The Five Giants: A Biography of the Welfare State* (London: Fontana).

Timms, N. (1964) *Psychiatric Social Work in Great Britain (1939-1962)* (London: Routledge & Kegan Paul).

Timms, N. (1966) *Social Casework: Principles and Practice* (London: Routledge & Kegan Paul).

Timms, N. (1997) 'Taking social work seriously: the contribution of the functionalist school', *British Journal of Social Work*, **27**(5): 273–37.

Titmuss, R. M. (1951) *Problems of Social Policy* (London: HMSO).

Topalov, C. (1994) 'The invention of unemployment: language, classification and social reform, 1880–1910', in Guillemard, A-M., Lewis, J., Ringen, S. and Salais, R. (eds) *Comparing Social Welfare Systems in Europe:* Volume 1: *Oxford Conference: France-United Kingdom* (Paris: MIRE): 493–507.

Townsend, P. (1962) *The Last Refuge: A Survey of Residential Institutions and Homes for the Aged* (London: Routledge & Kegan Paul).

Trattner, W. I. (1999) *From Poor Law to Welfare State: A History of Social Welfare in America* (6th edn) (New York: Free Press).

Treudly, M. B. (1940) 'The "benevolent fair": a study of charitable organization among women in the first third of the nineteenth century', *Social Service Review*, 14: 509–22.

Tripodi, T. and Miller, H. (1966) 'The clinical judgement process: a review of the literature', *Social Work*, 11(7): 63–9.

Truth and Reconciliation Commission (2002) *Truth and Reconciliation Commission of South Africa Report: Seventh Volume* (Cape Town: TRC); http://www.doj.gov.za/trc/report/finalreport/victims_main_vol7.pdf.

Tsang, A. K. T. and Yan, M.-C. (2001) 'Chinese corpus, western application: the Chinese strategy of engagement with western social work', *International Social Work*, 44(4): 421–34.

TSWR (Theorising Social Work Research) (2000) http://www.elsc.org.uk/socialcareresource/tswr/tswrindex.htm (accessed 29 July 2004).

Tulva, T. (1997) 'Developing social work in Estonia', in Tulva, T. (ed.) *Some Aspects of Estonian Social Work and Social Policy* (Tallinn: Department of Social Work, Tallinn Institute of Educational Sciences): 5–14.

Tunstill, J. (2000) 'Child care', in Hill, M. (ed.) *Local Authority Social Services: An Introduction* (Oxford: Blackwells): 59–84.

Tutvedt, Ø. (1995) 'Historical development of social work in Norway', in Tutvedt, Ø. and Young, L. (eds) *Social Work and the Norwegian Welfare State* (Oslo: NotaBene, Ø.K.S.): 19–32.

Ulsteen, A. M. (1995) 'From a one year vocational course to a three year college education: the Norwegian Council of Women's School of Social Work 1920-1984', in Tutvedt, Ø. (ed.) *40 År for Velførerdsstaten: Norges kommunal-og sosialhøgskoles Historie 1950–1990* (Oslo: NKSH): 192.

Unsworth, C. (1979) 'The balance of medicine, law and social work in mental health legislation, 1889–1959', in Parry, N., Rustin, M. and Satymurti, C. (eds) *Social Work Welfare, and the State* (London: Edward Arnold).

Utting, W. (1991) *Children in Public Care: A Review of Residential Child Care* (London: HMSO).

Vaizey, J. ([1959]1986) 'Scenes from institutional life', in *Scenes from Institutional Life and Other Writings* (London: Weidenfeld & Nicolson): 13–88.

van Drenth, A. and de Haan, F. (1999) *The Rise of Caring Power: Elizabeth Fry and Josephine Butler in Britain and the Netherlands* (Amsterdam: Amsterdam University Press).

Verma, R. (1991) *Psychiatric Social Work in India* (New Delhi: Sage).

Vick Report (1945) *London County Council Remand Homes: Report of the Committee of Inquiry* (Cmd 6594) (London: HMSO).

Vickery, A. (1977) *Caseload Management: A Guide for Supervisors of Social Work Staff* (London: National Institute for Social Work).

Vincent, A. (1992) 'Citizenship, poverty and the real will', *Sociological Review:* 702–25.

Vladinska, N. (1994) 'Tendencies in the development of social work/social pedagogy education in Bulgaria', IASSW *Papers from the 1994 Congress: Papers giving a Review of the Situation in a Particular Country* (Manchester: Department of Applied Community Studies, Manchester Metropolitan University): Paper 6.

Waddan, A. (2003) 'Redesigning the welfare contract in theory and practice: Just what is going on in the USA?' *Journal of Social Policy,* **32**(10): 19–35.

Wagner Report (1988) *Residential Care: A Positive Choice* (London: HMSO).

Wagner, G. (1979) *Barnardo* (London: Weidenfeld & Nicolson.)

Walker, W. M. and Jones, H. (1984) 'Appendix: A short history of social administration and social work in the college', in Jones, H. (ed.) *Issues in Social Welfare* (Cardiff: University College): 145–53.

Walkowitz, J. R. (1980) *Prostitution and Victorian Society: Women, Class and the State* (Cambridge: Cambridge University Press).

Walton, R. G. and El Nasr, M. M. A. (1988) 'Indigenization and authentization in terms of social work in Egypt', *International Social Work,* **31**(2): 135–44.

Ward, E. (1962) 'The Australian Association of Social Workers', *Social Work (UK),* **19**(3): 10–14.

Warner Report (1992) *Choosing with Care: The Report of the Committee of Inquiry into the Selection, Development and Management of Staff in Children's Homes* (London; HMSO).

Warner, A. (1894) *American Charities* (New York: Crowell).

Waterhouse Inquiry (2000) *Lost in Care – Report of the Tribunal of Inquiry into the Abuse of Children in Care in the Former County Council Areas of Gwynedd and Clwyd since 1974* (London: TSO); http://www.doh.gov.uk/lostincare/20102a.htm.

Webb, B. (1926) *My Apprenticeship* (1971 Penguin edn) (Harmondsworth: Penguin).

Webb, S. A. (2001) 'Some considerations on the validity of evidence-based practice in social work', *British Journal of Social Work,* **31**(1): 57–79.

Welshman, J. (1999) 'The social history of social work: the issue of the "problem family"', 1940–70', *British Journal of Social Work,* **29**(3): 457–76.

Whang, I. -Y. (1988) 'Social services programmes for the poor in a newly industrialising country: experience in South Korea', in Rondinelli, D. A. and Cheems, G. S. (eds) *Urban Services in Developing Countries: Public and Private Roles in Urban Development* (London: Macmillan – now Palgrave Macmillan).

Whitaker, D. S. and Archer, J. L. (1989) *Research by Social Workers: Capitalizing on Experience* (London: CCETSW).

White, G. C. (1959) 'Social settlements and immigrant neighbors, 1886-1914', *Social Service Review*, **33**(1): 55–66.

Wieler, J. (1988) 'A life dedicated to humanity: Alice Salomon under Nazi rule (1933–7) and in exile (1937–48)', *International Social Work*, **31**(2): 69–74.

Wilensky, H. L. and Lebeaux, C. N. (1965) *Industrial Society and Social Welfare: The Impact of Industrialization on the Supply and Organization of Social Welfare Services in the United States* (New York: Free Press).

Williams Report (1967) *Caring for People: Staffing Residential Homes* (London: Allen & Unwin).

Williams, K. and Williams, J. (1995) 'Keynes', in George, V. and Page, R. (eds) *Modern Thinkers on Welfare* (London: Prentice Hall): 69–83.

Willmott, P. (1992) *A Singular Woman: The Life of Geraldine Aves 1989–1986* (London: Whiting & Birch).

Willmott, P. (1996) '1895–1945: The first fifty years', in Baraclough, J., Dedman, G., Osborn, H., and Willmott, P. (eds) *100 Years of Health Related Social Work 1895–1995: Then – Now – Onwards* (Birmingham: BASW Trading): 1–20.

Wills, W. D. (1964) *Homer Lane: A Biography* (London: Allen & Unwin).

Wills, W. D. (1971) *Spare the Child: The Story of an Experimental Approved School* (Harmondsworth: Penguin).

Wills, W. D. (1973) 'Planned environment therapy- what is it?', in Klare, H. J. and Wills, D. *Studies in Environment Therapy* (vol. 2) (London: Planned Environment Therapy Trust).

Winch, D. (1987) *Malthus* (Oxford: Oxford University Press).

Witkin, S. (1991) 'Empirical clinical practice: a critical analysis', *Social Work*, **36**(2): 158–63.

Wolfensberger, W. (1972) *The Principlpe of Normalisation in Human Services* (Toronto: National Institute on Mental Retardation).

Wood Report (1929) *Report of the Interdepartmental Committee on Mental Deficiency, 1925–29* (Cd 3545) (London: HMSO).

Woodroofe, K. (1962) *From Charity to Social Work in England and the United States* (London: Routledge & Kegan Paul).

Woolf, S. (1986) *The Poor in Western Europe in the Eighteenth and Nineteenth Centuries* (London: Methuen).

Wootton, B. (1958) *Social Science and Social Pathology* (London: Allen & Unwin).

Yelaja, S. A. (1970) 'Towards a reconceptualization of the social work profession in India', *Applied Social Studies*, **2**(1): 21–6.

Yelaja, S. A. (ed.) (1971) *Authority in Social Work: Concept and Use* (Toronto: University of Toronto Press).

Yimam, A. (1990) *Social Development in Africa 1950–1985: Methodological Perspectives and Future Prospects* (Aldershot: Avebury).

Young, A. F. and Ashton, E. T. (1956) *British Social Work in the Nineteenth Century* (London: Routledge & Kegan Paul).

Younghusband, E. L. (1947) *Report on the Employment and Training of Social Workers* (1st Younghusband Report) (Dunfermline: Carnegie UK Trust).

Younghusband, F. I (1051) *Social Work in Britain* (2nd Younghusband Report) (Dunfermline: Carnegie UK Trust).

Younghusband, E. L. (1959) *Report of the Working Party on Social Workers in the Local Authority Health and Welfare Services* (3rd Younghusband Report, Chair: Younghusband) (London: HMSO).

Younghusband, E. (1963) 'Tasks and trends in education for social work: an international appraisal', *Social Work (UK)*, **20**(3): 4–11.

Younghusband, E. (1981) *The Newest Profession: A Short History of Social Work* (Sutton: *Community Care*/IPC Business Press).

Zarb, G. (ed.) (1995) *Removing Disabling Barriers* (London: Policy Studies Institute).

Zhang, M. and Kilpatrick, A. C. (1996) 'Change in China: social work and social development', in IASSW, IFSW and HKSWA (eds) *Participating in Change – Social Work Profession in Social Development Proceedings of the Joint World Congress of the International Federation of Social Workers and the International Association of Schools of Social Work; Volume 3* (Hong Kong: HKSWA): 102–4.

Zonabend, F. (1996) 'An anthropological perspective on kinship and the family', in Burgière, A., Klapisch-Zuber., Segalen, M. and Zonabend, F. (eds) *A History of the Family:* Volume 1: *Distant Worlds, Ancient Worlds* (English translation of *Histoire de la Famille*, 1986) (Cambridge: Polity): 8–68.

Author Index

Subject Index

Note: The UK and its constituent countries, and the USA and its constituent states are not indexed, since they are referred to throughout; cities are only indexed where an organisation within them is referred to.